Praise for Patrick Smith

"A brilliant writer, Patrick Smith provides a laugh-a-page tour of a misunderstood industry—a journey into the world of aviation, stripped of the mumbo-jumbo and filled with humor and insight."
—*Christine Negroni, aviation writer and author of* Flying Lessons

"Deliciously stylish and informative. A soaring accomplishment, and an indispensable book for anyone who travels by air, which means everyone."
—*James Kaplan*

"Patrick Smith is extraordinarily knowledgeable about modern aviation and communicates beautifully in English, not in pilot-ese. Smith is the ideal seatmate, companion, writer, and explainer."
—*Alex Beam*, Boston Globe

"I wish I could fold up Patrick Smith and put him in my suitcase. He seems to know everything worth knowing about flying."
—*Stephen J. Dubner, coauthor of* Freakonomics

"Brilliantly down to earth and reassuring."
—*Cath Urquhart*, The Times *(London)*

"Trenchant and insightful."
—*Joe Sharkey*, The New York Times

"What a pleasure it is reading Patrick Smith's surprisingly elegant explanations and commentary. The world needs somebody writing E. B. White simple and sensible about a topic everyone has a question about."
—*Berke Breathed*

"Wonderful."

"*Ask the Pilot* actually makes flying fun. Patrick Smith manages to demystify the experience and remind us of the magic of aviation. Also he has a great sense of humor—which is critical when you are wedged into seat 14D on a regional jet."

COCKPIT
CONFIDENTIAL

EVERYTHING YOU
NEED TO KNOW ABOUT
AIR TRAVEL

Questions, Answers & Reflections

PATRICK SMITH

 sourcebooks

This publication is designed to provide accurate and authoritative information in regard to the subject matter covered. It is sold with the understanding that the publisher is not engaged in rendering legal, accounting, or other professional service. If legal advice or other expert assistance is required, the services of a competent professional person should be sought. —*From a Declaration of Principles Jointly Adopted by a Committee of the American Bar Association and a Committee of Publishers and Associations*

All brand names and product names used in this book are trademarks, registered trademarks, or trade names of their respective holders. Sourcebooks, Inc. is not associated with any product or vendor in this book.

Published by Sourcebooks, Inc.
P.O. Box 4410, Naperville, Illinois 60567-4410
(630) 961-3900
Fax: (630) 961-2168
www.sourcebooks.com

Library of Congress Cataloguing-in-Publication data is on file with the publisher.

Printed and bound in the United States of America.
VP 10 9 8 7 6 5 4 3 2 1

CONTENTS

Airfoiled: how huge airplanes stay aloft • But isn't it more complicated? • On speed: what the hell is a knot? • A primer on parts • What
are those upturned wingtips for? • What are those canoe-shaped pods
under the wings? • Can a jetliner perform aerobatics? • How does a
jet engine work? • What's a turboprop? • What is that hole under the
tail? • Do planes run their engines at the gate? • How much does a
jetliner cost? • Boeing v. Airbus: which is better and safer? • Which
planes will get me there fastest? • Which have the longest range?
• How much does a jetliner weigh? • When it's "too hot to fly" •
Contrails • Air travel and the environment

Turbulence: everything you need to know • Wake turbulence • What's that trail of mist coming from the wing? • What is windshear? • Engine stalls • Can we glide to a landing? • Pressurization: facts and fallacies • Regional jets: are they safe? • How much fuel is on board? • Why and when do pilots jettison fuel? • Lightning: facts and fallacies • Oh my god, there's duct tape on my plane • Air traffic: how close is too close? • When metal meets feather • Icing and deicing • The truth about toilet water • Broken parts and maintenance protocols • Preflight inspections • Geriatric jets

Preflight preparations • Why do planes take off into the wind? • Why do we bounce, bump, and jig during climb? • Engine failure on takeoff • The climbout cutback • How fast are we going at takeoff and touchdown? • Runway numbers • Challenging airports • Aborted landings: everything you need to know • Instrument approaches • Why do some pilots land more smoothly than others? • Reverse thrust • What's that sudden roar all about? • The nuts and bolts of weather delays • Four bad ideas to fix congestion • An ATC primer: how pilots communicate en route • Navigation basics: BLOWN, BAABY, and LAYED • Why do flights to Europe travel so far north? • FUK, DAM, HEL: those mysterious airport codes

Captain, copilot, first officer? Who are these people? • Becoming an airline pilot • Training: everything you need to know • Pilot salaries, truth and fiction • The seniority system blues • Pilot shortage: the real story • A pilot's schedule, and the cross-country shuffle • This is your captain sleeping: the menace of fatigue • Regional pilots: are they safe? • Women and minorities • The truth about cockpit automation • How passengers can (or can't) gauge a pilot's skill • Captain Sully: heroics or hype? • Pilots and alcohol • Those fancy watches and mysterious black bags • Cockpit cuisine: first class fare and ramen noodles • Flying naked? • Globetrodden: pilot perks, and the yin and yang of travel

Window shades, tray tables, and seat backs • The barking dog: strange noises on the Airbus • The facts and fallacies of cabin air • Do pilots tinker with the oxygen levels? • Overheated cabins and those hot, stuffy takeoffs • Opening an exit during flight • Why are the windows so small? • The glorious glory • Dogs and cats below • The story on cell phones and PEDs • Those damn dings • Listening in on cockpit chatter • Public address madness and the babble of the safety briefing • Class struggles: first, business, economy, and beyond • The trials and tribulations of boarding, and how to make it better • A round of applause

Terrorism perspective: the golden age of air crimes • Fear and reason: encouragement for nervous flyers • What pilots dread • Emergencies, real and imagined • Where airlines fear to tread • The ten worst disasters of all time • Foreign airline safety • The myth of the Immaculate Qantas • Budget carrier safety • Flight and punishment • Exploding tires and other nightmares • Could a nonpilot land a jetliner? • Parachutes for passengers? • The truth about midair collisions • Runway congestion: cause for alarm? • The legacy of September 11 • The folly of a barricaded cockpit • Shoulder-fired missiles • "Soft walls" and other hooey • Conspiracy Nation

Service woes: taking on the world • Why are airlines such terrible communicators? • Which are the largest carriers? • The upside for consumers: routes and fares • Airfares à la carte: the pros and cons of unbundling • Tarmac delays and the "Passenger Bill of Rights" • The magic mojo of Southwest Airlines • Which are the oldest airlines? • Code-share confusion • Where do flight numbers come from? • Red-eye rationale: why do flights to Europe always go at night? • Size matters: big planes on short hauls • The longest hauls • The poetry of airliner names

Author's Notes
and Acknowledgments

When I began this book, it was intended to be little more than a mildly refreshed edition of its predecessor, *Ask the Pilot: Everything You Need to Know about Air Travel*, published in 2004. The more I revised, the more it grew and changed. Eventually it became an entirely new book. The framework is similar and I've retained some of the chapter names, but the material within is vastly different. Virtually everything has been updated or expanded in some way, and about 70 percent of the material is entirely new.

The contents are drawn from more than three hundred articles and columns originally written for the online magazine *Salon*, beginning in 2002 under the brand *Ask the Pilot*. The Q&A sequences were provided mostly by my readers at *Salon*, to whom I am deeply grateful for their enthusiasm and encouragement over the years.

I have done my best to ensure long-term timeliness of the information, but please bear in mind that commercial aviation is a landscape—or skyscape if you'd rather—of ever-shifting facts and statistics. Airlines come and go; planes are bought and sold; routes are swapped and dropped. Now and then comes a tragedy.

Special thanks to my agent, Sophia Seidner, and to Shana Drehs at Sourcebooks. Logistical, proofreading, and creative support was provided by Julia Petipas. Acoustic accompaniments by Bob Mould, Grant Hart, Greg Norton, and the Jazz Butcher Conspiracy.

All thoughts and opinions herein are the author's own and do not necessarily reflect those of any airline, agency, or entity.

For further information and additional reading, please visit www.askthepilot.com.

Patrick Smith
Somerville, Massachusetts

INTRODUCTION

The Painter's Brush

More than ever, air travel is a focus of curiosity, intrigue, anxiety, and anger. In the chapters that follow I will do my best to provide answers for the curious, reassurance for the anxious, and unexpected facts for the deceived.

It won't be easy, and I begin with a simple premise: everything you *think* you know about flying is wrong. That's an exaggeration, I hope, but not an outrageous starting point in light of what I'm up against. Commercial aviation is a breeding ground for bad information, and the extent to which different myths, fallacies, and conspiracy theories have become embedded in the prevailing wisdom is startling. Even the savviest frequent flyers are prone to misconstruing much of what actually goes on.

It isn't surprising. Air travel is a complicated, inconvenient, and often scary affair for millions of people, and at the same time it's cloaked in secrecy. Its mysteries are concealed behind a wall of specialized jargon, corporate reticence, and an irresponsible media. Airlines, it hardly needs saying, aren't the most forthcoming of entities, while journalists and broadcasters like to keep it simple and sensational. It's hard to know who to trust or what to believe.

I'll give it my best shot. And in doing so, I will tell you how a plane stays in the air, yes. I'll address your nuts-and-bolts concerns and tackle those insufferable myths. However, this is not a book about flying, per se. I will not burden readers with gee-whiz specifications about airplanes. I am not writing for gearheads or those with a predisposed interest in planes; my readers don't want to see an aerospace engineer's schematic of a jet engine, and a technical discussion about cockpit instruments or aircraft hydraulics is guaranteed to be tedious and uninteresting—especially to me. Sure, we're all curious how fast a plane goes, how high it flies, how many statistical bullet points can be made of its wires and plumbing. But as both author and pilot, my infatuation with flight goes beyond the airplane itself, encompassing the fuller, richer drama of getting from here to there—the "theater" of air travel, as I like to call it.

For most of us who grow up to become airline pilots, flying isn't just something we fell into after college. Ask any pilot where his love of aviation comes from, and the answer almost always goes back to early childhood—to some ineffable, hard-wired affinity. Mine certainly did. My earliest crayon drawings were of planes, and I took flying lessons before I could drive. Just the same, I have never met another pilot whose formative obsessions were quite like mine. I have limited fascination with the sky or with the seat-of-the-pants thrills of flight itself. As a youngster, the sight of a Piper Cub meant nothing to me. Five minutes at an air show watching the Blue Angels do barrel rolls, and I was bored to tears. What enthralled me instead were the workings of the airlines: the planes they flew and the places they went.

In the fifth grade I could recognize a Boeing 727-100 from a 727-200 by the shape of the intake of its center engine (oval, not round). I could spend hours cloistered in my bedroom or at the dining room table, poring over the route maps and timetables of Pan Am, Aeroflot, Lufthansa, and British Airways, memorizing the names of the foreign capitals they flew to. Next time you're wedged in economy, flip to the route maps in the back of the inflight magazine. I could spend hours studying those three-panel foldouts and their crazy nests of city-pairs, immersed in a kind of junior pilot porno. I knew the logos and liveries of all the prominent airlines (and many of the nonprominent ones) and could replicate them freehand with a set of colored pencils.

Thus I learned geography as thoroughly as I learned aviation. For most pilots, the world beneath those lines of the route map remains

a permanent abstraction, countries and cultures of little or no interest beyond the airport fence or the perimeter of the layover hotel.
For others, as happened to me, there's a point when those places
become meaningful. One feels an excitement not merely from the
act of moving through the air, but from the idea of *going somewhere.*
You're not just flying, you're *traveling.* The full, beautiful integration
of flight and travel, travel and flight. Are they not the same thing? To
me they are. One can inspire the other, sure, but I never would have
traipsed off to so many countries in my free time—from Cambodia
to Botswana, Sri Lanka to Brunei—if I hadn't fallen in love with
aviation *first.*

If ever this connection struck me in a moment of clarity, it was
a night several years ago during a vacation to Mali, in West Africa.
Though I could write pages about the wonders and strangeness of
West Africa, one of the trip's most vivid moments took place at the
airport in Bamako, moments after our plane touched down from
Paris. Two hundred of us descended the drive-up stairs into a sinister
midnight murk. The air was misty and smelled of woodsmoke. Yellow
beams from military-style spotlights crisscrossed the tarmac. We were
paraded solemnly around the exterior of the aircraft, moving aft in
a wide semicircle toward the arrivals lounge. There was something
ceremonial and ritualistic about it. I remember walking beneath the
soaring, blue-and-white tail of Air France, the plane's auxiliary turbine screaming into the darkness. It was all so exciting and, to use a
politically incorrect word, exotic. And that incredible airplane is what
brought us there. In a matter of hours, no less—a voyage that once
would have taken weeks by ship and desert caravan.

The disconnect between air travel and culture seems to me wholly
unnatural, yet we've seen a virtually clean break. Nobody gives a
damn anymore how you get there—the means coldly separated from
the ends. For most people, whether bound for Kansas or Kathmandu,
the airplane is a necessary evil, incidental to the journey but no longer
part of it. An old girlfriend of mine, an artist who would have no
trouble appreciating the play of light in a seventeenth-century painting by Vermeer, found my opinions utterly perplexing. Like most
people, she analogized airplanes merely as tools. The sky was the

canvas, she believed; the jetliner as discardable as the painter's brush. I disagree, for as a brush's stroke represents the moment of artistic inspiration, what is travel without the *journey*?

We've come to view flying as yet another impressive but ultimately uninspiring technological realm. There I am, sitting in a Boeing 747, a plane that if tipped onto its nose would rise as tall as a 20-story office tower. I'm at 33,000 feet over the Pacific Ocean, traveling at 600 miles per hour, bound for the Far East. And what are the passengers doing? Complaining, sulking, tapping glumly into their laptops. A man next to me is upset over a dent in his can of ginger ale. This is the realization, perhaps, of a fully evolved technology. Progress, one way or the other, mandates that the extraordinary become the ordinary. But don't we lose valuable perspective when we begin to equate the commonplace, more or less by definition, with the tedious? Aren't we forfeiting something important when we sneer indifferently at the sight of an airplane—at the sheer impressiveness of being able to throw down a few hundred dollars and travel halfway around the world at nearly the speed of sound? It's a tough sell, I know, in this age of long lines, grinding delays, overbooked planes, and inconsolable babies. To be clear, I am not extolling the virtues of tiny seats or the culinary subtlety of half-ounce bags of snack mix. The indignities and hassles of modern air travel require little elaboration and are duly noted. But believe it or not, there is still plenty about flying for the traveler to savor and appreciate.

I'm hesitant to say that we've developed a sense of entitlement, but it's something like that. Our technological triumphs aside, consider also the industry's remarkable safety record and the fact that fares have remained startlingly cheap, even with tremendous surges in the price of fuel. Sure, years ago, passengers could enjoy a five-course meal served by a tuxedoed flight attendant before retiring to a private sleeping berth. My first airplane ride was in 1974: I remember my father in a suit and tie and double helpings of fresh cheesecake on a ninety-minute domestic flight. The thing was, getting on a plane was expensive. This will be lost on many people today, young people especially, but once upon a time, college kids didn't zip home for a few days over Christmas. You didn't grab a last minute seat for $99 and pop over to Las Vegas—or to Mallorca or Phuket—for a long weekend. Flying was a luxury, and people indulged sporadically, if at all. In 1939, aboard Pan Am's *Dixie Clipper*, it cost $750 to fly round-trip between New York and France. That's equal to well over $11,000 in today's money. In 1970, it cost the equivalent of $2,700 to fly from New York to Hawaii.

Things changed. Planes, for one, became more efficient. Aircraft like the 707 and the 747 made long-haul travel affordable to the masses. Then the effects of deregulation kicked in, changing forever the way airlines competed. Fares plummeted, and passengers poured in. Yes, flying became more aggravating and less comfortable. It also became affordable for almost everybody.

I have learned never to underestimate the contempt people hold for airlines and the degree to which they hate to fly. While some of this contempt is well deserved, much of it is unfair. Today a passenger can, in a backpack and flip-flops, traverse the oceans for the equivalent of a few pennies per mile, in near-perfect safety and with an 85 percent chance of arriving on time. Is that really such an awful way to travel? Meanwhile, if you're that insatiably eager to revisit those luxurious indulgences of aviation's golden years, well, you can do that too, by purchasing a first or business class ticket—for less than what it cost fifty years ago. ✈

1 PLANE TRUTH

Things about Wings and Why Knots

Elementary question: So how do these enormous airplanes, carrying tons of passengers and cargo, stay in the air to begin with?

Yes, this forms the kernel of every layperson's curiosity about airplanes. But while the idea of getting hundreds of thousands of pounds of machinery smoothly into the sky would seem a marvel, if not a miracle, how it all happens is surprisingly elementary and easy to demonstrate. Next time you're on the highway in your Toyota, hold your arm out the window, perpendicular to the car and parallel with the ground. Bend your hand upward slightly, biting into the airflow, and what happens? You've made a wing, and your arm "flies." And it will remain flying for as long as you keep your hand at an adequate angle, and keep driving at a fast-enough speed. It flies because the air is holding it up. With an airplane it's no different. Granted, you're not getting the Toyota off the ground, but now imagine your hand is really, really big, and the car has enough horsepower to go really, really fast. Becoming airborne is all about procuring the right surpluses among the four competing forces of flight: that is, enough thrust over drag, and enough lift over weight. Or as Orville Wright put it: "The airplane stays up because it doesn't have time to fall."

There's also something in flying 101 known as Bernoulli's Principle, named for Daniel Bernoulli, an eighteenth-century Swiss mathematician who never saw an airplane. When forced through a constriction or across a curved surface, a fluid will accelerate and its pressure will simultaneously decrease. Our fluid is air, which moves faster over the top of the wing, which is curved (less pressure), than it does along the flatter surface below (higher pressure). The result is an upward push; the wing floating, if you will, on a high-pressure cushion.

I'll be chided for a less-than-nuanced explanation, but truly that's the gist of it: Bernoulli's pressure differential, together with the simple, hands-out-the-window deflection of air molecules, provide the indispensable component of flight: lift.

Loss of lift is called a stall. Again, the basic idea is easily demonstrated back on the highway: tilt your hand a little too steeply, or brake the Toyota below a certain point, and your arm ceases to fly.

But one look at the details of a wing tells me there's more going on.

And there is. Your arm flies—heck, even a brick can be made to fly if you stick enough air under it—but it's not particularly *good* at it. The wings of a jetliner need to be very, very good at it. Wings achieve optimum economy during cruise flight. That occurs at high altitudes and just shy of the sound barrier for most jets. But they also need to be efficient at low altitudes and speeds. Getting all of this right is grist for the engineers and their wind tunnels. The lateral cross section of a wing, around which the air does its thing, is called an airfoil, and it's meticulously sculpted. Not only in profile, but also spanwise—the shape and thickness changing from front to back, and from root to tip, in accordance with the type of aerodynamic calculations neither you nor I could fully understand.

Wings are augmented with an array of supplemental components—namely flaps, slats, and spoilers. Flaps trail backward and downward, enhancing the airfoil's curvature for safe, stable flight at lower speeds. (Airliners take off and land with flaps extended, though exact settings will vary.) There are inboard and outboard subsets of flaps, which themselves can be segmented horizontally. Slats roll forward from a wing's forward edge and perform a similar function. Spoilers are

2

rectangular planks that spring from the wing's upper surface. A raised spoiler interrupts airflow across the wing, destroying lift while adding copious amounts of drag. In flight they are used to increase rates of descent; on touchdown they assist in deceleration.

I remember one of my first times on an airplane, in a window seat on a 727, just behind the wing, and how the entire wing seemed to disassemble itself during descent. Big, triple-slotted flaps came barreling down, the spoilers fluttering and waving, the slats dropping into position. Magically, almost, you could see right *through* the very center of the wing, like through the bones of some skeletonized animal, with houses and trees appearing where the sections had slid apart.

You've probably noticed that a jetliner's wings are angled rearward. When a wing cuts through the sky, molecules of air accelerate across its camber. As this acceleration reaches the speed of sound, a shock wave builds along the surface, potentially killing lift. Sweeping the wings backward induces a more agreeable, spanwise flow. On faster planes you'll find a sweep greater than 40 degrees; the slowest have almost no sweep at all. Angling the wings upward from the root, meanwhile, counteracts a lateral rolling and swerving tendency known as yaw. This tilt, most easily seen from a nose-on perspective, is called dihedral. The Soviets, ever the good contrarians, used to apply an opposite version called anhedral, canting their wings downward.

The wing is everything. A plane is built around its wings the way a car is built around a chassis or a bicycle around a frame. Great big wings produce great big amounts of lift—enough to get a max weight 747, at nearly a million pounds, off the ground once it hits about 170 knots.

What's a knot?

In his essay "A Supposedly Fun Thing I'll Never Do Again," David Foster Wallace is on a cruise ship, where he's repeatedly perplexed by mention of "knots," unable to figure out what they are. I figure he was bluffing. Wallace was a math whiz, and the answer is easy enough:

a knot, used both at sea and in the air, is a mile per hour. Except it's a nautical mile, not a statute one. Nautical miles are slightly longer (6,082 feet versus 5,280). Thus a hundred knots is slightly faster than a hundred miles per hour. Origins of the word itself go back to when lengths of knotted rope were tossed from a ship to figure distances. A nautical mile represents 1/60 of a degree of longitude along the equator. With 60 miles to each degree, we compute 360 degrees and 21,600 nautical miles of equatorial Earthly circumference.

Flaps and slats aside, I'm baffled by the other moving parts of a plane's exterior. I see panels that move up and down, ones on the tail that go side to side...

When a bird needs to maneuver, it does so by twisting its wings and tail, something pioneer aviators emulated by incorporating wing-bending in early aircraft. But airplanes today are made from aluminum and high-strength composites, not wood, fabric, or feathers. Operated hydraulically, electrically, and/or manually via cables, various move-able contrivances are fitted that help us climb, descend, and turn.

Atop the rear fuselage is the tail, or vertical stabilizer, which func-tions exactly as its presence suggests—by keeping the plane straight. Hinged to the tail's back edge is the rudder. The rudder complements but does not control turns; its function is chiefly one of stability, tem-pering a plane's side-to-side swerve, or yaw. Some rudders are divided into sections that move together or separately, depending on airspeed. Pilots move the rudder by means of foot pedals, though an apparatus known as a yaw damper does most of the work automatically.

Beneath the tail, or occasionally attached to it, are two small wings. These are the horizontal stabilizers, the moveable rear por-tions of which are called elevators. The elevators command a plane's nose-up/nose-down pitch, as directed by the forward or aft motion of the pilot's control column, or joystick.

Ailerons, located at the trailing edges of the wings, are responsible for turns. Pilots steer via the control wheel or stick, which directs the ailerons up or down. They are interconnected and apply opposing forces: when the aileron on the left goes up, the one on the right goes down. A raised aileron reduces lift on that side, dropping the respective wing, while a lowered one causes the reverse. The smallest twitch of an aileron provides a good deal of turn, so you won't always spot them moving. It might look as though a plane is banked without anything having budged, but in fact the ailerons have done their thing, if ever so slightly. Large planes have two ailerons per wing, inboard and outboard, working in pairs or independently, depending on speed. Ailerons are often linked to the aforementioned spoilers, which partially deploy to aid turning.

So as you can see, even a simple maneuver might require a whole choreography of moving parts. But before you picture a hapless pilot kicking his feet and grasping madly for levers, keep in mind that individual pieces are interconnected. A single input to the steering wheel or column will cause any combo of movements outside.

Adding to the confusion, rudders, elevators, and ailerons are equipped with smaller tabs that operate independently from the main surfaces. These "trim" tabs fine-tune the motions of pitch, roll, and yaw.

If you're still with me, and before committing this all to memory, you'll be thrilled to know there are idiosyncratic variants of almost everything just described. One plane I flew had spoilers used only after landing, others that assisted with turning, and others still for inflight deceleration. Certain Boeing models are equipped not only with conventional trailing-edge wing flaps, but also ones at the leading edge, as well as slats. The Concorde had no horizontal stabilizers, so it had no elevators. But it did have "elevons." We'll save those, along with "flaperons," for another time.

Many planes have those little upturned fins at the end of their wings. What are they for?

At a wing's tip, the higher pressure beneath the wing meets the lower pressure above it, sending out a turbulent discharge of air. Winglets, as they're affectionately called, help smooth this mixing, decreasing drag and, in turn, improving range and efficiency. Because planes have different aerodynamic fingerprints, winglets aren't always necessary or cost-effective. For instance, the 747-400 and A340 have them, while the 777 does not, even though it too is a long-range widebody. Because fuel economy wasn't always the priority that it is today, and because the advantages of winglets weren't fully understood until fairly recently, older models were designed without them. For these planes—a list that includes the 757 and 767—they are available as an option or retrofit. An airline considers whether the long-term fuel savings is worth the cost of installation, which can run millions per plane. It depends on the flying. In Japan, Boeing has sold a number of 747s, used specifically on high-capacity, short-range domestic routes, with winglets *removed*. Winglets provide minimal efficiency gain on shorter flights, and removing them means the plane is lighter and easier to maintain.

Aesthetics are a personal thing. I find winglets attractive on some jets, like the A340, and awkward on others, like the 767. You see them in different forms. Some are large and jaunty, while others are just a tweak. With a "blended winglet," the wing tapers gradually with no harsh angles. Planes like the 787 and Airbus A350 use a more integrated style, sometimes referred to as a "raked wingtip."

What are those long, canoe-shaped pods that jut from the underside of a wing?

They're just coverings—streamlining devices called fairings. While they help prevent the formation of high-speed shock waves, mostly their purpose is a nonessential one: smoothing the airflow around the flap extension mechanisms inside.

There was a case not long ago when a group of passengers became alarmed after noticing that one of these fairings was missing from their aircraft. They refused to fly because—as the media reported the incident—"a piece of the wing was missing." In reality, the fairing had been removed for repairs after being damaged by a catering truck. Flying without a fairing might entail a slight fuel-burn penalty, but the plane remains perfectly airworthy. (Whether any part is allowed to be missing, and what the penalty might be, is spelled out in the plane's Configuration Deviation List [*see page 54*].)

Can a jetliner fly aerobatically? Could a 747 perform a loop or fly upside down?

Any airplane can perform more or less any maneuver, theoretically, from loops to barrel rolls to a reverse inverted hammerhead Immelman. (During a demonstration flight in the late 1950s, a Boeing 707 was intentionally rolled upside down.) However, the ability to do so is mostly a function of excess thrust or horsepower, and commercial planes generally lack enough engine strength relative to their weight. In any case, it's not a good idea. Airliner components are not designed for aerobatics and could suffer damage—or worse. Plus, the cleaners would be up all night scrubbing out coffee stains and vomit.

Maybe that makes you wonder, how can *any* plane fly upside down given what I said earlier about a wing being curved on top and flat on the bottom, resulting in a pressure differential that produces lift? If you're flying upside down, wouldn't lift act in the opposite direction, forcing the plane toward the ground? It would, to an extent. But as we've already seen, a wing creates lift in *two* ways, and Bernoulli's pressure differential is the less critical. Simple deflection is a lot more important. All a pilot needs to do is hold the right angle, deflecting enough air molecules, and the negative lift from an upside-down airfoil is easily offset by the kiting effect.

You've written that your duty isn't to burden readers with jargon. "A discussion of how a jet engine works," you've said, "is guaranteed to be uninteresting." Well, if you don't mind, how *does* a jet engine work?

Picture the engine's anatomy as a back-to-back assembly of geared, rotating discs—compressors and turbines. Air is pulled in and directed through the spinning compressors. It's squeezed tightly, mixed with vaporized kerosene, and ignited. The combusted gases then come roaring out the back. Before they're expelled, a series of rotating turbines absorbs some of the energy. The turbines power the compressors and the large fan at the front of the nacelle.

Older engines derived almost all of their thrust directly from the hot exploding gases. On modern ones, that big forward fan does most of the work, and you can think of a jet as a kind of ducted fan, spun by a core of turbines and compressors. The most powerful motors made by Rolls-Royce, General Electric, and Pratt & Whitney generate in excess of 100,000 pounds of thrust. The thrust is tapped to supply the electrical, hydraulic, pressurization, and deicing systems. Hence, you'll often hear jet engines referred to as "powerplants."

What is a turboprop?

All modern, propeller-driven commercial airliners are powered by turboprops. A turboprop engine is, at heart, a jet. In this case, for better efficiency at lower altitudes and along shorter distances, the compressors and turbines drive a propeller instead of a fan. Loosely put, it's a jet-powered propeller. There are no pistons in a turboprop engine, and the "turbo" shouldn't elicit confusion with turbocharging in the style of an automobile, which is completely different. Turboprops are more reliable than piston engines and offer a more advantageous power-to-weight ratio.

Jets and turboprops run on jet fuel, which is basically refined kerosene—a permutation of the stuff in camping lanterns. It's manufactured in different grades, but the flavor used by airlines is called Jet-A. Televised fireballs notwithstanding, jet fuel is surprisingly stable and less combustible than you'd think, at least until atomization. You can stick a lit match into a puddle and it will not ignite. (Neither Patrick Smith nor the publisher shall be responsible for injuries or damage caused in connection to this statement.)

I notice a hole up under the tail that emits some kind of exhaust. What is this?

That's the APU (auxiliary power unit), a small jet engine used to supply electricity and air conditioning when the main engines aren't running, or to supplement them when they are. All modern airliners have an APU, and it is typically located in the rear fuselage under the tail. If you're boarding through the old style airstairs and notice a hissing, jet-like noise similar to the sound of ten thousand hairdryers, that's the APU.

It also provides high-pressure air for starting the main engines. The internal batteries on larger planes aren't powerful enough to initially rotate an engine's compressors. Instead they are spun by air plumbed from the APU. The first commercial jetliner with an APU as standard equipment was the Boeing 727, which debuted in 1964. Prior to that, an external air source, referred to as an "air cart" or "huffer," would be hooked into the plane's pneumatic ducting. You might see one of these carts today on occasions when a plane is dispatched with its APU inoperative, used to get the first engine going. The running engine then becomes the air source for the remaining engine(s).

Most turboprops are started electrically rather than pneumatically. If there's no APU and ship's batteries aren't sufficient, something called a GPU (ground power unit) provides the juice. Towed behind a small tractor, the GPU looks like one of those generators used at roadside construction sites.

If the APU is supplying ground power, then why do you often see the engines turning while a plane waits at the gate?

You don't. Planes almost never run their engines at the gate. What you see is the wind spinning the first stage fan. Even a moderate breeze can rotate that fan quite rapidly. If this seems impossible because a plane is cornered against a building or facing the wrong direction, that's because the wind is coming *from behind*. On newer engines, the majority of intake air is blown *around* the core of compressors and turbines, providing a clear shot at the fan blades from the rear.

So how much does an airliner cost exactly?

Would you believe $200 million for a single new Airbus A330 or Boeing 777? Or $70 million for a new 737? Even the little regional planes most of you can't stand are multimillion-dollar machines. A $20 million sticker price isn't out of the question for a high-end regional jet or turboprop (and you can remember that the next time you're walking up the stairs and cracking a joke about rubber bands). The price for secondhand aircraft differs markedly with age, upgrades, and upkeep. A lot depends on the engines, which alone can sell for millions apiece, and maintenance: how long before an overhaul is due, and what kind of overhaul? A used 737 can be had for $2 million or $20 million, depending.

Airlines do not own all, or sometimes even any, of their planes outright. They lease them from banks and leasing companies, making regular payments not unlike the way you'd finance a car. There would be no other way to afford them.

Is there a difference in the quality of Boeing aircraft versus Airbus? I get the impression Airbus planes are made more cheaply.

I hate this question, and it comes up all the time in slippery forms. Descriptions like "made more cheaply" belittle the complexity of an airliner, no matter the maker. No plane is cheaply made. Boeings and Airbuses are certainly different in many ways. They abide by different philosophies of construction and operation, and both have their own pleasant or annoying quirks. And occasional controversies: Airbus has been criticized for relying on control automation that, in certain circumstances, cannot be overridden by the pilot. Boeing, for its part, was dogged by rudder malfunctions that caused at least two fatal 737 crashes in the 1990s. Still, there is no statistical safety difference that merits citing, and opinions on which is the "better" plane get into the nuts and bolts of the systems—the kinds of details that'll have you (and me) yawning fast and that do *not* reveal themselves as bangs, moans, rattles, or anything else detectable by a passenger. For pilots, it comes down to personal preference and, in a way, style, more than quality or lack thereof. It's not unlike comparing Apple to PC; each has its fans and detractors.

Should I look for a specific plane to get me to my destination faster?

Speed at higher altitudes is indicated by something called Mach number. Mach is the speed of sound (Ernst Mach is your man), and Mach *number* is a percentage of that speed. Long-haul planes fly slightly faster than short-haul planes. A 747, A380, or 777 will fly between .84 and .88 Mach (84 to 88 percent of the speed of sound). For smaller jets like the 737 or A320, the range is between .74 and .80 Mach. On the 767 I fly, cruising speed is anywhere from .77 to .82 Mach. Optimum speed is different for every flight. If the plane is on time, or if fuel burn is a factor, we'll be planned at whatever Mach is most fuel-efficient. If we're running late, and so long as fuel isn't an issue, we'll probably go a little faster. The recommended Mach is given to us as part of the flight plan.

On a thirteen-hour journey between New York and Tokyo, these differences matter. A slight Mach advantage saves several minutes of flying time. But on shorter hauls it's negligible, and there's no point in choosing one plane over another for the sake of punctuality. In any case, ATC (air traffic control) constraints are the primary factor in determining speed, not aircraft capabilities. On short flights especially, controllers routinely ask pilots to speed up or slow down.

The border between subsonic and supersonic, near which most planes cruise, is not an aerodynamic triviality. In a poor man's version of Einstein's speed of light conundrum, required energy increases dramatically as you cross the sound barrier. Though not an outright obstacle of physics, it's a gigantic pain in the wallet. For supersonic flight, a completely different wing is required, and fuel use soars. Remember the Concorde? It wasn't the tragic crash near Paris in 2000 that hastened the plane's obsolescence so much as its ghastly operating costs. For these reasons, despite all the other technological advances we've seen, the cruising speeds of commercial jets have not really changed since their inception. If anything, the twenty-first century airliner travels slightly *slower* than its counterpart of thirty years ago.

Which planes have the longest range?

The Boeing 777-200LR has the longest duration of any commercial jetliner—some twenty hours' worth, allowing it to span 9,000 nautical miles and then some without refueling. Almost every major city pair on Earth is connectable with this astoundingly long-legged aircraft (*see longest flights, page 276*). Runner-up is the A340-500, first flown by Emirates and Singapore Airlines. Current variants of the A380, 777, and 747 have comparable but slightly lesser capabilities.

Understand that endurance, which is to say hours aloft, is the more accurate metric for measuring range, not miles, and this can vary with altitude, cruise speed, and other factors. Also, a plane's size isn't always a good indicator of how long (or far) it can fly. The old Airbus A300, probably the best example, was built specifically for short- to medium-haul markets even though it could accommodate 250 people. Meanwhile, there are nine-passenger executive jets that can stay aloft for eleven hours. Neither is it fair to say out of hand that one plane has greater reach than another. Does an Airbus A340 outdistance a Boeing 747? Some do, some don't. Technical options, such as engine types and auxiliary fuel tanks, help determine endurance. Watch the dashes. There's not just a single A340; there are the A340-200, -300, -500, and -600. At Boeing you'll discover -200s, -400s, -800s, -LRs (long range), -ERs (extended range), and so forth. And a larger suffix might not tell the whole story. An A340-500 is a smaller plane than the A340-600, but it has a longer range.

A 777-200LR outlasts the substantially larger 777-300ER. Still with me? If you enjoy graphs and charts abounding with asterisks and fine print, go to the manufacturers' websites and knock yourself out.

How much do planes weigh?

There are weight limits for the different operational regimes, including limits for taxiing, taking off, and landing. The Airbus A380's maximum takeoff weight exceeds one million pounds. A Boeing 747's weight can be as high as 875,000 pounds. For a 757, it might be 250,000 pounds, and for an A320 or 737, it's around 170,000. A fifty-passenger turboprop or regional jet will top out around 60,000. Those are maximums. The actual, allowable takeoff weight varies with weather, runway length, and other factors.

Passengers are not required to divulge the quantitative specs of their waistlines, obviously, so instead, airlines use standard approximations for people and luggage. The values—190 pounds per person (including carry-ons) and 30 pounds per checked bag—are adjusted slightly higher during winter to account for heavier clothing (please don't ask me about trans-climate routes). The boarding tallies are added to something called the BOW (basic operating weight), another fixed value that accounts for the plane itself, replete with all furnishings, supplies, and crew. Once fuel and cargo are added in, the result is the total gross "ramp" or taxi weight. Fuel used for taxiing is subtracted to reveal the takeoff weight.

This will probably surprise you, but in the case of a fully loaded 747, four hundred passengers and their suitcases—about 75,000 pounds together—make up only around 10 percent of the total bulk. Fuel, rather than people or their belongings, is the greater factor, sometimes accounting for a third or more of a plane's sum heft. Because of this, pilots calculate their kerosene in terms of pounds, not gallons. Everything from initial fueling to en route burn is added or subtracted by weight, not volume.

Both weight and its distribution are important. A plane's center of gravity, which shifts as fuel is consumed, is calculated prior to flight and must remain within limits for takeoff and landing. Pilots are trained in the particulars of weight and balance, but the grunt work is taken care of by the load-planners and dispatchers.

We were flying out of Phoenix one day, and the temperature topped 105 degrees. Several passengers were bumped. The airline told us it was too hot for the plane to fly fully loaded.

Hot air is less dense than cold, negatively affecting both lift and engine performance. The takeoff roll will be longer and the climb shallower, and in very hot temperatures, a plane may no longer meet the safety margins for a particular runway—climb gradient parameters and the distance needed to stop if takeoff is aborted. A maximum allowable weight is determined for every takeoff based on weather and runway length. Going a short distance with limited fuel is unlikely to be a problem, but full tanks or a heavy payload can put you up against the limits, and cargo or people will sometimes need to be bumped.

In addition, some planes have maximum operating temperatures stipulated in their manuals. At a certain threshold, aerodynamic penalties become excessive and components begin to overheat. These limits tend to be quite high, around 50 degrees C (122 degrees F), but every once in a while flights will be grounded outright.

As it works for temperature, it works for altitude. The higher you climb, the thinner the atmosphere, degrading aerodynamic efficiency and output of the engines. High-altitude airports often entail payload penalties for takeoff. Mexico City sits at 7,400 feet and is a great candidate, as are Denver, Bogota, Cuzco, and many others. For years, before the advent of higher performance planes, South African Airways' New York–Johannesburg flight could go nonstop only in one direction, and this was part of the reason. The eastbound leg from JFK took advantage of a long runway at sea level. On the return, Johannesburg's 5,500-foot elevation entailed a sanction. Topping off the tanks meant having to leave people or freight behind, so the flight would call for fuel in the Cape Verde Islands or Dakar.

Once aloft, a flight may initially be too heavy to reach the most fuel-efficient altitude and will "step climb" its way as fuel is burned off. How high you can fly at any given time is predicated not only on the physical ability to reach an altitude, but also on maintaining applicable stall margins once it gets there.

Why do some planes leave those white trails in the sky?

Contrails are formed when humid jet exhaust condenses into ice crystals in the cold, dry, upper-level air—it's not unlike the fog that results when you exhale on a cold day. Contrails are clouds, you could say. Water vapor, strange as it might sound, is a byproduct of the combustion within jet engines, which is where the humidity comes from. Whether a contrail forms is contingent on altitude and the ambient atmospheric makeup—mainly temperature and something known as vapor pressure.

I refuse to devote valuable page space to the so-called "chemtrail" conspiracy theory. If you know what I'm talking about and wish to argue the matter, feel free to email. If you don't know what I'm talking about, don't worry about it.

Much is being made of air travel's impact on the environment, particularly with respect to emissions. Is it possible to reconcile frequent flying with a pro-planet consciousness?

This is a tough one for me. I'm probably greener than most people, abiding best I can by the three Rs of good stewardship: reduce, reuse, recycle. I don't own a car, and much of the furniture in my apartment was scavenged from curbsides and refurbished by hand. I've replaced my incandescent light bulbs with compact fluorescents. Then I go to work and expel hundreds of tons of carbon into the atmosphere. Am I a hypocrite or what?

Commercial aviation is under increasingly virulent attack for its perceived eco-unfriendliness. In Europe especially, powerful voices have been lobbying for the curtailment of air travel, proposing heavy taxes and other disincentives to restrict airline growth and discourage people from flying. ("Binge flyers" is the derogatory nickname for Europeans who take advantage of ultra-cheap airfares to indulge in short-stay leisure junkets.) How much of this outcry is fair and how much is gratuitous airline-bashing is debatable. Airlines are easy targets these days, but in the hierarchy of environmental threats, they are perhaps disproportionately villainized.

I'm the first to agree that airlines ought to be held accountable for their fair share of ecological impact, but that's the thing: globally, commercial aviation accounts for only about *2 percent* of all fossil fuel emissions. Commercial buildings, for one, emit a far higher percentage of climate-changing pollutants than commercial planes, yet there is little protest and few organized movements to green them up. It's similar with cars. Americans have staggeringly gluttonous driving habits, yet rarely are we made to feel guilty about them. U.S. airlines have increased fuel efficiency 70 percent over the past thirty years, 35 percent since 2001 alone, mostly through the retirement of fuel-thirsty aircraft. Average fuel efficiency of the American automobile, on the other hand, has stayed stagnant for at least three decades.

The sticking point, though, is that the true measure of aviation's environmental impact goes beyond simple percentages. For one thing, aircraft exhaust—containing not only carbon dioxide, but also nitrogen oxides, soot, and sulfate particles—is injected directly into the upper troposphere, where its effects aren't fully understood. Separately, experts contend that the presence of those aforementioned contrails propagates the development of cirrus clouds. Clouds breed clouds, you could say, and cirrus cover has increased by 20 percent in certain traffic corridors, which in turn influences temperature and precipitation. As a rule of thumb, experts recommend multiplying that previously cited 2 percent fossil fuel figure by another 2½ to get a more accurate total of the industry's greenhouse contributions. Using this formula, airlines now account for about 5 percent of the problem.

That's still not much, but civil aviation is growing rapidly around the world. China alone is planning to construct over forty large airports. In the United States, the number of annual passengers, already hovering at a billion, is anticipated to double by 2025, at which point greenhouse gases from planes would rise to as much as five times current levels. If indeed we begin reducing the carbon output from other sources, as we keep promising to, the output from aviation will rise drastically as a percentage of the whole.

The reason for all of this growth is that hopping on a plane is relatively cheap and easy. That may change. Air travel will always be an economic necessity, but the kinds of flying we've become used to might not always be possible should petroleum prices climb drastically, as many predict they will. We'll still have airplanes, but the binge flyers will be long gone in the face of higher fares.

Several carriers are experimenting with biofuel alternatives to jet fuel. Air Canada, Qantas, United, and All Nippon Airways are among those that have operated revenue flights powered completely or partly by biofuel. In the meantime, many airlines allow passengers to purchase inexpensive carbon offsets when booking online. Or, for a small fee, there are third-party organizations that will offset the estimated CO_2 of your journey, investing the money in sustainable energy projects.

Now forget emissions for a minute and let's talk about other kinds of pollution:

One thing that always shocks me is the amount of material waste—namely plastics, paper, Styrofoam, and aluminum—thrown away by airlines and their customers. Take the number of trays, cups, soda cans, snack wrappers, and discarded reading material produced during the average flight, and multiply it by the forty thousand or so daily commercial departures around the world.

Simple measures would go a long way toward reducing and reusing. For instance, why not offer passengers the option of receiving a cup with their beverage? My can of soft drink or juice *always* comes with a cup, dropped onto my tray before I have a chance to say no, even though it would be perfectly acceptable to drink from the container. And the packaging of airline food (what still exists of it) is nothing if not extravagantly wasteful. The typical inflight meal or snack consists of more petroleum-derived plastic than actual food.

Not all airlines ignore the waste problem. Virgin Atlantic's onboard recycling program asks passengers to hand in glass bottles and cans and leave newspapers on their seats to enable recycling. At American Airlines, cans are recycled, with the money going to charity, and trash from domestic flights is separated and recycled after landing. Delta recycles all aluminum, plastic, and paper products from flights into its Atlanta megahub, with proceeds going to Habitat for Humanity. But while a few carriers are stepping forward, the industry-wide effort has, for the most part, been pretty halfhearted.

The Airplane in Art, Music, and Film

Air travel is such a visual thing. Take a look sometime at the famous photograph of the Wright Brothers' first flight in 1903. The image, captured by bystander John T. Daniels and since reproduced millions of times, is about the most beautiful photograph in all of twentieth-century iconography. Daniels had been put in charge of a cloth-draped 5 x 7 glass plate camera stuck into Outer Banks sand by Orville Wright. He was instructed to squeeze the shutter bulb if "anything interesting" happened. The camera was aimed at the space of sky—if a dozen feet of altitude can be called such—where, if things went right, the Wrights' plane, the *Flyer*, would emerge in its first moments aloft.

Things did go right. The contraption rose into view, and Daniels squeezed the bulb. We see Orville, visible as a black slab, more at the mercy of the plane than controlling it. Beneath him, Wilbur keeps pace, as if to capture or tame the strange machine should it decide to flail or aim for the ground. You cannot see their faces; much of the photo's beauty lies in not needing to. It is, at once, the most richly promising and bottomlessly lonely image. All the potential of flight is encapsulated in that shutter snap; yet we see, at heart, two eager brothers in a seemingly empty world, one flying, the other watching. We see centuries of imagination— the ageless desire to fly—in a desolate, almost completely anonymous fruition.

I own a lot of airplane books. Aviation publishing is, let's just say, on a lower aesthetic par than what you'll find elsewhere on the arts and sciences shelves. The books are loaded with glam shots: sexily angled pictures of landing gear, wings, and tails. You see this with cars and motorcycles and guns too—the sexualization of mechanical objects. It's cheap and it's easy, and it misses the point. And unfortunately, for now, respect for aircraft has been unable to rise above this kind of adolescent fetishizing.

What aviation needs, I think, is some crossover cred. The Concorde and the 747, with their erudite melding of left- and right-brain sensibilities, have taken it close. Still, you won't find framed lithographs of 747s in the lofts of SoHo or the brownstones of Boston, hanging alongside romanticized images of the Chrysler Building and the Brooklyn Bridge. And I may not feel vindicated until commercial aviation gets its own ten-part, sepia-toned Ken Burns documentary.

Until then, when it comes to popular culture, movies are the place we look first. One might parallel the 1950s dawn of the Jet Age with the realized potential of Hollywood— the turbine and Cinemascope as archetypal tools of promise. Decades later, there's still a cordial symbiosis at work: a lot of movies are shown on airplanes, and airplanes are shown in a lot of movies. The crash plot is the easy and obvious device, and more than thirty years later, we're still laughing at Leslie Nielsen's lines from the movie *Airplane*. But I've never been fond of movies *about airplanes*. For most of us, airplanes are a means to an end, and often enough, the vessels of whatever exciting, ruinous, or otherwise life-changing journeys we embark on. And it's the furtive, incidental glimpses that best capture this—far more evocatively than any blockbuster disaster script: the propeller plane dropping the spy in some godforsaken battle zone or taking the ambassador and his family away from one; the beauty of the B-52's tail snared along the riverbank in *Apocalypse Now*; the Air Afrique ticket booklet in the hands of a young Jack Nicholson in *The Passenger*; the Polish Tupolevs roaring in the background of Krzysztof Kieslowski's *The Decalogue IV*.

Switching to music, I think of a United Airlines TV ad that ran briefly in the mid-1990s—a plug for their new Latin American destinations. The commercial starred a parrot, which proceeded to peck out several seconds of George Gershwin's "Rhapsody in Blue" on a piano. "Rhapsody" has remained United's advertising music and makes a stirring accompaniment to the shot of a 777 set against the sky.

We shouldn't forget the late Joe Strummer's reference to the Douglas DC-10 in the Clash's "Spanish Bombs," but it's the Boeing family that's the more musically inclined. I can think of at least four songs mentioning 747s (Nick Lowe's "So It Goes" being my favorite).

Somehow, the Airbus brand doesn't lend itself lyrically, though Kinito Mendez, a merengue songwriter, paid a sadly foreboding tribute to the Airbus A300 with "El Avion" in 1996. "How joyful it could be to go on flight 587," sings Mendez, immortalizing American Airlines's popular morning nonstop between New York and Santo Domingo. In November 2001, the flight crashed after takeoff from Kennedy airport, killing 265 people.

My formative years, musically speaking, hail from the underground rock scene, covering a span from about 1981 through 1986. This might not seem a particularly rich genre from which to mine out links to flight, but the task proves easier than you'd expect. "Airplanes are fallin' out of the sky..." sings Grant Hart on a song from Hüsker Dü's 1984 masterpiece *Zen Arcade*, and three albums later, his colleague Bob Mould shouts of a man "sucked out of the first class window!" Then we've got cover art. The back side of Hüsker Dü's *Land Speed Record* shows a Douglas DC-8. On the front cover of the English Beat's 1982 album, *Special Beat Service*, band members walk beneath the wing of British Airways VC-10 (that's the Vickers VC-10, a '60s-era jet conspicuous for having four aft-mounted engines). The Beastie Boys' 1986 album *Licensed to Ill* depicts an airbrushed ex-American Airlines 727.

The *Columbia Granger's Index to Poetry* registers no fewer than twenty entries under "airplanes," fourteen more for "air travel," and at least another five under "airports," including poems by Frost and Sandburg. John Updike's *Americana and Other Poems* was reviewed by *Kirkus* as "a rambling paean for airports and big American beauty." Subjecting readers to my own aeropoems is probably a bad idea, though I confess to have written a few, which you're free to Google at your peril. Maybe it was the cockpit checklists that inspired me, free-verse masterpieces that they are:

Stabilizer trim override, normal
APU generator switch, off
Isolation valve, closed
Autobrakes…maximum!

2 ELEMENTS OF UNEASE

Turbulence, Windshear, Weather, and Worry

HIGH ART: HISTORY, HYPE, AND THE WORLD'S BIGGEST PLANES

In the mid-1960s, aerodynamicists at Boeing faced a momentous task. Their assignment: to build the largest commercial jetliner ever conceived—one that would feature twice the tonnage and capacity of any existing plane—and make it pretty. Where to begin?

Well, specifically, you begin in the front and in the back. "Most architects who design skyscrapers focus on two aesthetic problems," explains the architecture critic Paul Goldberger in an issue of *The New Yorker*. "How to meet the ground and how to meet the sky—the top and the bottom, in other words." Thinking of a jetliner as a horizontal skyscraper, we see that its beauty is gained or lost chiefly through the sculpting of the nose and tail. The engineers at Boeing understood Goldberger's point exactly, and the airplane they came up with, the iconic 747, is an aesthetic equal of the grandest Manhattan skyscraper.

It's perhaps telling that today, strictly from memory, with only the aid of a pencil and a lifetime of watching airplanes, I am able to sketch the fore and aft sections of the 747 with surprising ease and accuracy. This is not a testament to my drawing skills, believe me. Rather, it's a natural demonstration of the elegant, almost organic flow of the jet's profile.

The tail rises to greater than 60 feet. Though it's essentially a six-story aluminum billboard, there's something sexy in the fin's cant, like the angled foresail of a schooner. Up front, it's hard to look at a 747 without focusing on the plane's most recognizable feature—its second-story penthouse deck. The 747 is often—and unfairly—described as "bubble-topped" or "humpbacked." In truth, the upper-deck annex is smoothly integral to the fuselage, tapering forward to a stately and assertive prow. The plane looks less like an airliner than it does an ocean liner in the classic *QE2* mold. There is something poetic and proud even in the name itself—the rakish tilt of the 7s and the lyrical, palindromic ring: seven-forty-seven.

The 747 was built for a market—high capacity, long haul—that technically didn't exist yet. By the end of the 1960s, no shortage of people craved the opportunity to travel nonstop over great distances, but no plane was big enough, or had enough range, to make it afford-able. Boeing's 707, a kind of 747 in miniature, had ushered in the Jet Age several years earlier, but its economies of scale were limited. Juan Trippe, the visionary leader of Pan Am who'd been at the vanguard of the 707 project, persuaded Boeing that not only was an airplane with twice the 707's capacity possible—it was a revolution waiting to happen.

He was right, even if vindication didn't come easy. Boeing took a chance and built Trippe his superjet, nearly bankrupting itself in the process. Early-on engine problems were a costly embarrassment, and sales were alarmingly slow at the outset. But on January 21, 1970, Pan Am's *Clipper Victor* (*see Tenerife story, page 229*) made the maiden voyage on the New York–London milk run, and the dynamics of global air travel were changed forever. It's not a stretch to consider the advent of the 747 as the most crucial turning point in the history of civil aviation. For the first time, millions of flyers were able to cover tremendous distances at great speed—at affordable fares. Fast-forward forty years, and the 747 is one of the bestselling airliners of all time. Of all passenger jets still in production, only its little brother, the 737, has sold more copies.

In the second grade, my two favorite toys were both 747s. The first was an inflatable replica, similar to those novelty balloons you buy at parades, with rubbery wings that drooped in such violation of the real thing that I taped them into proper position. To a seven-year-old, the toy seemed enormous, like my own personal Macy's float. The second was a plastic model about 12 inches long. Like the balloon, it was decked out in the livery of Pan Am. One side of the fuselage was made of clear polystyrene, through which the entire interior, row by row, could be viewed. I can still picture exactly the blue and red pastels of the tiny chairs.

Modeled in perfect miniature near the toy plane's nose was a blue spiral staircase. Early version 747s were outfitted with a set of spiral stairs connecting the main and upper decks. It gave the entranceway the look and feel of a lobby, like the grand vestibule of a cruise ship. In 1982, on my inaugural trip on a real 747, I beamed at my first glimpse of that winding column. Those stairs are in my blood—a genetic helix spinning upward to a kind of pilot Nirvana. (Alas, later-variant 747s adopted a traditional, ladder-style staircase.)

In the 1990s, Boeing ran a magazine advertisement for its 747. The ad was a two-pager, with a nose-on silhouette of the plane against a dusky sunset. *"Where/does this/take you?"* asked Boeing in staggered script across the centerfold. Below this dreamy triptych the text read: "A stone monastery in the shadow of a Himalayan peak. A cluster of tents on the sweep of the Serengeti plains. The Boeing 747 was made for places like these. Distant places filled with adventure, romance, and discovery." I so related to this syrupy bit of PR that I clipped it from the magazine and kept it in a folder. Whenever it seemed my career was going nowhere (which was all the time), I'd pull out the ad and look at it.

The nature and travel writer Barry Lopez once authored an essay in which, from inside the hull of an empty 747 freighter, he compares the aircraft to the quintessential symbol of another era—the Gothic cathedral of twelfth-century Europe. "Standing on the main deck," Lopez writes, "where 'nave' meets 'transept,' and looking up toward the pilots' 'chancel.' ... The machine was magnificent, beautiful, complex as an insoluble murmur of quadratic equations."

No other airplane could arouse a comparison like that. The 747 is arguably the most impressive and inspirational work of art—call it industrial art, if you must—ever produced by commercial aviation.

☆ ☆ ☆

On the other side of the Atlantic, however, designers seem to be thinking in different directions. "Air does not yield to style" is a refrain attributed some years ago to an engineer at Airbus, the European collective that is Boeing's main competitor. Right or wrong, he was addressing the fact that modern aircraft designs have become so bland and uninspired as to be nearly indistinguishable from one another. In addition to the 747, Jet Age romantics recall the provocative curves of the Caravelle, the urbane superiority of Concorde, the gothic confidence of the 727. Planes don't look like this anymore. They're a lot less distinctive. And this, we're told, is because in the name of efficiency and economy, they *have* to be.

But is this really the case, or is Airbus being lazy? The 747 is one of several good-looking planes to emerge from Boeing since the 1970s, yet Airbus has given us only one true head-turner—its long-range A340. It has produced a line of aircraft at once technologically exquisite and visually banal. At best, Airbus's philosophy seems centered around a belief that not enough people think air travel is boring. (It's a peculiar cultural juxtaposition—the Americans elite and tasteful, trumping those boorish Europeans. Who knew?)

I was once standing in an airport boarding lounge when a group of young women, seated near a window, began giggling as a small jetliner passed by the window. "Check out that goofy plane," said one of them. It was an Airbus A319, which you have to admit looks vaguely, well, dwarfish—as if it popped from an Airbus vending machine or hatched from an egg.

Bad enough, but the pinnacle of aesthetic disregard was achieved upon rollout of Airbus's biggest and most ballyhooed creation: the enormous, double-decked A380. With a maximum takeoff weight of more than a million pounds, the Airbus A380 is the largest, most powerful, and most expensive commercial plane in history.

And possibly the ugliest. There is something grotesquely anthropomorphic about the front of the A380, its abruptly pitched forehead calling to mind a steroidal beluga. The rest of the plane is bloated, swollen, and graceless. It's big for big's sake, yet at the same time conveys an undignified squatness, as if embarrassed by its own girth. It is the most self-conscious-looking airliner I've ever seen.

And is it really *that* big? When the 747 debuted in 1970, it was more than double the size and weight of its closest competitor. The Airbus A380 weighs in at only about 30 percent heavier than a 747. Meanwhile, its well-publicized capacity limits of eight-hundred-plus passengers is likely to be seen only in rare, high-density configurations. With airlines concentrating on first- and business-cabin amenities, most A380s are set up for about five hundred riders—slightly more than most 747s. The A380 is big; revolutionary it's not.

Though you wouldn't know it listening to the media. The puffery got going in spring 2005, when the A380 took to the air for its maiden test flight. "The most anticipated flight since Concorde leapt from the pavement in 1969," cried one news report. "Straight into the history books," said another of the "gargantuan double-decked superjumbo." Oh, the humanity. Over on the Airbus website, they were channeling Neil Armstrong, inviting visitors to listen to the "first words of chief test pilot Jacques Rosay."

☆ ☆ ☆

And what of the future? While the A380 was being doused with champagne and hyperbole, the 747 was flying into its fourth decade of operation. The bulbous new 'Bus wasn't much to look at, but it was loaded with high-tech gadgetry and the lowest seat mile operating costs ever seen. The 747's last substantial redesign had been in 1989, and for all its history, it was rapidly approaching obsolescence. Would the A380 soon be the only true jumbo jet?

Finally, in November 2005, as if the ghost of Juan Trippe himself (he died in 1981) had drifted down for a pep talk, Boeing made the move it should have made sooner, announcing that it would, after several false starts, go ahead and produce an advanced 747, designated the 747-8. (The nomenclature is a departure from Boeing's usual ordered suffixing of -100, -200, -300, etc., but a wily overture to Asia, where the bulk of sales were expected and where the number eight is considered fortunate.) The plane entered service in early 2012. The freighter version, introduced by Luxembourg-based Cargolux, was first. Lufthansa debuted the passenger variant later in the year.

The passenger 747-8 has a fuselage stretch of 12 feet and room for about thirty-five additional seats. Those are minor enlargements, but extra seating is secondary. Boeing's real mission was to upgrade the plane's internal architecture to cutting-edge standards, drawing from advancements already in place on the 777 and 787. Airlines can bank on a 12 percent fuel efficiency advantage and an eye-popping 22 percent trip cost advantage over the Airbus.

The big question, though, is whether there is room out there for *two* jumbo jets. It remains to be seen whether the 747 and A380 can coexist in an industry in which long-haul markets have steadily fragmented, trending toward smaller planes, not bigger ones. The need for an ultra-high-capacity aircraft is still out there, but not in the numbers of times past.

One way that Boeing has hedged its bets is by showcasing a freighter option right from the start. Cargo variants typically arrive later, not first. The 747's well-established history as an outstanding cargo-hauler ensures a certain sales buffer, should the passenger model stumble. And if the whole thing flops? Boeing has put up about $4 billion for the 747-8, with most of the R&D borrowed from prior, already-funded projects. Airbus spent three times that amount concocting the A380 from scratch.

But in my opinion, the best thing about the new 747 is the obvious one: the way it looks. Prominent tweaks include a futuristically raked wing, an extended upper deck, and scalloped engine nacelles that cover the engine and reduce noise, but from every angle, it remains true to the original profile. If anything, it's prettier.

As a kid, watching a whole generation of planes go ugly in front of me, I often wondered: why can't somebody take a classic airliner, apply some aerodynamic nip and tuck, imbue it with the latest technology, and give it new life? Not as a retro novelty project, but as a viable, profitable airliner. The 747-8 *is* that plane. Boeing's back-to-the-future gamble may or may not make a profit, but either way it's still pretty slick.

Over in Toulouse, Airbus swears that its A380 is no white elephant. And how can we not agree? Look at that forehead again; that's not doing justice to the grace of elephants. Does air yield to style? Maybe that's the wrong question, for obviously it yields to a little imagination and effort.

☆ ☆ ☆

Epilogue: It was a friend of mine, not me, who became the first pilot I knew to fly a 747, setting off for Shanghai and Sydney while I flew to Hartford and Harrisburg. The closest I've gotten is the occasional upstairs seating assignment. The upper deck is a cozy room with an arched ceiling like the inside of a miniature hangar. I'll recline up there, basking in the self-satisfaction of having made it, at least one way, up the spiral stairs.

I had an upper-deck seat to Nairobi once on British Airways. Prior to pushback I wandered into the cockpit unannounced, to have a look, thinking the guys might be interested to learn they had another pilot on board. They weren't. I'd interrupted their checklist, and they asked me to go away and slammed the door. "Yes, we do mind," said the second officer in a voice exactly like Graham Chapman's.

What Plane Is That? An Airfleets Primer

Almost every jetliner sold in the world today comes from one of two camps: the storied Boeing Company, founded in Seattle in 1916, or the much younger Airbus consortium of Europe. It wasn't always this way. For years we had McDonnell Douglas, Lockheed, and various throw-ins from North America and abroad: Convair, British Aerospace, Fokker. All those companies are gone now.

And we shan't neglect the Russians. Things are quieter now, but the Soviet design bureaus of Antonov, Ilyushin, and Tupolev assembled tens of thousands of aircraft over the decades. While the bulk of these were Western knockoffs turned Cold War pumpkins, hundreds remain in service, and a handful of newer prototypes have been introduced.

America's first jet was the Boeing 707, third in commercial service behind England's star-crossed Comet and the Soviet Tu-104. The 707 debuted between Idlewild and Orly (that's New York and Paris) with Pan Am in 1959. Boeing has since given us the 727 through 787. The number sequencing is merely chronology and has nothing to do with size. There also was a kind of short-bodied 707 called a 720. The 717 designation (see below), was reserved for a military version of the 707 but never used in that capacity.

The original Airbus product, the A300, didn't debut until 1974. Subsequent models range from small twins like the A320 to long-ranging widebodies like the A330 and A340. The numbers follow a pattern similar to Boeing's, but they jumped a few and haven't kept as firm with the chronology. The A350, for example, is still under development, while the A380 has been flying since 2007. The A360 and A370 were skipped entirely; who knows why?

Minor variations of the Airbus numbering system are enough to drive a plane-spotter mad. The A300-600 is really just an extended A310. An A319 is nothing more (or less) than a smaller A320. It was shortened even further as the A318, then stretched again into an A321. This mishmash of numbers, in this traditionalist's opinion, cheapens everything. That each model wasn't simply given a "dash" suffix is irritating. On our side of the ocean, a 737-900 is still a 737.

But then, when Boeing bought McDonnell Douglas and took over that company's production lines, it took the MD-95, which was really just a souped-up MD-90, which was really just a souped-up MD-80, which was really just a souped-up DC-9, and rechristened it the Boeing 717. The DC-9, first flown in 1965, was now brand new, as it were, as the 717. That just isn't right. McDonnell Douglas, for its part, had previously abandoned its popular DC prefix and switched to MD, scrambling up the digits for good measure. Everyone's heard of a DC-9, but what the heck is an MD-80, MD-83, or MD-88? Answer: a modernized DC-9. Everyone's heard of the DC-10, but what's an MD-11? Answer: a modernized DC-10.

A lot of older planes carried non-numerical designations. Names, in other words. Most were good choices, understated and dignified: Constellation, Trident, Vanguard—and most memorably, Concorde. There was something so wonderfully evocative about the sound of that word: Concorde. It described the plane perfectly: sleek, fast, stylish, a little bit haughty and probably out of your league. Others used names in conjunction with numbers, like Lockheed's L-1011 TriStar. There was also the British Aerospace One-Eleven, which in its proper spelled-out form was both a name *and* a number.

The 787 falls in the name-number combo category, though I'm not especially fond of the "Dreamliner" designation. Somehow the imagery there is a little too wobbly and ethereal. People don't want their planes nodding off. It could have been worse, though. Back in 2003, before Boeing had settled on a name, Dreamliner was in contention with three other possibilities. They were: Global Cruiser, Stratoclimber, and eLiner. Global Cruiser sounds like a yacht or a really big SUV. Stratoclimber sounds like an action hero, and eLiner is almost too awful to contemplate—sort of like "iPlane."

Regional jets—RJs as they're known—come primarily from Canada's Bombardier and Embraer of Brazil. China, Russia, and Japan have recently entered the field. Oddly, for all of their prowess in the big-plane market, American manufacturers have never developed an RJ. Older regional planes, including several turboprop models, have been exported from Canada (de Havilland), Sweden (Saab), Holland (Fokker), the UK (British Aerospace), Germany (Dornier), Spain (CASA), and Indonesia (IPTN). Even the Czechs (LET) manufactured a popular seventeen-seater.

Turbulence scares me to death. Do I have reason to be afraid?

Turbulence: spiller of coffee, jostler of luggage, filler of barf bags, rattler of nerves. But is it a crasher of planes? Judging by the reactions of many airline passengers, one would assume so; turbulence is far and away the number-one concern of anxious passengers. Intuitively, this makes sense. Everybody who steps on a plane is uneasy on some level, and there's no more poignant reminder of flying's innate precariousness than a good walloping at 37,000 feet. It's easy to picture the airplane as a helpless dinghy in a stormy sea. Boats are occasionally swamped, capsized, or dashed into reefs by swells, so the same must hold true for airplanes. Everything about it seems dangerous.

Except that, in all but the rarest circumstances, it's not. For all intents and purposes, a plane cannot be flipped upside-down, thrown into a tailspin, or otherwise flung from the sky by even the mightiest gust or air pocket. Conditions might be annoying and uncomfortable, but the plane is not going to crash. Turbulence is an aggravating nuisance for everybody, including the crew, but it's also, for lack of a better term, normal. From a pilot's perspective it is ordinarily seen as a convenience issue, not a safety issue. When a flight changes altitude in search of smoother conditions, this is by and large in the interest of comfort. The pilots aren't worried about the wings falling off; they're trying to keep their customers relaxed and everybody's coffee where it belongs. Planes themselves are engineered to take a remarkable amount of punishment, and they have to meet stress limits for both positive and negative G-loads. The level of turbulence required to dislodge an engine or bend a wing spar is something even the most frequent flyer—or pilot for that matter—won't experience in a lifetime of traveling.

Altitude, bank, and pitch will change only slightly during turbulence—in the cockpit we see just a twitch on the altimeter—and inherent in the design of airliners is a trait known to pilots as "positive stability." Should the aircraft be shoved from its position in space, its nature is to return there, on its own. I remember one night, headed to Europe, hitting some unusually rough air about halfway across the Atlantic. It was the kind of turbulence people tell their friends about. It came out of nowhere and lasted several minutes, and was bad enough to knock over carts in the galleys. During the worst of it, to the sound of crashing plates, I recalled an email. A reader had asked me about the displacement of altitude during times like this. How many feet is the plane actually moving up or down, and side to side? I kept a close watch on the altimeter. Fewer than forty feet, either way, is what I saw. Ten or twenty feet, if that, most of the time. Any change in heading—that is, the direction our nose was pointed—was all but undetectable. I imagine some passengers saw it differently, overestimating the roughness by orders of magnitude. "We dropped like 3,000 feet in two seconds!"

At times like this, pilots will slow to a designated "turbulence penetration speed" to ensure high-speed buffet protection (don't ask) and prevent damage to the airframe. This speed is close to normal cruising speed, however, so you probably won't notice the deceleration from your seat. We can also request higher or lower altitudes or ask for a revised routing. You're liable to imagine the pilots in a sweaty lather: the captain barking orders, hands tight on the wheel as the ship lists from one side to another. Nothing could be further from the truth. The crew is not wrestling with the beast so much as merely riding things out. Indeed, one of the worst things a pilot could do during strong turbulence is try to fight it. Some autopilots have a special mode for these situations. Rather than increasing the number of corrective inputs, it does the opposite, desensitizing the system.

Up front, you can imagine a conversation going like this:

Pilot 1: "Well, why don't we slow it down?" [*dials a reduced Mach value into the speed control selector*]

Pilot 2: "Ah, man, this is spilling my orange juice all down inside this cup holder."

Pilot 1: "Let's see if we can get any new reports from those guys up ahead." [*reaches for the microphone and double-checks the frequency*]

Pilot 2: "Do you have any napkins over there?"

There will also be an announcement made to the passengers and a call to the cabin crew to make sure they are belted in. Pilots often request that flight attendants remain in their seats if things look menacing up ahead.

Predicting the where, when, and how much of turbulence is more of an art than a science. We take our cues from weather charts, radar returns, and, most useful of all, real-time reports from other aircraft. Some meteorological indicators are more reliable than others. For example, those burbling, cotton-ball cumulus clouds—particularly the anvil-topped variety that occur in conjunction with thunderstorms—are always a lumpy encounter. Flights over mountain ranges and through certain frontal boundaries will also get the cabin bells dinging, as will transiting a jet stream boundary. But every now and then it's totally unforeseen. When we hit those bumps on the way to Europe that night, what info we had told us not to expect anything worse than mild chop. Later, in an area where stronger turbulence had been forecast, it was perfectly smooth. You just don't know.

When we pass on reports to other crews, turbulence is graded from "light" to "extreme." The worst encounters entail a postflight inspection by maintenance staff. There are definitions for each degree, but in practice the grades are awarded subjectively.

I've never been through an extreme, but I've had my share of moderates and a sprinkling of severes.

One of those severes took place in July 1992, when I was captain on a fifteen-passenger turboprop. It was, of all flights, a twenty-five-minute run from Boston to Portland, Maine. It had been a hot day, and by early evening, a forest of tightly packed cumulus towers stretched across eastern New England. The formations were short—about 8,000 feet at the tops, and deceptively pretty to look at. As the sun fell, it became one of the most picturesque skyscapes I've ever seen, with buildups in every direction forming a horizon-wide garden of pink coral columns. They were beautiful and, it turned out, quite violent—little volcanoes spewing out invisible updrafts. The pummeling came on with a vengeance until it felt like being stuck in an upside-down avalanche. Even with my shoulder harness pulled snug, I remember holding up a hand to brace myself, afraid my head might hit the ceiling. Minutes later, we landed safely in Portland. No damage, no injuries.

So that I'm not accused of sugarcoating, I concede that powerful turbulence has, on occasion, resulted in damage to aircraft and injury to their occupants. With respect to the latter, these are typically people who fell or were thrown about because they weren't belted in. About sixty people, two-thirds of them flight attendants, are injured by turbulence annually in the United States. That works out to about twenty passengers. Twenty out of the 800 million or so who fly each year in this country.

Anecdotal evidence suggests that turbulence is becoming more prevalent as a byproduct of climate change. Turbulence is a symptom of the weather from which it spawns, and it stands to reason that as global warming intensifies certain patterns, experiences like the one I had over Maine will become more common.

Because turbulence is so unpredictable, I am known to provide annoying, noncommittal answers when asked how best to avoid it.

"Is it better to fly at night than during the day?" Sometimes.

"Should I avoid routes that traverse the Rockies or the Alps?" Hard to say.

"Are small planes more susceptible than larger ones?" It depends.

"They're calling for gusty winds tomorrow. Will it be rough?" Probably, but who knows.

"Where should I sit, in the front of the plane or in the back?"

Ah, now that one I can work with.

While it doesn't make a whole lot of difference, the smoothest place to sit is over the wings, nearest to the plane's centers of lift and gravity. The roughest spot is usually the far aft—the rearmost rows closest to the tail.

As many travelers already know, flight crews in the United States tend to be a lot more twitchy with the seat belt sign than those in other countries. We keep the sign on longer after takeoff, even when the air is smooth, and will switch it on again at the slightest jolt or burble. In some respects, this is another example of American overprotectiveness, but there are legitimate liability concerns. The last thing a captain wants is the FAA breathing down his neck for not having the sign on when somebody breaks an ankle and sues. Unfortunately, there's a cry-wolf aspect to this; people get so accustomed to the sign dinging on and off, seemingly without reason, that they ignore it altogether.

Just after takeoff we were tossed around very roughly. The captain told us we'd been hit by "wake turbulence." What is this, and how dangerous is it?

If you can picture the cleaved roil of water that trails behind a boat or ship, you've got the right idea. With aircraft, this effect is exacerbated by a pair of vortices that spin from the wingtips. At the wings' outermost extremities, the higher-pressure air beneath is drawn toward the lower pressure air on top, resulting in a tight, circular flow that trails behind the aircraft like a pronged pair of sideways tornadoes. The vortices are most pronounced when a plane is slow and the wings are working hardest to produce lift. Thus, prime time for encountering them is during approach or departure. As they rotate—at speeds that can top 300 feet per second—they begin to diverge and sink. If you live near an airport, stake out a spot close to a runway and listen carefully as the planes pass overhead; you can often *hear* the vortices' whip-like percussions as they drift toward the ground.

As a rule, bigger planes brew up bigger, most virulent wakes, and smaller planes are more vulnerable should they run into one. The worst offender is the Boeing 757. A mid-sized jet, the 757 isn't nearly the size of a 747 or 777, but thanks to a nasty aerodynamic quirk it produces an outsized wake that, according to one study, is the most powerful of any airplane.

To avoid wake upsets, air traffic controllers are required to put extra spacing between large and small planes. For pilots, one technique is to slightly alter the approach or climb gradient, remaining *above* any vortices as they sink. Another trick is to use the wind. Gusts and choppy air will break up vortices or otherwise move them to one side. Winglets (*see winglets, page 5*) also are a factor. One of the ways these devices increase aerodynamic efficiency is by mitigating the severity of wingtip vortices. Thus a winglet-equipped plane tends to produce a more docile wake than a similarly sized plane without them.

Despite all the safeguards, at one time or another, every pilot has had a run-in with wake, be it the short bump-and-roll of a dying vortex or a full-force wrestling match. Such an encounter might last only a few seconds, but they can be memorable. For me, it happened in Philadelphia in 1994.

Ours was a long, lazy, straight-in approach to runway 27R from the east, our nineteen-seater packed to the gills. Traffic was light, the radio mostly quiet. At five miles out, we were cleared to land. The traffic we'd been following, a 757, had already cleared the runway and was taxiing toward the terminal. We'd been given our extra ATC spacing buffer, and just to be safe, we were keeping a tad high on the glide path. Our checklists were complete, and everything was normal.

At around 200 feet, only seconds from touchdown, with the approach light stanchions below and the fat white stripes of the threshold just ahead, came a quick and unusual nudge—as if we'd struck a pothole. Then, less than a second later, came the rest of it. Almost instantaneously, our 16,000-pound aircraft was up on one wing, in a 45-degree right bank.

It was the first officer's leg to fly, but suddenly there were four hands on the yokes, turning to the left as hard as we could. Even with full opposite aileron—something never used in normal commercial flying—the ship kept rolling to the right. There we were, hanging sideways in the sky; everything in our power was telling the plane to go one way, and it insisted on going the other. A feeling of helplessness, of lack of control, is part and parcel of nervous flyer psychology. It's an especially bad day when the *pilots* are experiencing the same uncertainty.

Then, as suddenly as it started, the madness stopped. In less than five seconds, before either of us could utter so much as an expletive, the plane came to its senses and rolled level.

Sometimes when a plane is landing, I see a long trail of mist coming from the wingtip. What is this?

As air flows around a wing at high velocity, its temperature and pressure change. If humidity levels are high enough, this causes the cores of the wingtip vortices described in the previous question to condense and become visible, writhing behind the plane like gray, vaporous snakes. Moisture will condense around other spots too, such as the flap fairings and engine attachment pylons. You'll witness what appears to be a stream of white smoke pouring from the top of an engine during takeoff. This is water vapor caused by invisible currents around the pylon. Other times, the area just above the surface of the wing will suddenly flash into a white puff of localized cloud. Again, this is condensation brought on by the right combo of humidity, temperature, and pressure.

What is windshear?

One of those buzzwords that scare the crap out of people, windshear is a sudden change in the direction and/or velocity of the wind. Although garden-variety shears are extremely common and almost never dangerous, encountering a powerful shear during takeoff or landing, when airplanes operate very close to their minimum allowable speeds, can be dangerous. Remember that a plane's airspeed takes into account any existing headwind. If that velocity suddenly disappears or shifts to another direction, those knots are lost. Shears can happen vertically, horizontally, or both, as in the case of a microburst preceding a thunderstorm. Microbursts are intense, localized, downward-flowing columns of air spawned by storm fronts. As the air mass descends, it disperses outward in different directions.

Windshear got a lot of press in the 1970s and 1980s, when relatively little was known about them. The crash of Eastern flight 66 in New York in 1975 is considered the watershed accident after which experts began to study the phenomenon more carefully. Since then, windshear has become relatively easy to forecast and avoid. Major airports are now equipped with detection systems, as are planes.

Pilots are trained in escape maneuvers and can recognize weather conditions that might be hazardous for takeoff or landing.

Over the Atlantic in a 747, we heard a loud bang, followed by a vibration through the cabin. The captain informed us we'd suffered an engine stall.

This would have been a "compressor stall," a phenomenon where airflow through the engine is temporarily disrupted. The compressors of a jet or turboprop consist of a series of rotating airfoils—each blade is, in essence, a tiny wing—and if air stops flowing smoothly around these airfoils or back flows between the sequential stages, your compressor is stalling. It *can* damage an engine, but chances are it won't.

Miscellaneous engine peculiarities, compressor stalls included, can sometimes put on a show. Aside from a bang, you might see a long tongue of flame shooting from the back, or even the front, of the cowling. Tough as it might be to accept, the engine is neither exploding nor on fire. This is the nature of a jet. Any time the engine is running, fuel is combusting, and certain anomalies will unleash this combustion rather boldly.

The stalling compressors of an Alaska Airlines 737 once made the news when, by chance, a burst of flame was captured by somebody's camcorder on the ground. The video was alarming, but the stall was effectively harmless. And when this sort of thing happens at the gate or during taxi, passengers have been known to initiate their own evacuations. One such panic took place aboard a Delta plane in Tampa, Florida. A stampede of frightened passengers made for the exits, refusing to heed flight attendant commands. Two people were seriously hurt.

If *all* of a jet's engines were to fail, can the plane glide to a landing?

While it may surprise you, it's not the least bit uncommon for jets to descend at what a pilot calls "flight idle," with the engines run back to a zero-thrust condition. They're still operating and powering crucial systems, but providing no push. You've been gliding many times without knowing it. It happens on just about every flight.

Obviously an idle-thrust glide is different from the engines quitting outright, but even then, the glide itself would be no different. There's no greater prospect of instant calamity than switching off the engine in your car when coasting downhill. The car keeps going, and a plane will too. In fact, the power-off performance of a large jet is better than that of a light Piper or Cessna. It needs to glide at a considerably higher speed, but the ratio of distance covered to altitude lost—close to 20:1—is almost double. From 30,000 feet, you could plan on a hundred miles worth of glide.

Total engine loss is about as probable as a flight attendant volunteering to give you a shoe-shine, though it *has* happened. Culprits have included fuel exhaustion, volcanic ash, and impacts with birds. In several of these incidents, crews glided to a landing without a single fatality or injury. In other cases, one or more engines were restarted before reaching the ground.

How is a plane pressurized, and why?

Pressurization is one of those things that few folks understand and that many fear needlessly. Something about the word "pressurization" causes people to picture the upper altitudes as a kind of barometric hell. I've been asked, "If the plane wasn't pressurized, would my eyes pop out?"

Cruising in an airplane is not the same as dropping to the Marianas Trench in a deep-sea diving bell. The cabin is not pressurized to keep your eyes in but to allow you to breathe normally at high altitudes, where the air is thin and oxygen levels are very low. The system uses air drawn from the compressors in the engines and regulated through valves in the fuselage to squeeze the rarified, high-altitude air back together, recreating the dense, oxygen-rich conditions at sea level. (Or close to it. Pressurizing all the way to sea level is unnecessary and would put undue stress on the airframe, so the atmosphere in a jet is actually kept at the equivalent of 5,000 to

8,000 feet, meaning that you're breathing as you would in Denver or Mexico City—minus the pollution.)

That's all there is to it.

Great, you're thinking, but what about a *loss* of pressurization: the plastic masks dropping, people screaming…

Yes, a cabin decompression is potentially dangerous. During cruise, depending on the altitude, there's a differential of somewhere between 5 and 8 pounds per square inch between the pressure inside the plane (high) and the pressure outside (lower). You can think of the fuselage as a sort of balloon, with up to 8 pounds of force pushing against every inch of it. Introduce a hole or a leak into the picture, and you've got a problem. Loss of pressure means loss of oxygen, and if this happens explosively, such as from a bomb, the resultant forces can damage or outright destroy the plane.

However, the overwhelming majority of decompressions are not the explosive kind, and they are easy for a crew to handle. Odd things have happened, such as the bizarre Helios Airways accident in 2005, but crashes or fatalities from pressure problems are extremely uncommon, even with a fairly rapid decompression brought on by a hole or puncture.

If cabin pressure falls below a certain threshold, the masks will deploy from the ceiling, exposing everybody to the so-called "rubber jungle." Should you ever be confronted by this spectacle, try to avoid shrieking or falling into cardiac arrest. Instead, strap your mask on and try to relax. The plane will be at a safe altitude shortly, and there are several minutes of backup oxygen for everybody.

Up front, the pilots will don their own masks and commence a rapid descent to an altitude no higher than 10,000 feet. If the descent feels perilously fast, this isn't because the plane is crashing: it's because the crew is doing what it's supposed to do. It might be jarring, but a high-speed emergency descent is not unsafe by itself.

One afternoon I was working a flight from South America to the United States. All was quiet high over the Caribbean, when suddenly there was a loud whooshing sound that seemed to come from nowhere and everywhere at once. I could feel my ears popping, and sure enough, a glance at the instruments showed we were quickly losing pressurization. The captain and I put our masks on, took out the book, and began to troubleshoot. Part of that troubleshooting involved one of those steep descents. Commencing such a drop is a multistep process: set 10,000 in the altitude window; select "flight level change" from the autoflight panel; increase the speed command to a point slightly below maximum; deploy the speedbrakes; retard the thrust levers to idle... To the passengers, I'm sure it felt like a roller coaster, but everything was carefully coordinated. The autopilot was engaged the whole time, and no limits were exceeded.

Should a pressure loss occur over mountains or other high terrain, pilots will follow predetermined depressurization routes, sometimes called "escape routes," that allow for a more gradual descent, in stages. Even if crossing the Andes or the Himalayas, there is *always* the opportunity to reach a safe altitude before supplemental O_2 runs out.

I often travel from Louisville to New York, but the only flights serving this route are puddle jumper regional jets. I'm reluctant to fly on these planes because I feel they're unsafe. Are they?

The short answer is no. No commercial aircraft is unsafe or anything remotely close to it. The long answer is more nuanced. Whether regional aircraft are, on some level, *less safe* than mainline jets is open to debate. There is no practical reason why anybody should outright avoid smaller planes, but it's still a debate worth having:

Size, strictly speaking, isn't the issue. I can't speak to claustrophobia or absence of legroom, but there is almost nothing about an airplane's size that correlates one way or the other to the likelihood of it crashing. A modern turboprop or regional jet can cost tens of millions of dollars, and if you haven't noticed, that money isn't going into catering and sleeper seats; it's going toward the same high-tech avionics and cockpit advancements you'll find in a Boeing or Airbus. These planes might be small, but quaint they are not. And, so you know, pilots bristle at the term "puddle jumper" the same way an environmental scientist bristles at "tree hugger."

Of course, a plane is only as safe as the crew flying it, and there has been controversy over the training and experience levels of regional pilots. With wages and working conditions at regional carriers notoriously substandard, it has become increasingly difficult for these companies to recruit and retain experienced pilots. New hires have been brought aboard with surprisingly low flight time totals. More about this in chapter four (*see regional pilots, page 117*).

Love them or hate them, RJs are here to say. In the United States, RJs now account for more than 50 percent of all flights. There are literally dozens of different "Express" and "Connection" affiliates hitched up with the majors. Unbeknownst to most travelers, these carriers operate independently from the majors, sharing little more than a flight number and paint job. They are subcontractors, with entirely separate management structures, employees, and training departments.

I've been on flights where we circled for an hour before landing. How much fuel is on board for these situations? Do airlines cheat to save money?

If you're impressed by big numbers, you'll be grabbing for the highlighter when you find out a 747 tops off its tanks at just over 45,000 total gallons. It takes around 11,000 to fill a 737 or A320. A fifty-seater with propellers might hold less than a thousand gallons. Paltry in comparison, but still enough to drive your car from Washington to California six times. Fuel is stored in the wings, in the center fuselage, and even in the tail or horizontal stabilizers. The cargo jet I used to fly had eight separate tanks, and much of my job was moving their contents around to keep them balanced.

Flights rarely depart with full tanks, however, as lugging around excess tonnage is expensive, impractical, and limits cargo or passenger payload. The amount to be carried is a somewhat scientific undertaking, with some hard-and-fast rules. Crews do not ballpark the load with a cursory glance at a gauge, as you might do in a car before a road trip. It's the dispatchers and flight-planning staff who do the calculating, in strict accordance to a long list of regulations. They are intricate, especially when flying internationally, and can vary from country to country (a plane is beholden to its nation of registry, plus any local requirements if they're more stringent), but the U.S. domestic rule is a good indicator of how conservatively things work: There must always be enough to carry a plane to its intended destination, then to its designated alternate airport(s), and then for at least another 45 minutes. The resulting minimum is nonnegotiable. Sometimes, if weather criteria so dictate (the particulars are very specific), two or more alternates need to be filed in a flight plan, upping the total accordingly. If traffic delays are expected, even more will be added. And although dispatchers and planners devise the figures, the captain has the final say and can request more still. Carrying surplus fuel costs money, but not nearly as much as the hassles of diverting.

The preflight paperwork includes a detailed breakdown of anticipated burn, which is carefully tracked once the flight is underway. Remaining fuel is compared to predetermined target values as the flight progresses from waypoint to waypoint. The totals are monitored by the crew and dispatchers, the latter receiving updates via datalink transmission. You have a solid idea, well in advance, of exactly how much fuel you'll be landing with. If for some reason that number drops below or close to what's legally required (unexpected headwinds, a mechanical issue), there's ample time to plan a diversion.

Do airlines cheat to save money? You'll periodically come across scandalous-sounding news stories describing planes dispatched with "reduced fuel loads," allegedly resulting in unsafe situations when these flights are hit with delays and holding patterns. Carriers are, in some situations, cutting back on the carriage of extra fuel, which is heavy and expensive to haul around. But note the word *extra*. It's the above-and-beyond fuel that airlines look to reduce, not regulatory fuel. While these cutbacks allow for less wiggle room, they are not dangerous. The penalty isn't crashing; it's having to divert earlier than you'd like, with logistical hassles for passengers and crew.

Given all of that, the idea of running the tanks dry would seem far-fetched. Yet a small number of fuel depletion accidents have occurred. Understanding how and why they occurred would entail pages of boring (for both of us) analysis that I haven't the space to explore. These were once-in-a-billion mishaps. Most of them happened decades ago, and suffice it to say the stories were a lot more complicated than an airline being cheap or a copilot waking from a nap and exclaiming, "Holy shit, we're almost out of gas."

I understand that planes can jettison fuel. Is this done to lighten the load for landing? Sometimes you can see it pouring from the wingtips just before touchdown.

People will sometimes complain to authorities about what they take to be streams of jet fuel trailing behind airplanes low to the ground. What they're actually looking at are trails of water vapor—the condensed cores of the vortices spinning from the wingtips (*see wakes and vortices, page 36*). This is common when humidity is high. You will sooner see sacks of hundred-dollar bills being heaved overboard than fuel being spit away for no good reason.

And then, yes, it's to lighten the load. The maximum weight for takeoff is often greater than the one for landing—for a few reasons, the obvious one being that touching down puts higher stresses on an airframe than taking off. Normally, a suitable amount of fuel is burned away en route. Now, let's say something happens after takeoff and a plane must return to the airport. If the trouble is urgent enough, the crew will go ahead and land heavy. But almost always there's time to get within landing limits, and rather than tossing passengers or cargo overboard, the easiest way of doing this is to jettison fuel through plumbing in the wings. (I once had to dispose of more than 100,000 pounds this way over Northern Maine after an engine malfunction, a procedure that took many minutes and afforded me a lavish night's stay at the Bangor Airport Hilton.) Dumping takes place at a high enough altitude to allow the kerosene to mist and dissipate long before it reaches the ground, and no, engine exhaust will not set the discharge aflame.

Not all airliners have this capability—just the bigger ones. The 747, the 777, the A340, and the A330 all can dump fuel. A 737, an A320, or an RJ cannot. These smaller jets must circle or, if need be, land overweight. For some, landing and takeoff limits are the same, in which case it doesn't matter.

Know that nine times out of ten, a plane dumping fuel and executing a precautionary return is not in the throes of an actual emergency. The term "emergency landing" is used generically by passengers and the press. Crews must formally declare an emergency to air traffic control and will do so only in situations when time is critical, there's the possibility of damage or injury, or aircraft status is uncertain. The great majority of precautionary landings, even those when fire engines are lined up along the runway, are just that: precautionary.

What happens when lightning hits an airplane?

Planes are hit by lightning more frequently than you might expect—an individual jetliner is struck about once every two years, on average—and are designed accordingly. The energy does not travel through the cabin electrocuting the passengers; it is discharged overboard through the plane's aluminum skin, which is an excellent electrical conductor. Once in a while there's exterior damage—a superficial entry or exit wound—or minor injury to the plane's electrical systems, but a strike typically leaves little or no evidence. In 1963, lightning caused a wing explosion aboard a Pan Am 707 over Maryland. Afterward, the FAA enforced several protective measures, including fuel tank modifications and the installation of discharge wicks aboard all aircraft.

In 1993, I was captaining a thirty-seven-seater when lightning from a tiny embedded cumulonimbus cell got us on the nose. What we felt and heard was little more than a dull flash and a thud. No warning lights flashed, no generators tripped off line. Our conversation went:

> "What was that?"
> "I don't know." [*shrug*]
> "Lightning?"
> "Might have been."

Mechanics would later find a black smudge on the forward fuselage.

On more than one flight, I have seen what appears to be silver duct tape affixed to one part of the plane or another. Tell me it isn't so.

Photos of what are taken to be duct-tape repairs are periodically passed around through email and posted on blogs, putting people in a frenzy. It always looks worse than it is. The material isn't duct tape at all, but a heavy-duty aluminum bonding tape known as "speed tape," used to patch superficial, noncritical components until more substantive repairs can be made later on. You'll see it on flap fairings, winglets, gear doors, and the like. Speed tape costs hundreds of dollars per roll and is able to expand and contract through a wide range of temperatures.

Midway across the ocean, I watched as a 747 approached us and flew close alongside for several minutes. It was just to the left and beneath us, so close that you could see people through the windows. I often see planes passing at such alarming proximity. Are these near misses?

This is a great illustration of what I like to call PEF, or Passenger Embellishment Factor, the phenomenon that accompanies so many accounts of dodgy takeoffs, supposed near misses, and so on. Earmark this page for the next time you're subject to a water cooler tale like this one.

Not to belittle your powers of observation, but distances aloft can be hard to judge, and passengers have an *extremely* common habit of underestimating separation with other aircraft. During cruise, planes will always be a minimum of 1,000 feet apart vertically or three miles horizontally. Flights on the transoceanic track systems (*see oceanic routings, page 87*) frequently encounter one another more or less as you describe. It can be startling—a 747 is a big ship, and even from a thousand feet away it looks awfully close—but it's perfectly safe and routine. The rules are different for takeoffs and landings. With simultaneous approaches to parallel runways, for instance, planes can be at the same altitude and a mile or less apart—though they remain under the very close watch of ATC and must also maintain visual contact with one another.

As for seeing people through the windows, this is classic PEF and something that I hear all the time. Even when an airplane is parked at the gate, a few feet away and stationary, it can be difficult to see anyone inside. Aloft, you have never been remotely close enough to another plane to see its occupants, trust me.

People have a habit of embellishing even the basic sensations of flight. They can't always help it—nervous flyers especially—but the altitudes, speeds, and angles are perceived to be far more severe than they really are. During turbulence, people sense that an airplane is dropping hundreds of feet at a time, when in reality the displacement is seldom more than ten or twenty feet—barely a twitch on the altimeter (*see turbulence, page 32*). It's similar with angles of bank and climb. A typical turn is made at around 15 degrees, and a steep one might be 25. The sharpest climb is about 20 degrees nose-up, and even a rapid descent is no more severe than 5 or 6 degrees nose-down.

I can see your letters: you will tell me that I'm lying, and how the plane you were on was *definitely* climbing at 45 degrees, and *definitely* banking at 60, and how you *definitely* saw people through the windows. And you're definitely wrong. Sorry to sound so bossy, and I wish that I could take you into a cockpit and demonstrate. I'd show you what a 45-degree climb actually looks like, turning you green in the face. In a 60-degree turn, the G forces would be so strong that you'd hardly be able to lift your legs off the floor.

How dangerous are collisions between airplanes and birds?

Bird strikes are common, and the damage tends to be minor or nonexistent—unless you're looking at it from the bird's point of view. As you'd expect, aircraft components are built to tolerate such impacts. You can see web videos of bird carcasses being fired from a sort of chicken-cannon to test the resistance of windshields, intakes, and so forth. I've personally experienced several strikes, and the result was, at worst, a minor dent or crease.

I should hardly have to mention, however, that strikes are occasionally dangerous. This is especially true when engines are involved, as we saw in 2009 when US Airways flight 1549 glided into the Hudson River after colliding with a flock of Canada geese. Modern turbofans are resilient, but they don't take kindly to the ingestion of foreign objects, particularly those slamming into their rotating blades at high speeds. Birds don't clog an engine but can bend or fracture the internal blades, causing power loss.

The heavier the bird, the greater the potential for harm. Flying at 250 knots—in the United States, that's the maximum allowable speed below 10,000 feet, where most birds are found—hitting an average-sized goose will subject a plane to an impact force of over 50,000 pounds. Even small birds pose a threat if struck en masse. In 1960, an Eastern Airlines turboprop went down in Boston after an encounter with a flock of starlings.

Your next question, then, is why aren't engines built with protective screens in front? Well, in addition to partially blocking the inflow of air, the screen would need to be large (presumably cone-shaped) and incredibly strong. Should it fail, now you've got a bird and pieces of metal going into the motor. The incidents above notwithstanding, the vast improbability of losing multiple engines to birds renders such a contraption impractical.

One sometimes hears of icing after an accident. How are ice and snow hazardous?

Ice or snow on an airplane is potentially very dangerous, especially when adhered to the wings. The devil isn't the added weight, but the way it disrupts the flow of air over and around a wing's carefully sculpted contours, destroying lift. You've also got slick runways to contend with and assorted other challenges.

On the Ground:

Ice or snow piles up on a plane parked at the gate the way it piles up on your car. But while a cursory brushing is a safe enough remedy for driving, it doesn't work for flying, when even a quarter-inch layer of frozen material can adversely alter airflow around the wing—highly important during takeoff, when speed is slow and lift margins are thin. To clean it away, planes are sprayed down with a heated mixture of water and glycol alcohol.

While it appears pretty casual to the passenger, the spraying procedure is a regimented, step-by-step process. Different fluid mixtures, varying in temperature and viscosity, are applied depending on conditions, often in combination. A plane might be hit with so-called Type I fluid to get rid of the bulk of accumulation, then further treated with Type IV, a stickier substance that wards off subsequent buildup. Pilots follow a checklist to ensure their plane is correctly configured for spraying. Usually the flaps and slats will be lowered to the takeoff position, with the APU providing power and the main engines shut down. The air-conditioning units will be switched off to keep the cabin free of fumes.

When deicing is complete, the ground crew will tell the pilots which types of fluid were used, as well as the exact time that treatment began. This allows us to keep track of something called a "holdover time." If the holdover time is exceeded before the plane has a chance to take off, a second round of deicing may be required. The length of the holdover depends on the kind of fluids used, plus the rate and type of any active precipitation (dry snow, wet snow, ice pellets; light, moderate, heavy). We have charts to figure it out.

Deicing fluid isn't especially corrosive, but neither is it the most environmentally friendly stuff in the world. And although it resembles apple cider or an apricot-strawberry puree, I wouldn't drink it; certain types of glycol are poisonous. At upward of $5 a gallon, it is also very expensive. When you add in handling and storage costs, relieving a single jet of winter white can cost several thousand dollars. Another method is to tow aircraft into specially built hangars equipped with powerful, ceiling-mounted heat lamps. In some ways, this is a greener technique, though it uses hideous amounts of electricity.

In the Air:

Snow will not stick to an airplane during flight. Ice, however, is another story. Owing to airflow and aerodynamic forces, it tends to adhere to the thinner, lower profile areas and not to larger expanses. It will build on the forward edges of the wings and tail, around engine inlets, and on various antennae and probes. Left unchecked, it can damage engines, throw propeller assemblies off balance, and rob the wings of precious lift. In a worst-case scenario, it can induce a full-on aerodynamic stall—the point when a wing essentially ceases to fly.

The good news is that all affected surfaces are equipped with devices to keep them clear. On propeller-driven planes, pneumatically inflated "boots" will break ice from the leading edges of the wings and horizontal tail. On jets, hot air from the engine compressors is used instead, bled to the wings, tail, and engine intakes. Windshields, propeller blades, and various probes and sensors are kept warm electrically. These systems use redundant power sources and are separated into independently functioning zones to keep any one failure from affecting the entire plane.

Airframe ice comes in three basic flavors: rime, clear, and mixed. Rime is the common one, appearing as a sort of white fuzz. The rate at which ice accretes is graded from "trace" to "severe." Severe icing, most commonly encountered when flying through freezing rain, is a killer. It's also quite rare, and it tends to exist in thin bands that are easy to avoid or fly out of. On the whole, inflight icing is considerably more of a threat to smaller noncommercial planes than it is to airliners. Even in the heaviest precipitation, seeing more than a trace amount of rime on a jetliner is uncommon.

Runway Hazards:

An icy runway is a slippery one, needless to say. Airports issue so-called "braking action reports" for each runway—even different portions of a runway—which pilots make careful note of, along with the latest wind and weather reports. Together, this data helps determine whether it's safe to arrive or depart. Because there must always be adequate rollout distance on landing, as well adequate room to stop following an aborted takeoff, operations are prohibited when braking reports fall below a certain value or when snow, ice, or slush exceed certain depths. Takeoff and landing speeds, as well as the power and flap settings to be used, are often different in snowy weather than they are in dry weather. And if you've ever looked closely at a runway, you'll see they are cut laterally by thousands of grooves spaced inches apart. This helps with traction, as do the sophisticated anti-skid systems found on modern planes.

I've made plenty of winter-weather landings. One thing that always surprises me is the way in which fresh snowfall can make a runway difficult to see and align yourself with. In normal conditions the runway sits in stark contrast to the pavement, grass, or whatever else is around it. When it's snowing, *everything* is white. Runways are outfitted with an array of color-coded lighting. Most of the time you pay only cursory attention to these displays. That is, until the moment you break from a low overcast, just a few hundred feet over the ground with a half-mile of visibility, and find yourself confronted with a landscape of undifferentiated whiteness. Those lights and colors are suddenly very helpful.

Accidents and Incidents:

There have been several tragedies over the years in which planes attempted takeoff with iced-over wings. Most recent was a 1991 USAir incident at LaGuardia. Nine years earlier was the infamous Air Florida disaster in Washington, DC, when in addition to ignoring buildup on the wings, the crew failed to run the engine anti-ice system, allowing frozen probes to give faulty thrust readings. On Halloween night in 1994, sixty-eight people died aboard American Eagle flight 4184, a crash attributed to a design flaw—since rectified—in the ATR-72's deicing system. Numerous other planes have gone skidding off the end of snowy runways. Culprits have included erroneous weather or braking data, an unstable approach continued when it should have been broken off, the occasional malfunction, or any combination of those things.

I can't tell you there will never be another ice-related accident. But I can assure you that airlines and their crews take icing a lot more seriously than they used to. We've learned a lot—much of it the hard way—and this has carried over into specific, formalized procedures that leave little to chance.

Are the contents of airplane toilets jettisoned during flight?

Several years back, I was on a train going from Malaysia into Thailand when I stepped into the restroom and lifted the toilet seat. I was presented with a mesmerizing view of gravel, dirt, and railroad ties, all passing rapidly beneath me. Those who travel will encounter this now and again, and maybe it's people like us who get these nutty myths off and running. The answer is no. There is no way to jettison the contents of the lavatories during flight.

Intentionally, that is. A man in California once won a lawsuit after pieces of "blue ice" fell from a plane and came crashing through the skylight of his sailboat. A leak, extending from a toilet's exterior nozzle fitting, caused runoff to freeze, build, and then drop like a neon ice bomb. If you think that's bad, a 727 once suffered an engine separation after ingesting a frozen chunk of its own leaked toilet waste, inspiring the line "when the shit hits the turbofan."

At the end of a flight, the blue fluid, along with your contributions to it, are vacuumed into a tank on the back of a truck. (The truck driver's job is even lousier than the copilot's, but it pays better.) The driver then wheels around to the back of the airport and furtively offloads the waste in a ditch behind a parking lot.

In truth I don't know what he does with it. Time to start a new urban legend.

Before boarding, we were told our flight was weight restricted because of a malfunctioning system. Whose decision is it to take off when something important isn't working?

Airplanes can depart with inoperative components—usually non-essential equipment carried in duplicate or triplicate—only in accordance with guidelines laid out in two thick manuals called the Minimum Equipment List (MEL) and Configuration Deviation List (CDL). Any component in these books is "deferrable," as we put it, so long as any outlined stipulations are met. These stipulations can be quite restrictive. One of the first things a crew does after signing in for a trip is scan the paperwork for deferrals, making note of any pertinent restrictions. A malfunctioning anti-skid system, for example, might require a longer runway for takeoff and landing. The books are not contrived to allow airlines an easy hand at flying around with defective equipment. Many things, as you'd hope, are not deferrable at all, and any malfunctioning item must be repaired in a set number of days or flight hours. The captain has the final say and can refuse to accept any deferral if he or she feels it is unsafe.

I've watched a pilot do his walk-around check from the terminal. This doesn't seem to be a very in-depth inspection.

The walk-around inspection, while useful, is a basic inspection not a whole lot different from checking your oil, tires, and wipers before a road trip. The most common discoveries are superficial dents, unlatched panels, minor leaks, and tire issues (cuts, scrapes, etc.). The more intensive preflight routine takes place in the cockpit. While you're bottlenecked in the jet bridge, the various cockpit instruments and systems are being tested. Maintenance personnel also perform preflight and postflight checks, both interior and exterior, with special inspections and sign-offs required for overwater flights. Watch a plane dock, and you might spot one or more mechanics fanning out beneath it while another heads up front to consult with the crew and review the logbook, ensuring everything is set for the next departure.

I'm concerned about flying on older planes. Should I be?

If your concerns rest with cabin accouterments or particle emissions from older-generation engines, go ahead and gripe. But statistically, with respect to accidents, there is little correlation between service time and safety. Commercial aircraft are built to last more or less indefinitely—which is one of the reasons they're so expensive—and it's common for a jet to remain in service for thirty years or more.

The older a plane gets, the more and better care it needs in the hangar, and inspection criteria grow increasingly strict. Factors include the plane's overall age, its total number of flight hours, and the accrued number of takeoffs and landings—"cycles" as they're called. The FAA recently implemented tough new inspection and record-keeping procedures for certain geriatric aircraft, covering things like corrosion, metal fatigue, and wiring.

Surprisingly—or maybe not—U.S. airline fleets are the oldest on average. Asian, European, and Middle Eastern airlines have the newest. Many of American Airlines's MD-80s were built in the 1980s. Delta Air Lines still cares for several DC-9s that date from the Age of Aquarius, acquired during its merger with Northwest.

"Retirement" is an ambiguous term with airplanes. Planes are sold, traded, or mothballed not because they've grown old and are falling apart, but because they've become uneconomical to operate. This may or may not be related to their date of construction. Take the case of Delta and American, who disposed of their MD-11s, yet plan to retain substantially older MD-80s and 767s for years to come. Aircraft are tailored to particular roles and markets, and there's a fragile balance—tiny, shifting percentages of expenses and revenues— between whether it makes or loses money. Poor performance means quick exit to the sales block. To another carrier with different costs, routes, and needs, that same aircraft might be profitable.

Revere Reverie: A Hometown Memoir

Sometimes, when I hear the whine of jet engines, I think of the beach.

I don't expect that to make sense to you—unless, like me, your childhood was defined by an infatuation with jetliners *and* summers spent at a beach directly below an approach course to a major airport.

That would be Revere Beach, in my case, just north of Boston, in the middle and late 1970s. Then, as now, the city of Revere was a gritty, in many ways charmless, place: rows of triple-deckers and block after block of two-story colonials garnished in gaudy wrought-iron. (Revere is a city so architecturally hopeless that it can never become gentrified or trendy in the way that other Boston suburbs have.) Irish and Italian families spoke in a tough, North Shore accent that had long ago forsaken the letter *R*. Shit-talking kids drove Camaros and Trans-Ams, the old country *cornuto* horns glinting over their chest hair.

Revere's beach was the first public beach in the United States. Like the rest of the city, it wasn't the kind of place that lent itself to niceties or sentimental descriptions. The roller coasters had long ago burned, and the boulevard was dotted by biker hangouts and the sort of honky-tonk bars that, as a kid, you never dared set foot in, no matter how bad you needed to use the bathroom. Seagulls swooped and gorged on the garbage toppling out of barrels and dumpsters.

But it had the sand, and water that was clean enough to swim in—with those long, flat, shimmering low tides that seemed to recede all the way past Nahant and into the horizon. We spent our summers here—nearly all of the weekends and many of the weekdays too. My parents would have the car packed by 10:00 a.m. I remember the folding chairs, the towels, and the endless supply of Hawaiian Tropic suntan lotion, its oily coconut aroma mixed with the hot stink of sunbaked Oldsmobile leather.

I swam, dug around for crabs, and endured the requisite mud-ball fights with my friends. But for me, the real thrill was the airplanes. Revere Beach's mile-long swath lines up almost perfectly with Logan International Airport's runway 22L, the arrivals floating past at regular intervals, so low you'd think you could hit them with one of the discarded Michelob bottles poking out of the sand. I'd bring a notebook and log each plane as it screamed overhead.

They'd appear first as black smudges. You'd see the smoke—the snaking black trails of a 707 or DC-8 as it finally turned up over Salem or Marblehead. Then came the noise. The little kids, and grown-ups too, would cover their ears. People today don't realize how earsplittingly loud the older-generation jets could be. And they were low, maybe 1,500 feet above the sand, getting lower and lower and lower until disappearing over the hill at Beachmont, just seconds from touchdown.

I remember all of them: TWA 707s and L-1011s in the old, twin-globe livery. United DC-8s and DC-10s in the '70s-era bow-tie colors. Flying Tigers DC-8s and 747s; Allegheny DC-9s and BAC One-Elevens. Eastern's 727 "Whisperjets" that did anything but whisper. Braniff, Piedmont, Capitol, and Seaboard World; TAP, North Central, Zantop, and Trans International. The term "regional jet" wouldn't exist for at least another decade. Instead we had "commuter planes." There was PBA and its Cessna 402s; Air New England's Twin Otters and FH-227s; and Bar Harbor's Beech-99s, Pilgrim, Empire, Ransome, and Downeast.

Fast-forward thirty years:

The arrivals pattern to 22L hasn't changed. It still passes directly over Revere Beach. After I finally became an airline pilot, one of my biggest thrills was being at the controls on a 22L arrival into BOS, looking down at the same beach from which I spent a childhood looking up. But other things are different.

The demographics of the city and its beach have changed,

for one. In the Revere of my youth, pretty much every last family was Italian, Irish, or some mix of the two. At the beach it was no different. Today, both the neighborhoods and the sand are a virtual United Nations of the North Shore. Those harsh, *R*-less accents are joined by voices in Hindi, Arabic, Portuguese, and Khmer. The muscle shirts, Italian horns, and shamrocks are still there, but those sunburned Irish complexions are contrasted against those from Somalia, Ghana, Haiti, and Morocco.

And overhead, those plumes of oily smoke are gone. The jets nowadays are cleaner, much quieter. And a lot less exciting. At age twelve, I could tell a DC-10 from an L-1011 when it was ten miles out. Every plane had its own distinct profile. Today's jets are often indistinguishable even at close range, and the endless procession of Airbuses and RJs just doesn't get the pulse going, or the sunbathers pointing, the way a 707 or a DC-8 would—its motors shrieking, black smoke spewing behind.

Revere itself has both gained and lost character over the years. The skies above, though, have mostly just lost it.

3 WHAT GOES UP...

Takeoffs, Landings, and the Mysterious Between

WHAT'S THE MATTER WITH AIRPORTS?

"Air travel has influenced the architecture and design of our cen-
tury to a perhaps greater degree than anything else, including even
the automobile."
                                    —John Zukowsky, from Building for Air Travel

For a whole host of reasons, airports are often bewildering, maddening places. There is much to be found in the modern-day terminal to
enrage, confuse, or vex the traveler. Where to begin?

Consider, for instance, the widespread phenomenon of teenage
girls carrying big fluffy pillows onto airplanes. When did this start,
and how did it become so popular? (Granted, it's a helpful idea, now
that many carriers no longer dispense even tiny, nonfluffy pillows on
all but the longest flights. The trouble is, people like me are out of
the club. Grown-up men can't walk through airports with giant fluffy
pillows unless we're willing to get laughed at. We're stuck with those
neck brace things.) Almost as confounding is the mania of Sudoku:
this generation's answer to crossword puzzles and, from what I can
see, the number-one pastime of bored flyers. (I'm not saying the
game isn't challenging. But so is high-diving or sword-swallowing.
That doesn't mean we should all be doing it.)

However, the most alarming trend to strike airports in the past
half-century has nothing to do with games, pillows, suicide hijackings,

or erotic pat-downs from TSA. No, the most troubling thing about airports is noise.

If American airports need to borrow one idea from their counterparts in Europe and Asia, it's that passengers need not be assailed by a continuous loop of useless and redundant public address announcements. Security alerts, boarding calls, traffic and parking directives—all playing simultaneously. At some airports, this sonic layering is unbearable. I have heard up to four announcements playing at once, rendering all of them unintelligible in a hurricane of noise.

Intensifying this bombardment are those infernal gate-side monitors blaring CNN Airport Network. Somewhere out there is a survey in which a majority of travelers insist that they enjoy and appreciate the chance to watch TV at the gate. That may well be true, and I am not suggesting they be denied this privilege outright. But a license to entertain and a license to *harass* are different things. If the TVs have a right to be there, shouldn't travelers have the right to get the heck away from them if they desire? That's what's missing. These yammering hellboxes are everywhere, and they cannot be turned off. There is no button, no power cord, no escape. Every gate has one, and they run twenty-four hours a day. Not even airport workers know how to shut them up. Then you've got the shrieking kids, the beeping carts, the cellphone chatter, and so on. It's an inescapable, multifront attack seeping into every nook and corner of the terminal, day and night.

The following list was inspired by a layover I had not long ago at Incheon International Airport (ICN), serving Seoul, Korea. Not to take away from perennial survey-toppers like Amsterdam's Schiphol or Singapore's Changi Airport (amenities at Changi include a movie theater, a swimming pool, and a butterfly garden), but Incheon stands as the most functional, attractive, and overall flyer-friendly airport I've ever visited. It's cavernous and immaculate, with a cathedral-like calm throughout. Security and immigration are a breeze; international transit is effortless. The staff at the multilingual information desks is disarmingly helpful. Amenities include free Internet, free showers, luggage storage, cellphone rental desks, a post office, and massage facilities. Relaxation areas, with sofas and easy chairs, are set away from the main thoroughfares. There's a cultural center, a museum, and a full-service hotel *inside* the secure zone, allowing travelers with extended layovers to rent a room without the need to clear immigration. Or, if you're feeling energetic, a tour desk arranges *free* excursions to Incheon City. If you're headed into Seoul, the airport's high-speed rail connection will have you downtown in under an hour. Why can't every airport be like this?

Fifteen Things No Terminal Should Be Without:

1. A fast, low-cost public transportation link to downtown

In a way, choosing a favorite airport is like choosing a favorite hospital: amenities aside, nobody really wants to be there in the first place, and the easier and faster you can get the hell out, the better. To that end, every terminal should have public transport links similar to those across Asia and Europe. The examples of Portland, Oregon, and Washington-Reagan notwithstanding, rail links in the United States aren't nearly as convenient—when they exist at all. At my hometown airport, Boston-Logan, my six-mile commute to the airport by public transportation takes almost an hour and requires two changes, including a ride on the Silver Line bus, which in addition to being at the mercy of automobile traffic requires, at one point, that the driver step out and manually switch power sources. Or how about JFK, where for hundreds of millions of dollars, they finally got the AirTrain completed—an interterminal rail loop that connects only as far as the Queens subway. It can take forty-five minutes up and down a Rube Goldberg assembly of escalators, elevators, and passageways just to get from one terminal to another, let alone all the way to Manhattan.

2. In-transit capabilities

It's a shame that American airports cannot, for whatever reasons, recognize the "in transit" concept. All passengers arriving from other countries, even if they're merely passing through on the way to a third country, are forced to clear customs and immigration, collect and recheck their luggage, and pass through security screening. It's an enormous hassle, unheard of in most of the world. And it costs our airlines millions of annual customers. Why change planes in the United States, where you'll have to stand in three different lines, be photographed and fingerprinted, recheck your bags, and face the TSA gauntlet, when instead you can transfer seamlessly in Frankfurt or Dubai? Indeed, this is part of what has made carriers like Emirates, Singapore Airlines, and others so successful.

3. Complimentary wireless Internet

What do we do at airports? We kill time. And there are few better and more productive ways of killing time than logging on to the web. Send an email to your mistress; read my blogs at askthepilot.com; Skype your friend in Slovenia. Many, if not most, major terminals have Wi-Fi access, but it's often expensive and cumbersome (few things in life are more irritating than those credit card payment pages). It should be everywhere, and it should be free.

4. Convenience stores

It appears the evolution of airport design will not be complete until the terminal and shopping mall become indistinguishable. I'm okay with Starbucks and souvenir kiosks, but it's the saturation of high-end boutiques that always confounds me. Apparently there isn't a traveler alive who isn't in dying need of a hundred-dollar Mont Blanc pen, a remote-control helicopter, or a thousand-dollar massage chair. And what's with all the luggage stores? Who on earth buys a suitcase *after* they get to the airport? What we really need are the same sorts of things we buy at CVS or the corner convenience store: basic groceries and dry goods, stationery, and personal care items. Brussels and Amsterdam are two places that do this right, with in-terminal food marts and pharmacies.

5. Power ports

I didn't realize that passengers have a right—nay, a duty—to mooch free electricity from their carrier of choice, but at this point it's a lost cause to argue. Airlines should throw in the towel and build more charging stations.

6. Showers and a short-stay hotel

No serious international terminal should be without a place to wash up or crash for a few hours. Passengers arriving from overseas can shower and change before their next connection. Those with longer waits can grab a nap in one of those pay-by-the-hour sleeping pods.

7. Play areas for children

Truth be told, airport play areas encourage toddlers to shriek and yell even more than they already do, but at least they're doing it in a localized area that's easy for the rest of us to avoid. Ideally, this spot should be in a soundproofed bubble six miles from the airport, but a space at the far end of the concourse is a reasonable alternative. The Delta terminal in Boston has a pretty cool kidport, but nothing tops the "Kids' Forest" at Amsterdam-Schiphol. I'd play there myself if nobody was watching.

8. Better dining options (i.e., fewer chain restaurants)

Chick-fil-A, Burger King, Sbarro. Airport cuisine isn't a whole lot different from the shopping mall food court. We need more independent restaurants serving actual food, ideally with a local bent.

The next time you're at LaGuardia, check out Rocco Manniello's Yankee Clipper restaurant over at the Marine Air Terminal. That's the circular building with the art deco doors and flying fish relief along its rooftop, adjacent to the Delta Shuttle. Rocco's is a cafeteria-style place on the left-hand side of the rotunda. It's good greasy spoon food with absolutely no corporate affiliation. (If Anthony Bourdain ever does a segment on airport food, Rocco's should be his first stop.)

The Marine Air Terminal was the launching point of the first-ever transatlantic and around-the-world flights, and the restaurant's walls are decorated with historic photographs. You can eat in or take your sandwich out to one of the wooden benches beneath the famous James Brooks *Flight* mural. Commissioned in 1952, Brooks's painting traces the history of aviation from mythical to (then) modern, Icarus to Pan Am Clipper. The painting's style is a less-than-shy nod at Socialist realism, and at the height of '50s McCarthyism, in a controversy not unlike that surrounding Diego Rivera's famous mural at Rockefeller Center, it was declared propaganda and obliterated with gray paint. Not until 1977 was it restored.

9. An information kiosk

Where is the Yankee Clipper restaurant? Where is the nearest ATM? Where is the nonexistent subway link to the city? Every arrivals hall ought to have personnel who can give directions, hand out maps, and make change.

10. A bookstore

Reading on planes is a natural, am I right? Why then is it so hard to find a proper bookstore at an airport? (Not all of us preload our reading material on a Kindle.) Not long ago, every major airport had a proper bookseller. Nowadays, they are harder and harder to find, and what passes as a bookstore is usually just a newsstand hawking a thin selection of business books, thrillers, and pop-culture trash. Believe it or not, travelers' tastes extend beyond Sudoku and the latest CEO biography. And naturally, said proper bookstore will be amply stocked with copies of *Cockpit Confidential*.

11. Sufficient gate-side seating

If the plane at the gate holds 250 people, there ought to be a minimum of 250 chairs in the boarding lounge. There is something uncivilized about having to sit on the floor while waiting to board. Do we sit on the floor when waiting for a table in a restaurant or at the doctor's office? When Changi was built in Singapore, the gates were outfitted with no fewer than 420 chairs, matching the number on the average 747.

12. Escalator etiquette

Americans haven't figured out how to behave on an escalator. If you're not in a hurry, you should *stand on the right* and enjoy the ride, allowing those of us with a flight to catch to *walk on the left*. Instead, we stand in the middle, hogging up both sides. Ditto for moving sidewalks. The point of the moving sidewalk is to expedite your passage, not to indulge your laziness. You're not supposed to *stand* on it; you're supposed to *walk* on it. And to take yet another page from the Europeans and Asians, what prevents us from fitting escalators and sidewalks with a motion trigger that shuts off the motor when nobody is on them? Our conveyors run constantly, riders or no riders, wasting huge amounts of energy.

13. A view

Why are so many architects intent on hiding the fact that airports are actually airports? Gate-side seating always faces *away* from the windows, and the windows themselves are sometimes intentionally opaqued or obstructed by barriers. Why? Plenty of people would enjoy the opportunity to sit and watch the planes go by. You needn't be an airplane buff to find this relaxing or even a little exciting. As a bonus, more windows mean more natural light—always welcome over harsh fluorescents.

Here in Boston, there was once a spectacular observation deck on the sixteenth floor of the control tower. It featured opposing sides of knee-to-ceiling windows and the best view in town. It's a scant two miles from Logan's perimeter seawall to the center of downtown, and you observed the city and its airport in a state of working symbiosis. Passengers relaxed on carpeted benches while kids and families came on the weekends, feeding coins into the mechanical binoculars and picnicking on the floor. It made the airport a destination unto itself, like a park or a museum, and encouraged a kind of civic togetherness seldom seen anymore. You can still find observation decks here and there, usually in Europe. Boston's was shuttered in 1989, ostensibly for security reasons.

14. Bring back the airstairs!

Have you ever taken a good look at a jet bridge (or Jetway, to use the proprietary term), that strange umbilicus connecting terminal to fuselage? One thing to notice is how ridiculously overbuilt they are. Do we really need all of that metal and cable and wire and hydraulics for what is, at heart, a simple gangway?

Of course, I'm opposed to jet bridges on principle. I prefer the classic, drive-up airstairs. Some of the international stations I fly to still employ those old-timey stairs, and I always get a thrill from them. There's something dramatic about stepping onto a plane that way: the ground-level approach along the tarmac followed by the slow ascent. The effect is like the opening credits of a film—a brief, formal introduction to the journey. By contrast, the jet bridge makes the airplane almost irrelevant; you're merely in transit from one annoying interior space (terminal) to another (cabin).

Save your emails. This is just me being romantic. The benefits to the jet bridge are obvious—inclement weather, disabled passengers, etc.—and I realize there's no going back.

15. Last but not least, some aesthetic flair

If an airport has one aesthetic obligation, it's to impart a sense of place: you are here and nowhere else. On this front, Europe and Asia again set the standard. I think of Lyon and its magnificent hall by Santiago Calatrava, or Kuala Lumpur with its indoor rainforest, where terminal design is a point of expressive pride—where it *makes a statement*, be it quietly stylish or architecturally stupendous.

Take the magnificent Suvarnabhumi (pronounced "Su-wanna-poom") airport in Bangkok, Thailand. Its central terminal is the most visually spectacular airport building I have ever seen. At night, as you approach by highway from the city, it looms out of the darkness like a goliath space station—a vision of glass and light and steel, its immense transoms bathed in blue spotlight. Or for sheer character, try the little airport in Timbuktu, Mali. Here you'll find a handsome, Sudanese-style building emulating the mud-built mosques ubiquitous in that country.

With scattered exceptions (Denver, San Francisco, Washington, Vancouver), there is nothing comparable in America. To the contrary, some of our most expensive airport renovations have been terrible disappointments. jetBlue's wildly overrated home at JFK, for example. Terminal 5—or "T5" as the carrier likes to call it—is a $743 million, 72-acre structure that opened in 2008 to considerable promotion and fanfare. Inside, the atrium food court and rows of shops conspire to make yet another airport feel like yet another mall. The Wi-Fi is free, and so is the noise and claustrophobia at the overcrowded gates. But it's the exterior that's the real tragedy. Although the streetside facade is at worst cheerless, the tarmac side is abominable—a wide, low-slung, industrial-brutalist expanse of gray concrete and ugly brown sheathing. Once again it looks like a shopping mall. Or, to be more specific, it looks like the *back* of a shopping mall. All that's missing are some pallets and dumpsters. The facility's only visual statement is one of not caring, a presentation of architectural nothingness, absolutely empty of inspiration—precisely what an airport terminal should *not be*. Is this the best we can do?

It's ironic that Eero Saarinen's landmark TWA Flight Center sits directly in front of T5, itself part of the jetBlue complex. Regarded as a modernist masterpiece, the Flight Center opened in 1962 and was the first major terminal built expressly for jet airliners. It is supposed to serve as an entryway lobby and ticketing plaza for T5, though for now it remains semi-derelict and only partly renovated. I wish they'd finish the thing so more people could appreciate what is widely considered the most architecturally significant airport terminal ever constructed. Saarinen, a Finn whose other projects included the Gateway Arch in St. Louis and the terminal at Washington-Dulles, described the interior as "all one thing." The lobby is a fluid, unified sculpture of a space, at once futuristic and organic. It's a kind of Gaudi inversion, a carved-out atrium reminiscent of the caves of

Turkish Cappadocia, overhung by a pair of cantilevered ceilings that rise from a central spine like huge wings.

And just to the north of T5 used to be the National Airlines Sundrome, designed by I. M. Pei. It opened in 1970 and was named in honor of National's yellow and orange sunburst logo and its popular routes between the Northeast and Florida. After National was folded into Pan Am, the terminal was taken over by TWA. Later it was used by jetBlue, then abandoned and torn down.

Pei and Saarinen, a half-minute walk from each other. Our airports ain't what they used to be.

Am I making too much of this? While terminal design and passenger friendliness are important, isn't it the operational aspects of an airport—the state of its runways, taxiways, and logistical infrastructure—that ultimately matter most? Indeed, but here too the situation is worrying, as any American who travels globally can attest. Once again, it's a funding issue. Our airports are failing, and nobody wants to pay for them. There's little in the federal budget, while airports and airlines lack the lobbying strength of the pharmaceutical industry or the military-industrial complex.

"Other parts of the world are more enlightened in their aviation policies than we are," said Greg Principato, North American president of the Airports Council International, speaking at a conference in 2012. He added that members of the U.S. Congress have a poor understanding of how the upkeep and renovation of U.S. airports needs to be funded. "They have a sense that airports are economically important," he explained, "but don't really understand why." Principato warns that the declining state of its airport infrastructure puts the United States "at risk of being turned into a feeder system for the global aviation network." ✈

How long does it take pilots to prepare for a flight, and what goes into that prep?

At my airline, sign-in time for domestic flights is sixty minutes prior to departure. For flights overseas, it's ninety minutes. That's pretty standard. When the flight is headed overseas, things start off in the crew lounge. After introducing ourselves, we gather up the paperwork and move to a cubicle to review it all. The paperwork contains the full flight plan (see below), all necessary weather reports and forecasts, and a slew of supplemental information. There are dozens of pages in total, covering everything from taxiway closures to the phone number of the layover hotel. (Some of this material is laser-printed on standard-size office paper, but most of it comes rolling off in splendorous dot matrix.) For transoceanic flights the route needs to be manually plotted, old school, on a chart. Once you're at the plane, your gear (headsets, manuals, clipboards, etc.) needs to be stowed and assembled, and the interior and exterior inspections completed. The cockpit systems and instruments have to be checked; the logbook has to be reviewed; and all of the route, wind, and performance data have to be loaded into the plane's flight management system (FMS). And don't forget the most important task of all: looking over the menu and deciding which entree you want for dinner.

Somewhere in there, the pilots and flight attendants will huddle up for a pre-departure crew briefing. Sometimes this meeting takes place in a designated briefing room before heading to the aircraft; otherwise it happens on the jet prior to boarding. It starts with an exchange of names. The captain then speaks for three or four minutes, going over the flight time, anticipated turbulence, arrival weather, and anything else pertinent or peculiar. Long-haul crews are sometimes together for a week or more. Aside from the practical aspects, the briefing is, if nothing else, an introduction to the people you'll be spending the next several days with.

On domestic flights all of this is quicker and more casual. The majority of the prep takes place in the cockpit, and the paperwork packet is much lighter. The gate agent will run most of it off the podium printer and hand it to the captain or first officer. The crew briefing is little more than the captain calling aside the lead flight attendant and going over the flight time, turbulence, and weather. Sixty minutes is more than ample time to prepare. There are no menus.

Airline pilots do not file flight plans—or plan their flights for that matter. Almost everything that needs to be researched, filed, or requested, from the flight plan itself to foreign overflight permissions, is taken care of backstage, so to speak, by teams of licensed dispatchers and planners working in the airline's operational control center, a sprawling facility that looks like the old mission control room at NASA. We shouldn't give dispatchers short shrift; their job is a critical one. Officially, responsibility for a flight is shared fifty-fifty between the captain and the dispatcher. From pushback to touchdown, a flight remains in constant contact with its dispatcher via radio or datalink.

And maybe you're wondering: What is a flight plan, anyway? Technically it's a document filed with air traffic control listing the operational vitals of a flight, such as aircraft type and registration, requested routing and altitudes, and flying time. The crew never sees this document, or even a copy of it, usually. What we do see and carry with us, however, as part of that great big paperwork packet, is a comprehensive printout, several pages long, containing not only these vitals but a highly detailed, waypoint-by-waypoint breakdown of the flight, start to finish, including everything from anticipated fuel burn figures to wind and temperature analyses to aircraft performance data. We call this document the flight plan. Really it's not, but in practice it is.

Why do planes take off and land into the wind?

In the aviator's world, there are two kinds of speed: speed relative to the air (airspeed) and speed relative to the ground (groundspeed). It's that first one that keeps a plane flying—the air pushing against the wing and holding it aloft. Remember in chapter one, sticking your arm out the window of the Toyota and getting it to fly? Well, you wouldn't need to be driving 60 miles per hour if, instead, you had 60 miles-per-hour worth of wind blowing straight at you. You wouldn't have to move; the wind would be doing all the work. Your arm, which is to say the wing, would be registering 60 miles per hour of airspeed, even as your groundspeed sits at zero. It's the same idea with an actual plane, the chief benefit being that taking off or landing into a headwind means that less runway is needed.

Because of air traffic constraints and noise abatement rules,

into-the-wind operations aren't always possible, and you're sometimes stuck with a crosswind or tailwind. Tailwinds are beneficial
during cruise, but not for takeoff or landing. Racing down a runway,
a plane will be pushed along by a tailwind, increasing groundspeed
and using up valuable real estate, with no benefit to actual flying
speed—that is, airspeed. For this reason, takeoff and landing tailwind
limits are usually very low, at a meager 10 knots or so.

Can you explain how a plane takes off and why it bumps, jigs, and turns, sometimes at steep angles, during climbout?

The plane accelerates to a predetermined speed, at which point
the pilots lift the nose to a specific angle and begin the climb. The
particular speed at which this happens, the amount of engine power
used, and the runway distance required are different for every occasion and are calculated beforehand. It depends not just on the weight
of the airplane, but temperature, wind, and other factors.

Inherently, takeoff is the more critical point than landing. Here,
the airplane is making the transition from ground to flight, and its
grip on the latter is much more tentative than it is when coming
down. It's landings that fearful flyers hate, but in deference to the
principles of lift, gravity, and momentum, this anxiety is misplaced.
Not that you should be, but if you insist on being nervous, takeoff is
your time—from just prior to liftoff through the first twenty seconds
or so of flight.

After breaking ground and raising the landing gear, the pilots
follow a profile of target speeds and altitudes at which they retract
the flaps—often in stages as the plane accelerates—all the while
banking and climbing to assigned headings altitudes. It can be
noisy, with multiple power changes, turns, and pitch adjustments.
If it feels unusually hectic, chances are good the crew is following a
noise abatement procedure on behalf of residents below. These can
require complicated profiles with low-altitude turns and steeper-
than-normal climbs.

Planes heading east might initially turn west after takeoff. Those headed south might at first go north, and so on. Your pilots aren't lost, they're simply following a published departure pattern. Airports can have dozens of these standard instrument departures (SIDs, as we know them). The one you fly will be assigned by ATC as part of your predeparture clearance. Taking off from runway 31L at JFK, for example, the SIDs require that you *always* make a sharp left turn to the south, regardless of your destination. The purpose is to keep flights adequately sequenced and separated, clear of obstructions, and clear of traffic from nearby airports. Eventually you'll be worked into the higher-altitude structure and sent in the proper direction, but expect a number of turns, sequential step climbs, and speed adjustments in the first several minutes of flight. And the last several as well—on arrival it happens the same way, except these patterns are called STARs (standard terminal arrivals).

What if, just at the second of liftoff, an engine quits?

Every airliner is certified for takeoff with one of its engine failing at the worst possible moment. From the passenger's perspective, this is just about that point when the plane's nose is lifting into the air. From the pilot's perspective, this moment is known as V1, or "takeoff decision speed," referring to the speed beyond which discontinuing the takeoff is no longer an option. V1 is different for every takeoff, as determined by weight, runway length, wind, temperature, and flap setting. If a malfunction of any magnitude occurs at or past this point, crews are trained to *continue the takeoff*, as per regulation planes must be capable of accelerating and climbing away, even with total failure of an engine. This guarantee extends beyond the airport perimeter to account for buildings, mountains, antennae, and whatever else. For each airport—indeed each runway—data are computed not only to ensure the ability to fly, but also to avoid off-airport obstructions.

Now, what about prior to that V1 point? With a full load, doesn't an aborted takeoff guarantee you'll be careening off the end of the runway? No. When all the numbers are crunched, two things are certain before any commercial jet begins to roll. First, as we just saw, the plane must be able to climb away safely following an engine failure at takeoff decision speed, V1. Second and no less important, the same jet must be able to come to a safe stop if the takeoff is aborted at any time *prior* to that speed. Think of V1 as a fulcrum. If there's a problem after V1, the crew knows the plane will fly and clear obstructions. If there's trouble before V1, it knows there's room to stop. This includes applicable penalties for ice, snow, or any other performance-altering peculiarities of a runway. And this is one of the reasons flights may be weight restricted when using short runways. Not because the runway is inadequate for takeoff, but because it's inadequate for an *aborted* takeoff.

Which isn't to say that no plane has ever aborted its takeoff and gone skidding off the end. It happens from time to time—meaning very infrequently. With hundreds of tons moving at hundreds of miles per hour, things don't always work out exactly the way the data says they will. To help the cause, modern airplanes are equipped with extremely sophisticated brakes *and* extremely sophisticated pilots.

Bigger planes have incredibly powerful engines and fancy high-lift devices (flaps, slats, and such) that allow them to take off and land at relatively low speeds. The leviathan A380, for example, has the same approach and landings speeds as the much smaller A320. It's wrong, therefore, to assume a bigger plane, by its nature, requires a longer runway than a smaller one. It might or it might not. A lightly loaded 747 might use *less* runway than a maxed-out 737, a quarter of its size.

During early climb, engine thrust is suddenly cut and it feels like the plane is falling. What is happening here?

The amount of thrust used for takeoff is always more than enough, so typically at a thousand feet or so, depending on the profile, it's reduced to what we call "climb power." This saves wear-and-tear on the engines and keeps the plane from exceeding low-altitude speed restrictions. The plane is neither descending nor decelerating; it's just not climbing as rapidly.

It might surprise you to learn that despite the impressive roar and acceleration, airliners seldom take off at full available power. Maximum thrust is used when conditions (weight, runway length, and weather) dictate, but normally they don't, allowing for a reduced setting. This is healthier for the engines, and the power is still there if you need it.

How fast is a plane going when it leaves the ground? And how about when it lands?

Time again for this book's two most important and annoying words: it depends. Certain planes always use higher speeds than others, but from there it differs with the usual suspects: weight, flap settings, wind, and temperature. To ballpark it, a regional jet might take off at 130 knots and land at 110 knots. An Airbus or Boeing could be doing 40 knots faster on either end. On the 757s and 767s that I fly, liftoff speeds fall anywhere between 140 and 170 knots. Touchdown speeds range between 130 and 150 knots. Landing speed will always be the slower of the two, and landing uses up considerably less runway than taking off.

Our pilot told us we were taking off on runway 31 at LaGuardia. How can there be thirty-one runways at the airport?

There aren't. The numbers correspond to the runway's magnetic (compass) orientation. Picture a 360-degree circle, with the cardinal points (north, south, east, and west) of 360, 180, 90, and 270. To figure out which way a runway is aligned, add a zero. Runway 31 is pointing 310 degrees, toward the northwest. The opposite end of the same strip would be designated 13, pointing 130 degrees, or southeasterly. Thus one runway is actually two runways. When laid in parallel, runways are given a letter suffix of L or R, designating left or right. (Taxiways, if you're wondering, use alphabetical or alphanumeric designations—A, N, KK, L3, and so on—referred to using the phonetic alphabet: Alpha, November, Kilo-Kilo, Lima-3.)

An airport can have several runways aligned in all manner of geometry—triangles, perpendiculars, parallels, crisscrossing, tic-tac-toe—or just one (which is to say two). Seen from above, Chicago's O'Hare looks like an aerial view of the Nazca Lines, with seven separate strips for a whopping fourteen total runways. There's no standard length, which like the dissimilar outfield fences of Major League Baseball stadiums, adds some, uh, character to particular airports. La Guardia and Washington-Reagan are known for short, less forgiving runways of about 7,000 feet. Runway 31L at JFK is more than twice that. Ten or eleven thousand feet is a classic "long" runway.

Excavated, paved, lighted, and instrumented for all-weather ops, building a runway is a much more serious undertaking than slapping down asphalt and painting stripes on it. The sixth runway at Denver International carried a tab of $165 million.

Where are the trickiest places for takeoffs and landings? Should flyers be wary of certain airports?

Maybe you've seen those "world's scariest landings" and "world's most dangerous airports" lists that pop up time to time on the web and elsewhere. Take them with a grain of salt, because no commercial airport is unsafe. If one were, no airline would be flying there. Pilots speak of certain airports as challenging, which is a completely different thing. As in any profession, some tasks—in this case, some takeoffs and landings—are more difficult and work-intensive than others, but they remain well within the capabilities of the people trained to perform them.

What makes an airport challenging is usually one of two things, either alone or in combination: runway length and surrounding terrain. Many Andean, Himalayan, or Rocky Mountain airports feature complicated arrival and departure patterns due to nearby peaks. New York's La Guardia, Chicago's Midway, and São Paulo's Congohnas airports are among those known for their stubby runways.

Those complicated patterns might be work-intensive, but that doesn't make them scary. Likewise for short runways. As we saw a few questions ago, a runway must always be long enough to ensure a safe takeoff. Landings work much the same way; a pilot does not eyeball the runway and conclude "that looks about right," then hit the brakes and hope for the best. Taking weight and weather into account—including penalties for a surface slickened by ice, snow, or rain—data must show that a plane can stop within a maximum of 85 percent of the total available distance. Takeoffs and landings are more scientific than people realize. We hear a lot about pilots needing to possess expert judgment and seat-of-the-pants skill. While that may be true, there is almost nothing subjective about choosing where to land or take off from.

It goes without saying, though, that shorter runways leave limited margin for error, and history records numerous overrun accidents, some of them fatal. During severe weather, things can get squirrelly. Low visibility, gusty crosswinds, and slippery surfaces can combine to throw an approach off kilter. The best way—indeed the right way—of dealing with an unstable approach is to discontinue it. Which brings us to the next question…

Just before touchdown, our flight powered up and aborted its landing. We banked around at severe angles before returning for a second approach. Many of us were frightened. How common is this, and why does it happen?

There you are, belted in for landing. The approach is smooth, the weather clear. Down, down, down you come. At 500 feet or so, you can make out the writing on billboards; touchdown is only seconds away. Then, without warning, the engines roar. The aircraft pitches up sharply and begins to climb, groaning and shuddering as the landing gear retracts and the flaps are reset. The ground falls away; the plane banks sharply. You grip the armrest. What the heck is happening? A long minute later, the PA crackles and the captain speaks. "As you're aware," he says, "we had to abandon our approach and make another circuit. We're circling back around for another approach and will be on the ground in about ten minutes." If you fly often, you have experienced this scenario at least once. The maneuver is called a go-around, and it holds a special place in the fearful flyer's pantheon of worries. I read about go-arounds all the time, luridly described in emails from terrified travelers who wonder if they've narrowly escaped with their lives.

The truth is pretty boring: go-arounds are fairly common and seldom the result of anything dangerous. In most cases it's a minor spacing issue: controllers aren't able to maintain the required separation parameters or the aircraft ahead has not yet vacated the runway. Not an ideal situation, but let's be clear: this is *not* a proverbial near miss. The reason you're going around is to *prevent* a near miss. Actual instances where a collision is narrowly averted do occur, but they are exceptionally rare.

Other times, traffic has nothing to do with it. A variant of the go-around, spoken of somewhat interchangeably, is the missed approach, when a plane pulls off the same basic maneuver for weather-related reasons. If, in the course of an instrument approach, visibility drops below a prescribed value or the plane has not made visual contact with the runway upon reaching the minimum allowable altitude, the crew must climb away (often followed by a diversion to an alternate airport). A go-around will also be initiated any time an approach becomes unstable. Glidepath deviations, a too-high rate of descent, severe crosswinds, a windshear alarm—any of these may trigger one.

As for the steepness or suddenness of the climb, that is the manner in which any go-around is executed. There's no need to dilly-dally around at low altitude. The safest direction is up—as quickly as practical. The abrupt transition from a gentle descent to a rapid climb might be noisy and jarring, but it's perfectly natural for an airplane.

For pilots, executing a go-around is very straightforward, but also quite work-intensive. The first step is advancing the power to go-around thrust, retracting flaps and slats to an intermediate position, and rotating to a target pitch—somewhere around 15 degrees nose-up. Once a climb is established, the landing gear is raised. Flaps and slats are then retracted, followed by additional power and pitch adjustments. Once at level-off, the FMS may need to be reprogrammed, the autoflight components reset, checklists run, the weather checked, and so on—all while taking instructions from air traffic control. There is a lot of talking and a rapid succession of tasks. This is one of the reasons you might not hear from the pilots for several minutes.

And when you finally do hear from the cockpit, the explanation is liable to be brief and, much as I hate to say it, maybe not as enlightening as it could be. The reality is, pilots and microphones aren't always a good mix (*see communications, page 257*). In our attempts to avoid technical jargon and simplify complicated situations, we have a proclivity for scary-sounding caricature. Granted, passengers do not need a dissertation on the nuances of ATC spacing restrictions or approach visibility minima, but statements like "We were a little too close to that plane ahead" paint a misleading, if not terrifying, picture. Later that night, passengers are emailing their loved ones (or me) with a tale of near death, whereas the pilots have probably forgotten about it.

How does a plane find the runway during lousy weather? Those foggy landings always scare me.

The standard procedure for bad-weather approaches is, and has been for decades, something called the instrument landing system, or ILS. A plane follows two guidance beams, one horizontal and one vertical, transmitted from antennae on the ground. With the two beams centered in a kind of electronic crosshair, an airplane descends to a designated height—usually about 200 feet above the ground, though sometimes higher or lower—at which the runway must be visible for landing. GPS, now in general use for en route navigation, is still an emerging technology when it comes to approach and landing.

To organize the flow of traffic, ATC will commonly assign ILS approaches even when the weather is good. But on occasions when you really need them, there are three categories of ILS—Cat I, Cat II, and Cat III (in pilot-speak we say "cat" not "category")—with different visibility and equipment requirements for each. Cat I is the standard. Cats II and III are more complicated and can take you all the way down to zero visibility—provided the runway, airplane, and pilots are equipped, authorized, and trained for it (this isn't always the case).

For departures it works similarly. When takeoff visibility drops to certain levels, the runway and the crew both require specific authorization. With the runway it's mostly about lighting and markings. For the crew it depends what minimums you're trained and approved for. We're in Amsterdam, and the visibility on runway 36R is 250 meters. Can we go? Better get the charts out and check.

Runway visibility is measured using something called RVR (runway visual range), where a series of light-sensitive machines arrayed along the runway provides values in feet or meters.

On a recent flight, we made a terrible landing. We touched down crooked and thumped onto the pavement with a bang. Why do some pilots land more smoothly than others?

Now and then a pilot doesn't land as smoothly as he intends to. Although passengers put a lot of stock in the smoothness of a touchdown, this is hardly an accurate benchmark of skill. Judging a flight by its landing is a bit like judging an entire paragraph by a single awkward word or punctuation mark. It's a small, if occasionally memorable, part of a much bigger picture. And a firm or "crooked" landing is often exactly what the pilot is aiming for. On short runways, the priority is getting the plane safely onto the ground within the touchdown zone, not finessing it. The correct technique in a crosswind is a slightly skewed alignment, with one set of tires hitting the ground before the other.

When a plane lands, it sounds like the engines rev up immediately after touchdown. I can't imagine how, but are they reversing?

Jet engines do reverse, and that's exactly what you're hearing. The pilot manually raises a lever, one for each engine, causing deflector panels to lift or slide into place. If you're seated with a view of the engines, you can see these deflectors quite clearly. Once they're positioned, which takes a second or two, engine power is increased—though only so far; full reverse thrust is only a fraction of available forward thrust. It's not a true, 180-degree redirection, but more of a semi-forward vector, like the effect of blowing into your cupped hand. (Turboprop engines reverse as well; the propeller blades rotate longitudinally, forcing air forward rather than backward.) The amount of power used ranges with runway length, brake settings, surface conditions, and, to an extent, which taxiway turnoff the pilots intend to use. Although reversing is helpful, it's the brakes that do most of the stopping, assisted by drag from the flaps and deployment of spoilers. That 85 percent runway length limit we talked about earlier is calculated *without* use of reverse. Whatever help it gives you is a bonus.

The old Douglas DC-8 came with a stipulation that permitted inflight reversal of its inboard engines to help with descents. No modern planes allow this; reversing in flight is strictly prohibited, and the reversers are locked out to prevent inadvertent deployment. Aerodynamically, I suppose you *could* reverse in flight, provided you did it symmetrically. Just as you *could* drive your Toyota backward down the interstate at 90 miles per hour. Chances are it's not going to end well.

While at cruising altitude, I periodically hear a loud rumbling, as if engine power is being increased. This lasts for a few minutes, and then it dies down. It sounds almost like taking off, yet the plane doesn't seem to be climbing.

This is either the gastrointestinal distress of the guy sitting next to you, or what's known as a "cruise climb," whereby the plane is ascending from one cruising altitude to a higher one, be it for traffic, weather, or better economy. Engine thrust is increased, resulting in a noisy rumble, but because the climb angle is a lot more gradual than it is on departure, you don't necessary feel it. This sound is most noticeable only to those seated aft of the engines. People in the forward rows might not hear it.

Where do weather delays come from, and why does the system seem to collapse when the climate goes bad?

Bad weather causes delays in two ways. The first is materially—the physical slowdown that inevitably results when human beings are forced to perform their duties in harsher than normal conditions. If it's raining or snowing, planes tend to be late taking off for the same reasons that people tend to be late getting to work or school: we and our vehicles move more slowly; simple tasks take longer.

The second way, which has greater repercussions and is harder to predict, is by blocking up the air traffic control system. "Weather delays" is frequently a misnomer. More correctly, it's a traffic delay—the product of aircraft saturation at departure point, destination, or someplace in between. Even in ideal weather the skies are crowded and delays common; throw in ice, snow, low runway visibility, strong crosswinds, slick surfaces, and so on, and you've substantially reduced the number of allowable arrivals and departures per hour. Runways need to be plowed or sanded, aircraft need to be sequenced into instrument approach patterns, crosswinds or low visibility might render one or more runways unusable, and so on. And as local traffic backlogs, the effects are soon felt hundreds or even thousands of miles away. A plane headed to New York City might be asked to fly a holding pattern over Pittsburgh. To avoid airborne gridlock, departing flights are sometimes kept on the ground until specified, preplanned release times.

One thing that makes ATC postponements maddening to airlines and passengers alike is their fluidity. They change hour to hour, minute to minute. Typical scenario: A crew is preparing for a noontime departure from Washington to Chicago. The plane is on the verge of pushing back when suddenly, owing to a line of thunderheads somewhere above Ohio, there comes word of a ground stop. The pilots are assigned a "wheels-up" time (*see glossary, page 283*) of 2:00 p.m., or two hours hence. Passengers are asked to disembark, with the plan to re-board at approximately 1:15. But then, fifteen minutes later, ATC calls back with a revised time: the plane is cleared to depart *immediately*. Unfortunately the passengers have all wandered off, browsing in the bookstore or standing in line at Starbucks.

Government statistics show us that better than eight out of ten flights arrives when it's supposed to. That's a strong number, and one that has been improving. Still, it's no secret that ATC bottlenecks continue to victimize tens of millions of flyers. The system is so precarious that backlogs develop even on clear sunny days. We hear lots of flak as to what's to blame for this—from antiquated air traffic control equipment to freeloading business jets clogging up airways—and how to fix it. It's an important conversation, but one that too often ignores the elephant in the room: the fact that airlines have pumped too many airplanes—particularly smaller regional jets—into an already stressed system. More takeoffs, more landings, more delays. Clearly we ought to modernize ATC—for instance by taking greater advantage of GPS technology to reduce the horizontal distance limits between aircraft. But, in the end, you can only squeeze as many planes into and out of a major airport as its runways and taxiways will allow. What is typically spun as an airspace issue is really an *airport* issue.

And we can't talk about delays without talking about the preponderance of regional jets. The number of flyers has more than doubled over the last thirty years, and so has the number of planes carrying them. Yet the size of these aircraft has been shrinking. In 1980, going from New York to Miami or Chicago, you stepped aboard a 275-seat L-1011 or, at the smallest, a 160-seat Boeing 727. Today, don't be shocked if you're riding in a 70-seat RJ. The average jetliner now has 140 or so seats—far fewer than it used to. The use of RJs, which carry up to ninety or so people, has increased 300 percent in the past ten years alone, and today these planes account for an astonishing 53 percent of all domestic departures. That's half of the traffic carrying about a quarter of the passengers—a highly inefficient ratio. At airports like LaGuardia and Washington-Reagan, it's not unusual to watch ten or more regional jets arrive or depart in a row.

Short of building dozens of new and bigger airports—about as likely as constructing a civilization on Venus—the most reasonable alternative is for airlines to consolidate flights and use larger planes.

Unfortunately, competitive forces make this almost as far-fetched. There are a lot more airlines than there used to be, and market shares have fragmented. Therefore, one of the most effective competitive tools is the ability to offer as many flights as possible to the busiest cities. More airlines providing more flights, on smaller planes.

And passengers, after all, are getting what they demand. When airlines come around asking for opinions, their customers invariably answer yes, absolutely, they want as many flights to choose from as possible. Instead of offering five departures a day between cities A and B, why not ten? If the demand isn't there to fill ten big planes, bring in RJs. In this way, frequency has become one of the holy grails of airline marketing; having more flights to pick from sells more tickets. It's an illusion, of course, when those flights don't actually leave or arrive when they're supposed to, but airlines sell it and people buy it.

But for the heck of it, let's try an informal poll. Instead of a choice between a dozen daily flights, a third of which land an average of 30 minutes late, how about picking between a half-dozen larger planes instead, with all of them landing on time? Apply this line of thinking systemwide, and I suspect many ATC bottlenecks would be eliminated. Not only that, but the larger economies of scale would save millions of gallons of fuel while reducing emissions. (It also could eliminate thousands of jobs, so I should be careful what I wish for.)

But what about other possible solutions, such as increased use of satellite airports, peak-period pricing schemes, and the construction of high-speed rail? Let's review some of the commonly suggested alternatives.

1. We need to modernize air traffic control.

Although enhancements are long overdue, they would primarily benefit the higher-altitude, en-route airspace sectors, with a lesser impact where it is needed most—in and around airports. Benefits would include shorter flight times, fuel savings, reduced emissions, and somewhat better traffic management during inclement weather. Those are all good things, but they neglect the reality that a runway can process only so many planes per hour.

2. So, why not build more runways?

For lots of reasons, not the least of which are the long and contentious battles that runway construction projects inevitably trigger between airport authorities, politicians, and anti-expansion neighborhood groups. At my hometown airport, Boston's Logan International, it took thirty years to get a badly needed, 5,000-foot stub of a runway completed. No less daunting are the funding and technical issues. Taxiways have to be constructed; complex lighting systems installed; navigational aids put in place; flight patterns developed and test-flown. Denver's newest runway cost $165 million. And Denver, at least, had the room. At LaGuardia, Newark, or Kennedy? Where would it fit?

3. How about encouraging carriers to serve underutilized satellite airports instead of saturated hubs?

This is one of the more annoying and persistent red herrings. To begin with, big, busy hubs are just that because of the number of passengers who connect there. People transfer from flight to flight— from small plane to big plane, from international to domestic. Satellite airports offer limited amounts of point-to-point, so-called O&D (origin and destination) traffic, such as leisure flights heading to Florida, but there are virtually no connecting options. Therefore, unless a carrier is going to move its entire operation into a satellite airport, the end result is actually more aircraft entering the system. If American Airlines were to begin flying from Stewart-Newburgh (located northwest of New York City) to London, it would not do so *instead* of flying from JFK, but *in addition* to flying from JFK. Or take the example of Southwest Airlines, which has capitalized by drawing millions of flyers into cities like Manchester, Providence, and Islip, providing an alternative to the hassles of Boston, Kennedy, and LaGuardia. Have its competitors at those crowded airports reduced their schedules in response? Heck no. If a certain number of passengers are siphoned away, the tendency isn't to eliminate flights outright; it's to reduce the size of the aircraft. A 767 becomes a 737; a

737 becomes an RJ. Airline competition is seldom a zero-sum game. The market splinters and keeps on growing.

These very same points are what make the high-speed rail "solution" similarly misunderstood. There's no reason to oppose trains on their own merits, but any effect on air traffic would be negligible. See Europe, where railways are fast, dependable, and ultra-convenient, yet the number of annual airline passengers is only marginally lower than it is in the United States.

4. If we accept that airline schedules are to blame, how about a fee system that charges them a premium to fly at the busiest times?

Peak-period pricing, this is called, and it's a popular and controversial idea, akin to levying heavy tolls on downtown automobile drivers as a way of alleviating traffic jams. In cities like London, apparently, such roadway disincentives have met with success. But jetliners are not cars, and airlines are not private motorists. The result would be higher fares with a minimal impact on congestion. With ticket prices as low as they are, it'd be relatively easy for airlines to pass along a modest rise to customers. You already pay extra to fly at the choicest times, and I suspect you'd be willing to pay more.

☆ ☆ ☆

Technology will not fix the problem. Neither will patronizing small airports, bleeding the airlines, or fantasizing about new runways. If you ask me, the only hope is a theoretical one, where carriers abandon their self-defeating fixation with frequency and break their berserk addiction to regional jets. Expecting airlines to consolidate in this fashion is a bit like expecting them to return to the days of three-cheese omelets in economy class, but I can't help throwing it out there. What we have instead is a new normal in which airlines and passengers are resigned to a certain, apparently acceptable level of inconvenience. It is what it is. Try to look on the bright side: 85 percent of all flights land on time. All things considered, that's a pretty strong number.

The idea of a "control tower" strikes me as anachronistic. To whom are pilots talking, and how do they communicate en route?

"The tower" is used colloquially to describe ATC in general, but towers themselves are responsible only for planes on the runways and those within the immediate airport area. There's a lot more to it. To give you some idea, let's follow a flight from start to finish across the United States. As we do, keep in mind that airplanes use an electronic unit known as a transponder to transmit location, speed, and altitude to an ATC radar screen. At many airports, the transponder-radar link is used to track planes along taxiways as well.

Departing from New York, bound for Los Angeles, our flight first obtains local weather info and flight plan clearances via cockpit datalink computer. When it's ready to leave the gate, the crew radios for pushback clearance, followed by another call for taxi instructions. A separate call is occasionally required for engine start clearance. Getting from gate to runway can involve four or five conversations on as many frequencies—clearance delivery, gate control, metering, ground control, and others—varying from airport to airport. Finally a flight will be cleared onto the runway, and for takeoff, by the control tower.

Moments after liftoff, we're handed over to departure control, which follows us on radar issuing turns, altitudes, and so forth as the plane is sequenced into the overlying route structure. A flight can progress through several departure subsectors, each on a different frequency. Once we reach higher altitude, we're guided by a series of Air Route Traffic Control Centers (ARTCC), commonly called "Center." New York Center, Denver Center, etc. They maintain huge swaths of sky, rendering them somewhat irrelevant to their namesake identifiers, and are often located far from an airport. Boston Center, for instance, in charge of airspace extending from Southern New England to the Canadian Maritimes, resides in a building in Nashua, New Hampshire. Centers too are broken down into subsectors, each in the hands of individual controllers.

Eventually, descending into LAX, the above happens more or less in reverse. Center first hands us to approach control, and if the weather is bad and arrivals are backing up, these are usually the folks who'll assign a holding pattern. Around the time you hear the landing gear plunking into position, the crew is given over to the tower for landing clearance, and then it's another conversational gambol with ground and gate control before docking in safely and, of course, on schedule.

Terminology changes when we leave the United States, but almost everywhere the basic sequence is the same.

Transoceanic flights are not normally under radar control, but they do follow specific, assigned routes. These routes, known in some areas as tracks, are made up of connected points of latitude and longitude, with a gateway fix at either end where you transition to and from the normal ATC environment. Flights are sequenced based on speed and time. At each latitude/longitude fix, a position report is made to the controlling agency whose jurisdiction you're in. The person with whom you're communicating can be thousands of miles away. The reports are made by voice using HF radio, or automatically via satellite datalink, and include the exact crossing time, altitude, remaining fuel, and estimated time to the next point.

English is the lingua franca of commercial aviation, and controllers and pilots are required to speak it the world over. But depending on the country, they might also use their local language. In Brazil, for example, you'll hear both English and Portuguese over the radio; controllers talk in English to foreign crews and in Portuguese to Brazilian crews. France, Spain, Russia, and many other countries do it the same way.

Flying from Seattle to San Diego, I was watching our progress on the seat-back screen. We did a lot of zigging and zagging rather than following a straight course. Why?

Despite the ubiquity of satellite GPS, the U.S. airspace system is still a ground-based one, and indirect routings remain common. Planes travel in connect-the-dots patterns oriented around decades-old navigational beacons known as very high-frequency omnidirectional range (VOR), or they follow long, often circuitous strings of point-in-space fixes. Crews use GPS to determine a VOR's equivalent position, creating virtual waypoints in lieu of homing to the physical beacon, but fundamentally it's the same thing. The FAA's much-touted (but poorly funded) NextGen project is intended to streamline and modernize all of this, but it's a long-term project that is just getting started.

Meanwhile, if you've ever paid attention to the air-ground communications through a plane's entertainment system (*see cockpit eavesdropping, page 162*), you've probably been mystified by the calls of controllers directing flights toward all kinds of strange, fantastical-sounding places. "United 626, proceed to ZAPPY," you'll hear. Or, "Southwest 1407, cleared direct to WOPPO." A look at a navigational chart reveals the entire United States—and the rest of the world for that matter—is overlaid by tens of thousands of point-in-space fixes that carry these peculiar five-letter monikers. I invented ZAPPY and WOPPO myself, but I'll bet they're out there somewhere. Most fix names are arbitrary, but once in a while they are coined in folksy reference to some geographic or cultural characteristic below. SCROD is a transatlantic gateway fix off the coast of Labrador, not far from OYSTR, PRAWN, and CRABB. Not far from where I live is one called BOSOX (think baseball). And so on. God only knows what's going on beneath BLOWN, BAABY, and LAYED, a trio of fixes over West Virginia and Pennsylvania.

Flights between the United States and Europe always go far to the north, up over northeastern Canada and close to Iceland. I assume this is to remain as near as possible to land in case of emergency?

It has nothing to do with emergencies. It's simply the shortest distance.

Between continents, airplanes follow what are called "great circle" routes, accounting for the earth's curvature. These routes won't make sense if you're looking at a traditional flat map, because when the earth is crushed from its natural round state into a horizontal one, it becomes distorted as the divisions of latitude and longitude stretch apart. (Depending on the layout used—what cartographers call "projection"— the distortion can be grotesque. Kids grow up believing that Greenland is about ten times larger than it really is, thanks to the preposterous polar dimensions of the commonly used Mercator projection.) If you have a globe handy, however, the logic of great circles is very apparent. Measuring with a piece of string, it's obvious that the shortest distance between New York and Hong Kong, for instance, is not westerly, as it would seem on a map, but pretty much straight north, up into the Arctic, and then straight south. Over the top, in other words.

That's the extreme, but the principle applies to many long-range pairings, and this is why passengers between America and Europe discover themselves not just high up, but high *up*—over Newfoundland, Labrador, and occasionally the icy realm of Greenland. Across the Pacific, same idea: a flight from Los Angeles to Beijing will touch the Aleutian Islands and the easternmost portions of Russia.

One night at Kennedy airport I gave what I thought were accurate instructions to a group of Muslims crouched on the floor looking for Mecca. It seemed to me they were facing more toward Bridgeport, Connecticut, so I suggested they adjust their prayer rugs a few south-eastward degrees. I should have known better, because the most efficient routing between New York and Mecca is not southeast, but northeast. Required to periodically align themselves with a point thousands of miles away, many Muslims know how this works. To face the holy Kaaba at Mecca, they employ what's called the *qibla*, which is the shortest distance to Mecca from where they're praying—a kind of Islamic great circle. My friends at Kennedy were searching for their *qibla*, only to find quibble instead with an itinerant pilot who was thinking flat when he should've been thinking round.

I'm intrigued by the three-letter codes for airports. Many make no sense.

The three-letter abbreviations are devised by IATA. That's the International Air Transport Association, the industry's worldwide trade and advocacy group. (There also are four-letter versions administered by ICAO, the civil air transport branch of the United Nations, but these are used only for navigation and technical purposes.) If the abbreviations aren't obvious, like BOS for Boston or BRU for Brussels, they can be fairly intuitive, such as London Heathrow's LHR or KIX for Osaka's Kansai International. Many of the outwardly arbitrary ones are carryovers from former names for the airport. MCO is derived from McCoy Field, the original name for Orlando International. Chicago O'Hare's identifier, ORD, pays honors to the old Orchard Field. Others are geographical associations or personal tributes, some more obscure than others. In Rio de Janeiro your plane will land at Galeão, on Governor's Island (Ilha do Governador), lending to GIG. On Maui, OGG is homage to Bertram Hogg (spoken with a silent H), Hawaii native and Pacific flying pioneer.

In one of those moments of American puritanical excess, a campaign was launched in 2002 to change the identifier for Sioux City, Iowa, from SUX to something less objectionable. The campaign failed and the letters, along with some pleasantly roguish charm, were retained. The Finns don't mind HEL as their capital city, and neither do the Syrians have a problem with DAM. Not being intimate with Japanese vulgarity, I'm unsure what that country's opinion is of FUK, the code for Fukuoka. To be safe, though, if ever you're traveling FUK-DAM-HEL, avoid speaking in acronyms while checking in.

4 FLYING FOR A LIVING

The Awe and Odd of a Life Aloft

THE RIGHT SEAT: PROPELLERS, POLYESTER, AND OTHER MEMORIES

Boston, 1991

I reach for the starter toggle, left engine. It's a scalding morning and there's no external air, so we're desperate to get the props turning. Out on the Logan asphalt in July, the little Beech 99 becomes a sweatbox, and passengers won't be pleased if their crew keels over from heatstroke.

These midsummer flights to Nantucket are the worst. We're always full, and the island-bound passengers are cranky and petulant. Today we're loaded to max weight, with fifteen passengers—all from tony Boston suburbs, decked out identically in mirrored aviator glasses, straw hats, and Tevas—and a luggage hold bursting with wicker from Crate & Barrel. After several minutes of organizing carry-ons and dusting off whichever unfortunate soul managed to trip over the center cabin wing spar, it's time to wipe off the sweat and get started. "Let's go," I say. There's a tattered checklist in my hand, soggy with perspiration.

The toggle clicks into place, and we immediately hear the grainy whine of the turbines. The propeller begins to spin, and a small white needle shows the fuel flow. But twenty seconds later there's a problem. There's no combustion. Great. So I release the switch and everything stops. We wait the allotted time so the starter won't overheat, repeat the checklist, and try again. Same result. The engine is turning, but it's not running. What's missing, I notice, is the click-click-click of the igniters. For some reason they aren't firing.

"Kathy," I say quietly, "can you see if there's a circuit breaker popped?" I can feel eyes on me. The first passenger row is only inches behind us, without so much as a curtain separating cockpit from cabin. "Ignition, left side?"

A diminutive blond, Kathy is my first officer and something of a celebrity around campus. She is one of only a few people I will meet over the years who, through no small effort, made the unusual vocational shift from flight attendant to pilot. She had worked the aisles at Delta before giving up the peanuts—and most of her salary—for propellers. Is this what she expected, I wonder: taking orders in a sweltering, thirty-year-old contraption not much larger than her car?

The breakers are secure, Kathy reports, running her hand across the panel the way one surfs for an errant wallpaper seam. She motions toward the backup radio, her eyebrows forming a question mark. I nod, and she twists in the frequency. "Maintenance, this is aircraft 804, are you there?" We'll wait ten minutes for the mechanics now, while the inside temp hits 106.

A turboprop engine is, at heart, a jet engine. Combusted gases spin the turbines; the turbines spin the compressors and the propeller. It's the combustion part that we're missing.

After an embarrassing PA to our aggrieved customers, who by now are checking the ferry schedule, I notice the woman directly behind me has a giant wicker beach bag balanced on her lap. Somehow we'd missed it. "I'm sorry," I say to her. "You'll need to stow that bag. It can't rest on your lap for takeoff."

"Takeoff?" she says. Then she pauses, lowering her aviators and clearing her throat. "Maybe you oughta see if you can get the fucking plane started before you worry about my fucking luggage."

As she glares at me with insolently pursed lips, the woman's glasses reflect the pained face of a very hot and very disappointed young captain—one who, barely past his twenty-fourth birthday, often finds that the hardest thing about his job is resisting the urge to take it for granted. I restrain myself and manage a smile, a brittle smirk. I restrain myself, not on behalf of Northwest Airlink, in whose employ I toil in kiln-like summer heat, but on behalf of the twelve-year-old kid I used to be, not all that long ago, whose dream of dreams was to someday wear the wings and epaulets of an airline pilot. If living out that dream means taking abuse along the way from an asshole passenger or two, well, that's the price I pay.

☆ ☆ ☆

Although I have only hazy memories of the day I first soloed a small airplane, I am able to recollect my first day as an airline pilot in uncannily vivid detail. It was October 21, 1990—a date promptly immortalized in yellow highlighter in my logbook. Despite the absurdly low salary I'd be earning, I could not have been happier. This cherished day involved a drive to Sears at 9:30 in the morning, an hour before my sign-in time, because I'd already lost my tie. (And then the clerk's face when I told him, "plain black" and "polyester, not silk.") Later, in a thickening overcast just before noon, I would depart on the prestigious Manchester, New Hampshire, to Boston route— the twenty-minute run frequented, as you'd expect, by Hollywood stars, sheikhs, and dignitaries.

There was no flight attendant, and I had to close the cabin door myself. Performing this maneuver on my inaugural morning, I turned the handle to secure the latches as trained, deftly and quickly in one smooth motion—in the process dragging the first three knuckles of my right hand across the head of a loose screw, cutting myself. Taxiing out, my fingers were wrapped in a bloody napkin.

It was oddly and improbably apropos that my inaugural flight would touch down at Logan International. Airline pilots, especially those new at the game, are migrants, moving frequently from city to city as the tectonics of a seniority list dictate. It's a rare thing indeed to find yourself based at the very airport you grew up with. And I mean that—"grew up with"—in a way that only an airplane nut will understand. On that afternoon in 1990, as I maneuvered past the Tobin Bridge and along the approach to runway 15R, I squinted toward the parking lots and observation deck from which, years earlier, I'd perched with binoculars and notebooks, logging the registration numbers of arriving aircraft.

Our company was a young regional upstart called Northeast Express, and we flew on behalf of Northwest Airlines, code-sharing their flights and using their colors. (Northeast, Northwest, it could be confusing to some of our passengers.) Although the airline was growing quickly, it was run with such austerity that we didn't even have legitimate uniforms. We were given surplus from the old Bar Harbor Airlines. The owner, Mr. Caruso, had also been the owner at Bar Harbor, and I suspect he had a garage full of remainders. Bar Harbor had been something of a legendary commuter airline in a parochial, New England sort of way, before finally it was eaten by Lorenzo's Continental. I remember as a kid in the late '70s, sitting in the backyard and watching those Bar Harbor turboprops going by, one after another, whirring up over the hills of Eastie and Revere.

A dozen years later, I was handed a vintage Bar Harbor suit—battleship gray wool, soiled and threadbare in the knees and elbows. The lining of my jacket was safety-pinned in place and looked as if a squirrel had chewed the lapels. Some poor Bar Harbor copilot had worn the thing to shreds, tearing the pockets and getting the shoulders soaked with jet fuel. I'm fairly sure it had never been laundered. Our hardware too—metal emblems for our hats and a set of wings—were tarnished hand-me-downs from Bar Harbor. Standing with my fellow new hires in our new (old) outfits for a group picture, we looked like crewmembers you might see stepping from a Bulgarian cargo plane on the apron at Entebbe.

The uniforms were doled out by a fellow named Harvey. Tall, gangly, and bald, Harvey was a fast-talking and distrustful sort who wore heavy, round glasses and chewed a long, unlit cigar. As he explained proper laundering techniques and recommended the use of vinegar to clean soot from our epaulets, his cigar rolled and bobbed like a counterweight, always seeming to perfectly balance the tilt of his head. "Keep your hats on," Harvey warned, his eyes bugging out. "Some of you guys look so young, you'll scare the passengers!" He smiled, and his teeth were the color of root beer.

One day, in the winter of '91, Harvey posted a tremendously exciting memo informing us of a uniform revamp. We'd swap our gray service station suits for brand new ones—handsome dark navy with gold stripes. We'd get new hardware too; the Bar Harbor eagle, which looked uncannily like the wings-akimbo bird once found on the caps of Göering or Himmler, was out. According to Harvey, our new threads were designed to keep the airline's image, not that it actually had one, "in accordance with Northwest specs." Ostensibly this made sense, since we were operating in their name and painting our planes in their livery, but the truth was Northwest Airlines couldn't have cared less if we wore banana-colored jumpsuits. It was just a way for Harvey to pull some navy blue wool over our eyes and sell some clothes.

My first airplane was the Beechcraft BE-99, aka the Beech 99, or just "the 99." Same as those old Bar Harbor planes I'd watched over Revere in the fifth grade. This was either sentimentally touching or gruesomely depressing, depending on how you looked at it. Some of the 99s were *precisely* the same ones, still with a -BH registration suffix painted near the tail. Unpressurized and slow, the plane was a ridiculous anachronism kept in service by a stingy and ultimately doomed airline. Passengers at Logan would show up planeside in a red bus about twice the size of the plane. Expecting a 757, they were dumped at the foot of a fifteen-passenger wagon built in 1968. I'd be stuffing paper towels into the cockpit window frames to keep out the rainwater while businessmen came up the stairs cursing their travel agents. They'd sit, seething, refusing to fasten their seat belts and hollering up to cockpit.

"Let's go! What are you guys doing?"

"I'm preparing the weight and balance manifest, sir."

"We're only going to goddamn Newark! What the hell do you need a manifest for?"

And so on. But hey, this was my dream job, so I could only be so embarrassed. Besides, the twelve grand a year was more than I'd been making as a flight instructor.

In addition to just enough money for groceries and car insurance, my job provided the vicarious thrill of a nominal affiliation with

Northwest Airlines. Our twenty-five turboprops, like Northwest's 747s and DC-10s, were painted handsomely in gray and red. Alas, the association ran no deeper—important later, when the paychecks started bouncing—but for now I would code-share my way to glory. When girls asked which airline I flew for, I would answer "Northwest," with a borderline degree of honesty.

My second plane was the Fairchild Metroliner, a more sophisticated nineteen-seater. It was a long, skinny turboprop that resembled a dragonfly, known for its tight quarters and annoying idiosyncrasies. At Fairchild, down in San Antonio, the guys with the pocket protectors faced a challenge: how to take nineteen passengers and make them as uncomfortable as possible. Answer: stuff them side by side into a 6-foot-diameter tube. Attach a pair of the loudest turbine engines ever made, the Garrett TPE-331, and go easy on the soundproofing. All of this for a mere $2.5 million a copy. (Somewhere out there is a retired Fairchild engineer feeling very insulted. He deserves it.)

As captain of this beastly machine, it was my duty not only to safely deliver passengers to their destinations, but also to hide in shame from those chortling and spewing insults: "Does this thing really fly?" and "Man, who did *you* piss off?"

The answer to that first question was sort of. The Metro was equipped with a pair of minimally functioning ailerons and a control wheel in need of a placard marking it "for decorative purposes only." It was sluggish, I'm saying, and crosswind landings could be tricky.

Like the 99, the Metro was too small for a cockpit door, allowing for nineteen backseat drivers whose gazes spent more time glued to the instruments than ours did. One pilot to remain nameless doctored up one of his chart binders with these prying eyes in mind. On the front cover, in oversized stick-on letters, he'd put the words HOW TO FLY, stowing the book on the floor in full view of the first few rows. During flight, he'd pick it up and flip through the pages, eliciting some hearty laughs—or shrieks. Another pilot thought it would be amusing to dangle a pair of velvet red dice from the overhead standby compass. That one had customers giggling, pointing, slapping him on the back, and sending letters to the FAA. Poor Eric lost a paycheck and earned a blemish on his record that would have recruiters at the major airlines affixing the wrong color stickies to his résumé.

The view of the cockpit was even more entertaining if, as occasionally was the case, somebody had spit-glued a magazine photo across the radar screen. Our radar units, mounted in the middle of the panel and visible all the way to the aft bulkhead, looked like miniature TV sets. At the end of a rotation, pilots would clip out a ridiculous picture from a newspaper or magazine, adhere it to the empty screen, and leave it for the next crew.

Next up came the De Havilland Dash-8. The Dash was a boxy, thirty-seven-passenger turboprop and the biggest thing I'd ever laid my hands on. A new one cost $20 million, and it even had a flight attendant. Only thirteen pilots in the entire company were senior enough to hold a captain's slot. I was number thirteen. I went for my checkride on July 7, 1993, about a month after my twenty-sixth birthday. For the rest of the summer, I would call the schedulers every morning, begging for overtime. Getting to fly the Dash was a watershed. This was the real thing, an "airliner" in the way the Metro or the 99 could never be, and of all the planes I've flown, large or small, it remains my sentimental favorite.

I flew the Dash only briefly, and Northeast Express would be around only for another year. Things began to sour in the spring of '94. Northwest, unhappy with our reliability, would not renew its contract with us. We were in bankruptcy by May, and a month later the airline collapsed outright. The end came on a Monday. I remember that day as vividly as I remember my bloody-knuckle inaugural in New Hampshire four years earlier. No, this wasn't the collapse of Eastern or Braniff or Pan Am, and I was only twenty-seven, with a whole career ahead of me. But just the same, it was heartbreaking, the sight of police cruisers circling our planes, flight attendants crying, and workers flinging suitcases into heaps on the tarmac. Thus the bookends of my first airline job were, each in their own way, emotional and unforgettable. But that second one I could have done without. ✈

Please clarify the terms *captain*, *first officer*, *pilot*, and *copilot*. What are the differences?

All modern aircraft are operated by a two-person crew consisting of a captain and a first officer. The latter is referred to colloquially as the copilot—a misleading and misunderstood term. The copilot is not on hand as a backup or a helpful apprentice. The captain does not say to his underling, "Here, son, how about you take it for a minute." Copilots are fully qualified to operate the plane in all regimes of flight, and they perform just as many takeoffs and landings as captains do. Pilots take turns at the controls. If a crew is going from New York to Chicago to Seattle, the captain will fly the first leg and the first officer will fly the second. The pilot not flying is still plenty busy with a long list of chores: communicating, programming the FMS and navigational equipment, reading checklists, and so forth. The captain has ultimate authority over the flight, and a larger salary to go with it, but he may not be the one physically steering the plane. (How he got to be captain is a function of seniority; more on that later.)

Captains wear four stripes on their sleeves and epaulets; first officers wear three. Outside North America, you'll notice slightly different uniform designs, sometimes with stars, crests, or other markings.

A few older aircraft still in service, such as the classic model 747, require a third pilot. This is the second officer, aka flight engineer, whose workstation, including a wall-mounted instrument panel, is on the right side of the cockpit behind the first officer. His job is the management of a multitude of onboard systems—electrical, hydraulic, fuel, pressurization, and others—as well as backing up the captain and first officer.

If you're wondering about the navigator, that's a job description that hasn't existed on western-built planes since the early 1960s. The last known navigator in the United States was the Howard Borden character from the old *Bob Newhart Show*.

Maybe the single most annoying habit of the media is when, in a discussion of virtually any aviation incident, reference is made to "the pilot." I fail to understand how, after decades of experience, the press cannot make it clear that there are, at a minimum, two evenly credentialed pilots in the cockpit. Use of the term "pilot" is fine, but only as a generic reference to either crewmember. To cite "the pilot," at the exclusion of *the other pilot*, is misleading and incorrect—not to mention rude to first officers like me.

Regulations require that long-haul flights carry augmented crews of three or four. This allows for a rotating series of rest breaks. It's slightly different from airline to airline, but usually flights between eight and twelve hours duration will bring along an extra first officer. All three pilots will be in the cockpit for takeoff and landing, but once at cruise they will begin swapping out, one at a time. Thus each pilot spends roughly one-third of the flight on break—sleeping, eating, watching movies, or otherwise relaxing. Flights exceeding twelve hours will carry *two* extra pilots, and they break in pairs. On a fourteen-hour flight, each team of two will work about seven hours.

The luxuriousness of crew rest facilities varies with airline and aircraft type. On bigger planes like the 747, 777, or A380, crews have surprisingly spacious quarters outfitted with bunks. They can be above deck, below deck, or squirreled away somewhere in the main cabin. Some are built into a removable, lower-deck pod reached via a ladder or staircase. (Q: Where is the captain? A: He is sleeping in the cargo compartment.) Flight attendants too are entitled to inflight breaks, though their digs aren't always as cushy as those for the pilots.

Here's a basic but perplexing question: How does somebody become an airline pilot?

In Europe and other parts of the world, so-called ab initio programs are increasingly popular, whereby carriers select, groom, and train young pilots from the ground up, so to speak. Little or no flying experience is prerequisite. More traditionally, however, commercial airlines will not hire a pilot without substantial prior experience. In the United States, the typical major airline applicant already possesses thousands of hours of flight time (including various FAA licenses and supplemental ratings) and a college degree to boot.

Accumulating that prior experience requires that a pilot choose one of two paths: civilian or military. Advantages to the military route include having your training costs covered by the government and that airlines tend to hire military pilots with fewer total hours than their counterparts who come up through civilian channels. Drawbacks include intense competition for a limited number of slots and mandatory service time lasting several years. Historically, upward of 80 percent of airline pilots were recruited from the armed forces, but that number has fallen to around 50 percent at the majors. At the regionals, it's around 15 percent.

The civilian route is a long, unpredictable, and extremely expensive slog.

Step one is primary flight training. At a minimum, you're going to need an FAA commercial pilot certificate, with multi-engine and instrument ratings. A flight instructor certificate (CFI) isn't a bad idea either. The good news is you can do this piecemeal, at your own pace, taking lessons at the local flight school an hour at a time. On the downside, it's going to cost tens of thousands of dollars and demand plenty of dedication. Alternately, you can enroll in one of many aviation colleges—Florida's Embry-Riddle Aeronautical University being the most popular—that combine primary training with a bachelor's degree. This is a faster, more consolidated, and even more expensive method.

The next step is to get as much flight time as possible. The fact that you've got a commercial pilot's license from the FAA might impress girls at a party (though it never worked for me), but it does *not* entitle the holder to a job with an airline—far from it. You still need to accumulate hundreds or even thousands of hours of logbook time before an airline will take you seriously. Prepare to spend at least a few years instructing, towing banners, or engaged in some other means of ad-hoc experience-building—the pilot equivalent of odd jobs, none of which pay well. Once you've hit 1,500 hours, you'll want to study up for what's called an Airline Transport Pilot (ATP) certificate, yet another FAA credential to help sharpen your competitive edge.

Oh, and if you haven't done the Embry-Riddle thing, you'll also be expected to have a college education. When it's not an outright requirement, airlines strongly prefer candidates with at least a four-year degree (though contrary to popular belief, it needn't be within a science-, math-, or technology-related field; there are plenty of airline pilots out there who majored in economics, music, literature, and philosophy).

After a while, provided you're resilient enough and haven't been hauled off to debtor's prison, you've got a nice, fat logbook and all the boxes checked. You're finally ready to apply for that airline job.

At a *regional* airline, I mean. To make a baseball analogy, you've graduated only as far as Triple-A. You can now look forward to several added years of little money and lots of hard work before a major will consider moving your application into the right pile—assuming any of them are hiring. There's a fair chance you'll be spending the rest of your career at this level. In decades past, flying for a regional was considered a temporary apprenticeship, a stepping-stone before moving on to a more rewarding career at a major. That progression, never a sure thing, is today even more of a gamble. The regional sector has expanded so greatly that a position at one of these companies, for better or worse, is looked upon not so much as a means to an end, but as a permanent career.

Here's how it unfolded for me:

Extreme parental generosity funded my initial training. With mom and dad footing the bill, I began taking flying lessons in my late teens, two or three times a week, at an airport outside Boston, working fast enough to obtain my commercial pilot's license by age twenty-one. (I took it easier on the academic side: I had an associate's degree from a local community college, eventually converting it to a four-year degree through a correspondence program.) From there, I became a flight instructor, accumulating 1,500 hours in various Pipers and Cessnas over a three-year span. My big break came in 1990, when I was hired as a first officer on a fifteen-seat regional turboprop, to the tune of about $850 a month (*see The Right Seat, page 91*).

That airline went bankrupt four years later. I then worked briefly at two other regionals before getting a job as a flight engineer (*see pages 98 and 141*) on a DC-8 freighter—my first jet. Four years after that, I was at last offered a position by the large passenger airline in whose employ I hope to remain for the rest of my career. I'd amassed about 5,000 flight hours and was thirty-five years old.

While that's a fairly standard résumé, it's the hiring trends more than anything else—the health of the airline industry and how many positions open through attrition and expansion—that determine where, when, and if a pilot finds a job. The regional sector has the highest rates of turnover and attrition, while the mainline carriers can go several years at a time—sometimes a decade or more—without taking on a single new pilot.

The application process is standard across the industry: Having met a carrier's minimum requirements, you submit an application and wait for the phone to ring. The rest is out of your hands. Aside from getting a written recommendation or two from pilots already on the property, there is little you can do to improve your chances. Networking, as understood in the corporate world, does not exist at airlines.

Tell us about training. What are the trials and tribulations of making the grade with an airline?

Once hired, airline training curricula are highly similar across the industry. Whether a pilot is learning to fly an RJ or a 777, the duration and structure of the regimen are about the same.

New-hires will spend a month or more at an airline's training center. The first thing all of them must endure is a weeklong course known as basic indoctrination, or "basic indoc." It's not as scary as the name implies—nobody gets his head shaved or is forced to do push-ups—but it's several tedious days devoted to administrative paperwork and learning company-specific rules and procedures. In addition to filling out insurance forms, you'll spend a lot of time going over something known as operations specifications (ops-specs, we call them), which is about as exciting as it sounds. Trainees can phone home and mesmerize their spouses with all they've learned about takeoff visibility criteria and the required ceiling minima when selecting alternate airports.

The hands-on airplane training takes around three weeks to complete. Which plane you're assigned to is determined by your bidding preferences, in-class seniority (determined by lottery or date of birth), and which vacancies happen to be available (more on that later in the chapter). Before you move on to the full-motion simulators, practice takes place in computerized cockpit mock-ups—high-tech mini-sims. These machines have fully working instruments and controls, but do not have visuals and do not physically move. You will get familiar with the plane's various systems, rehearse different malfunctions and emergencies, and "fly" instrument approaches galore.

"Systems" is pilot patois for a plane's internals—its electrical layout, its hydraulic and fuel plumbing, the workings of its autoflight components, and so forth. It used to be that flight crews underwent lengthy systems training in a classroom setting, but nowadays the emphasis is on self-study. The company will mail you a package of books and CDs, and you're expected to have a healthy systems knowledge *before* showing up for training. This takes strong self-discipline and the careful compartmentalizing of information—lots of it.

Then come the simulators. You've seen the sims on television—those giant paint-shakers with their creepy hydraulic legs. Everyone has heard how astoundingly true-to-life these contraptions are, and maybe you take this with a grain of salt. Don't. A session of mock disaster in "the box" is exceptionally true to life. The 3-D visuals, projected onto wraparound screens, aren't the most realistic—the renderings of terminal buildings and landscapes, for example, wouldn't win any CGI contests—but the airplane and its systems behave precisely as they do in the real world.

Each session lasts about four hours, not including the time spent on prep and debriefing. It might comprise a series of "snapshot" maneuvers, whereby the sim is repositioned for various drills, or it might follow the real-time pattern of an actual flight, gate to gate, complete with paperwork, radio calls, and so on. Captains and first officers training together are tested both individually and as a working team. Behind them sits a merciless instructor whose job it is to make them as miserable as possible.

That's being facetious. The instructor is a teacher, a coach, and the point here isn't to wash people out. Just the same, I'd rather be almost anywhere than sitting in a full-motion simulator. There are plenty of would-be pilots and aerogeeks out there who would sell their families into slavery for the chance to spend an hour in one of these damn boxes. (You can actually rent them out, though a sixty-minute block of time runs thousands of dollars.) Which is a bit ironic, because there is almost nothing on Earth I enjoy less. I hate simulators, and they hate me—which, if you think about it, is the optimum relationship.

Although flunking out completely is rare, every pilot will botch his or her share of maneuvers. It's not at all uncommon to need an extra sim period or two, and for certain exercises to be repeated. Washout rates at the major airlines are quite low—1 or 2 percent maybe—but never is success taken for granted. Fail a check-ride, and you'll be given another chance, sure. Fail it a second time, though, and things start to get uncomfortable. The majors tend to have an accommodating, gentlemanly approach to training. Regional carriers aren't always as patient and aren't known for their touchy-feely training environments.

After a final sim check, a pilot graduates to the actual aircraft for what we call IOE, or "initial operating experience." This is a series of revenue flights completed under the guidance and tutelage of a training captain. There are no warm-ups; your very first takeoff will be with a load of paying passengers seated behind you.

Those assigned to international routes also receive a brief course in long-range navigation. Additionally, there's "theater training" specific to airports or regions that are especially challenging. Parts of South America, for example, or Africa. For first officers, this is usually self-study, though for captains it entails flying there in the company of a training pilot before being allowed to do so on their own.

And finally it's over. Except that it's not, because pilot training never really stops. Once or twice each year (the frequency varies, depending on your seat and which programs your carrier is approved for) it's back to the training center for a refresher. Recurrent training, it's called—a mandatory rite of study and stress culminating in a multihour sim session. Assuming it goes okay, you're signed off and sent back to the line.

To give you an idea, here's a breakdown of one of my latest recurrent sim sessions:

We begin with a departure from Washington-Dulles. At the moment of liftoff, bang, the left engine fails and catches fire. For good measure, the instructor has set the weather at bare minimums for a Category 1 ILS approach, and asks that it be hand-flown, sans autopilot. Then, a quarter mile from touchdown, we're forced to go around when a 747 wanders errantly onto our runway. Next scenario: We're at 36,000 feet over the Andes, when suddenly there's a rapid decompression. This would be fairly straightforward over the ocean, but in this case, the high terrain means we have to adhere to a preprogrammed escape route and a carefully scripted diversion path. It gets busy. This was followed by a pair of windshear encounters—one each during takeoff and landing, a series of complicated GPS approaches, and an engine-out departure at Quito, Ecuador, where again mountainous terrain entails unusual and tricky procedures.

And that was just the first day. Practice? Is that the right word? Perhaps, though I can't imagine that this is how an outfielder might feel shagging flies before game-time. If nothing else, at least the time passes quickly. And when it was over, my sense of relief was exceeded only by a renewed resentment for those who believe that flying planes is easy and that modern aircraft basically fly themselves (*see automation myths, page 120*).

Wait, we're still not finished. You've also got random "line checks"—periodic spot checks whereby you'll work a trip in the company of a training captain—as well as unannounced jumpseat visits from the FAA. I love my job, but I do not, even a little bit, enjoy having to fly all the way from Europe with an FAA inspector peering over my shoulder for eight hours, scribbling unseen comments into a notebook.

And lastly, pilots must keep up to date with a never-ending flow of paperwork—an administrative blizzard of operational memos, bulletins, and revisions to our books. Seldom a day goes by without *something* changing.

Are pilots trained to fly more than one airplane at a time? Can the pilot of a 747 also fly a 757?

Yes and no; mostly no. Although management and training staff are occasionally cross-qualified, the rank and file is assigned to one specific aircraft. In a few instances, certification to fly different models is the same, as with the Airbus A330/A340 and Boeing 757/767, but these planes were designed with dual-qualification in mind and are exceptions to the rule. There are enormous differences between aircraft types, and switching from one to another entails a lengthy syllabus of classroom and simulator training. At the moment, I fly the 757 and 767. If you threw me into the cockpit of an Airbus A320, I'd be hard pressed to get an engine started.

Transitioning to another model, or upgrading from first officer to captain of the same model, pilots undergo a complete training regimen. Even if you've previously checked out on a particular plane, you'll sweat through an extensive requalification program.

Tradition holds that pilots earn very high salaries. Is this really so true anymore?

You'll often hear about pilots making upward of $200,000 a year. These are the fellows who airlines and pundits love to make examples of during contract negotiations. In truth, a very small portion of all pilots out there make this much—the gray-haired captains nearing retirement, on the highest rungs of a major carrier's seniority ladder. Seldom do you hear about the pilots making thirty, forty, or sixty thousand. Or, at the regionals, twenty thousand.

There are those of us who make a decent living, but believe me, it didn't come easy, and overall the profession isn't nearly as lucrative as it once was. According to the Air Line Pilots Association and U.S. Bureau of Labor Statistics, the average airline pilot salary in the United States fell 42 percent between 1977 and 2010. The biggest drop came in the years between 2002 and 2007, when carriers slashed wages by 20 percent or more. On top of this, pensions have been gutted and benefits cut.

Annual starting salaries at the majors are around $30,000. Even with yearly raises, it takes eight or ten years' tenure before you'll earn six figures. That is, provided a pilot is lucky enough to reach that level. Most who set their sights on the majors never get that far and have to settle for a career at the regionals, where the pay is considerably lower. A junior copilot on a RJ might earn as little as $19,000 a year. Senior captains top out around $100,000.

Readers should be cautious of sources citing "average" pilot salaries. Those averages might pertain only to certain sectors of the industry—the major carriers, for instance, neglecting the approximately 40 percent of airline pilots who work at the regionals. They also fail to explain that a given pilot is liable to be in his fifties by the time he earns his captain stripe and a respectable income, after decades of mediocre pay and perhaps a layoff or two.

Another thing to be leery of are quotes of hourly pay rates. While it's true that most pilots are compensated by the hour, these are *flight* hours, not work hours as most people think of them. A hundred dollars an hour might seem extravagant, but it is engineered to account for the off-the-clock ancillaries of the job: preflight planning, downtime between connections, and periods laying over in hotels. Only a portion of a typical multiday assignment is spent in the air. Over the course of a month, perhaps 80 hours of actual flying are recorded, but a pilot might be *on duty* for 250 hours and away from home for two weeks or more. This disparity spawns the idea that airline pilots work far less than the typical full-time employee. I once heard a radio commentator remark snarkily about pilots "only working seventy hours a month." A pilot works seventy hours a month the way a pro football player works an hour each week.

How much do *you* think a pilot should be paid? What is your passage worth? That's a tough one to answer, and it sets up a trap. Does a baseball player deserve $10 million a year? Or, turning it around, does a teacher or a social worker deserve $24,000? That's making a moral judgment on a market-determined product. Pilots aren't paid what they're worth; they're paid what they can *get*, through negotiation and collective bargaining. But, just for fun, pretend you're traveling from New York to San Francisco on an airline whose pilots are compensated by voluntary passenger dona-tions. A cup is passed around at the conclusion of each flight. How much is safe transport across the continent worth to you? How much would you put in the cup?

In practice, you're putting in about twelve dollars. When you aver-age out the pay rates of the biggest airlines, the captain of a Boeing 767 (a typical plane for this route) makes $190 per flight hour. The plane has 210 seats, and the flight lasts six hours. That hashes out to a contribution of $5.42 per seat. The average flight is 80 percent full, which brings it to $6.78 per passenger. The captain gets just under seven dollars of your fare. The first officer gets around $5.00.

Now let's try a regional. It varies with seniority, but you can expect the captain of a sixty-five-seater to make around $95 per flight hour. For a ninety-minute flight, you've given him $2.74. The copilot gets slightly better than a dollar.

Flying, it has been said, is a lot like acting, painting, or playing minor league ball (or trying your luck at writing a book). Reward awaits the fortunate, but countless others toil in extended purgatory for their art. The trick is to grab a seniority number (*see next question*) as quickly as possible and hope for the best. Rewards come later, not sooner, and though risks are inherent in many professions, aviation is especially unpredictable and unforgiving. Nevertheless, and despite the setbacks endured over the course of my own career, I'm obliged to admit that I enjoy my job tremendously. A berth at a major airline, at least when the ink is running black and people aren't flying planes into buildings, is still a good one.

How are pilots evaluated for raises or promotions? Who and what determines when a first officer becomes a captain?

This, and several questions that follow, require an understanding of the airline seniority system. In the United States and many other countries, all of a pilot's quality-of-life variables are determined via seniority bidding, based on date of hire. Our destiny has almost nothing to do with merit and everything to do with timing. Experience and skill, for all of their intangible value, are effectively meaningless. *Seniority* is the currency of value. Nothing is more important than, as we call it, our "number." We bid our preferences for position (captain or first officer), aircraft type, base city, monthly schedule, vacations, and so on. What we're ultimately assigned comes down to our relative position within the ranks: our number within the airline overall; our number in a particular base; our number within a specific aircraft category; our number, number, number.

First officers become captains only when a slot becomes available, and only when seniority permits them to. How talented you are, or how swell a person you are, will not earn you a faster track to the left seat. Neither will how many lives you managed to save in the throes of some emergency. Only your number can do that.

I should point out that not every pilot whose seniority permits an upgrade to captain will opt for it. The transition from first officer to captain means you're going from the top of one category to the bottom of another. You'll probably be getting a raise, but not necessarily, and once you account for schedule, the places you're likely to fly, and so on, you might have a better lifestyle remaining as a senior first officer than you would as a junior captain. Thus it's not terribly unusual to find copilots who are senior to, and more experienced than, many captains.

The seniority system is not as rigid in every country, though many follow all or part of the U.S. model. And with minor variations, flight attendants work within an almost identical framework. It's at once fair and unfair, the ultimate insult and the ultimate egalitarian tool—dehumanizing, maddening, and immensely important. It's important for the reasons just listed, and also because, if a pilot is laid off or his airline goes bust, his years of accrued tenure become meaningless. Seniority is never transferable from airline to airline. Any time a pilot changes airlines, he starts over at the *bottom* of the list, at probationary pay and benefits, regardless of experience. The long, slow climb begins again. This is industry standard, and there are no exceptions—not for Chesley Sullenberger, not for a former NASA astronaut, not for anybody. When the pilots of Eastern, Braniff, Pan Am, and a hundred other belly-up carriers suddenly found themselves on the street, their choice was an ugly one: start over as a rookie, as it were, or find another career.

If business is bad and airlines are contracting, seniority moves in reverse: captains become first officers; and *junior* first officers become cab drivers. In the rickety profit/loss roller coaster that is the airline industry, layoffs—furloughs, as we call them—come and go in waves, displacing thousands at a time. Following the 2001 terrorist attacks, more than ten thousand airline pilots were furloughed in the United States, yours truly among them. Many are yet to return. When it happens, a portion of an airline's pilot seniority roster, which is to say everybody at the bottom, per date of hire, is lopped away. If cutbacks determine that 500 flyers have to go, the 501st one hired now becomes the company's most junior—and most nervous— crewmember. Some pilots are fortunate, getting on at just the right time and sliding through a long, uneventful tenure. But it's not the least bit unusual to meet pilots whose résumés are scarred by three or more demotions or furloughs, some lasting several years.

Furloughees remain nominal employees, presumably to be sum- moned back when conditions improve or attrition warrants their return. When and if that day comes, assuming the airline that cut you loose stays in business, you're brought back to the fold in strict seniority order—the first pilot out is the last pilot back. How long can it take? My furlough lasted five and a half years.

Pilots can reduce the risk of furlough by embracing the lucrative but less-than-glamorous realm of cargo flying. If the greasy glare of warehouse lights at 4:00 a.m. doesn't cramp your style, you can hunker down on one of the more recession-resistant seniority lists at FedEx, UPS, Atlas Air, etc. You won't be signing autographs for little kids, and your circadian might graph out a little funny, but lay- offs aren't as common in the freight business.

If you're a youngster setting your sights on this mad business, expect that it *will* happen to you. When it does, try to relax; it's not the end of the world (yet). Don't join any religious cults and don't make voodoo dolls of your employer's corporate board. Don't take a job flying unexploded munitions out of Liberia, and, as gloomy as the future might seem, do not sell your wings and hat on eBay. The FBI won't like that, and you might need them again.

And not that you asked, but allow me to propose that the two greatest songs about furlough and unemployment are a couple of old school punk rock staples—the Clash's "Career Opportunities" and the Jam's "Smithers-Jones." The former, from the Clash's eponymous debut in 1977, is a raucous tear-down of the economic malaise in late '70s Britain. The latter, written by the Jam's Bruce Foxton, tells the story of a British workingman who arrives for work one morning, optimistic and "spot on time," only to be summoned into the office and summarily handed his walking papers.

> *"I've some news to tell you*
> *There's no longer a position for you*
> *Sorry Smithers-Jones."*

The song implodes around the word "Jones" in a crash of orchestral beauty. It also makes me nauseous and gives me the willies, because I know the feeling.

We keep being told of a looming shortage of pilots. How acute will this shortage really be?

The first step is to draw a sharp divide between the major carriers and their regional affiliates. It's the latter that may have a problem. The majors, able to cull from the top ranks of the regionals and the military, will always have a surplus of highly qualified candidates to choose from. No amount of attrition, expansion, or even the impending wave of retirements you sometimes hear about will come close to depleting this supply.

At the regionals it's a different story. Tenure at a regional was once assumed to be temporary. It was a job one took before—fingers crossed—moving on to a more lucrative slot with a legacy carrier. This progression was never guaranteed, but if nothing else, it served as a carrot that kept a supply of young, talented, and highly motivated pilots moving through the ranks. That was then. The regional sector is much, much larger than it used to be, and hiring by the majors has slowed to a trickle. Many pilots are figuring out that a job with a regional means a *career* with a regional—one with limited return for the cash and commitment it takes to get there. It's not an easy life, and the pay, as we've seen, is the kind of thing that causes people to skip their school reunions.

An aspiring aviator has to ask: Is it worth sinking $50,000 or more into one's primary flight training, plus the cost of a college education, plus the time it will take to build a competitive number of flight hours (a number that, in accordance with a recent FAA ruling discussed later in this chapter, is about to rise sharply)...only to spend years toiling at poverty-level wages, with at best a marginal shot at moving to a major? For many, the answer is no. A growing number of regional pilots are bailing out of the business altogether, while the replacement pool dwindles.

How much it dwindles remains to be seen. It's somewhat telling that virtually no regional carriers have raised their salaries or benefit packages to levels that would appear aimed at retaining or attracting pilots. Bear in mind too the willingness of pilots to suffer for their art, so to speak. There will always be pilots—some would say too many of them—happy to endure almost anything for the sheer thrill of the job. If you ask me, there will be plenty of experienced pilots out there in the foreseeable future hungry for work, and airlines big and small can continue to expect a hundred or more applications for every available job.

What is a pilot's schedule like?

There's almost no such thing as a typical schedule. In a given month, one pilot might spend ten days on the road logging sixty hours in the air; another pilot might be gone for twenty days, with ninety hours aloft. That's a big range, because seniority has enormous impact on where and when we fly, and because schedules are very flexible.

Every thirty days, around the middle of the month, we bid our preferences for the following month: where we'd like to fly, which days we'd like to be off, which insufferable colleagues we hope to avoid, etc. What we actually end up with hinges on seniority. Senior pilots get the choicest pickings; junior pilots get whatever is left over. A top-of-the-list pilot might be assigned a single, thirteen-day trip to Asia worth seventy pay hours; a bottom-dweller might get a long series of two- and three-day domestic trips scattered throughout the month. And if we hate what we get, it's always changeable. We can swap, drop, and trade with other pilots, even on short notice.

A lot of people assume pilots are assigned to specific destinations and fly there all the time. One of the more amusing questions I often get is: "What's your route?" Seniority permitting, it's possible to visit the same place over and over, if that's what you want, but normally it's a mixed bag. As I type this, my month ahead has scheduled layovers in Las Vegas, Madrid, Los Angeles, and São Paulo, totaling seventy-six pay hours and fourteen days away from home. Not bad, though I'm hoping to dump that Vegas trip for something better…we'll see.

Those at the very bottom are assigned to on-call "reserve" status. A reserve pilot has designated days off and receives a flat minimum pay rate for the month, but his or her workdays are a blank slate. The pilot needs to be within a stipulated number of hours from the airport—anywhere from two to twelve, and it can change day to day. When somebody gets sick, or is trapped in Chicago because of a snowstorm, the reserve pilot goes to work. The phone might ring at 2:00 a.m., and you're on the way to Sweden or Brazil—or to Omaha or Dallas. Among the challenges of life on reserve is learning how to pack. What to put in the suitcase when you don't know if your next destination will be tropical or freezing cold? (Answer: everything.)

At most carriers, cockpit crews are paired together for as long as a particular assignment lasts. If I've got four different trips on my schedule for the month, I'll fly with four different captains. Some airlines, though, use a different bidding system in which captains and copilots are matched up for the entire month.

And, just as there's no such thing as a typical schedule, there's no such thing as a typical layover. Domestic overnights can be as short as nine or ten hours. Overseas, it's usually a minimum of twenty-four hours, though forty-eight or even seventy-two hours aren't unheard of. I've spent up to five full days on a layover. On longer trips, crew-members will occasionally bring along family members (*see travel perks, page 133*).

For cabin staff it works the same way. A senior flight attendant might grab the same coveted layovers in Athens or Singapore that a senior captain does. There are, however, fewer duty-time restrictions and contractual protections for flight attendants, and they tend to work more days. A pilot might fly three or four multi-day trips in a month, while a flight attendant might fly seven.

Should you therefore extrapolate that the largest planes on the longest routes are operated by the most senior and most experienced crews? Not always. One factor is the airport you are based out of. The larger carriers typically offer six or seven base cities to choose from. Certain of these bases are more preferable to pilots than others, and so seniority becomes a relative thing. I'm based in New York, for example, which at my carrier tends to be the least desirable, and therefore the most junior, base. This allows me to fly international routes even though my overall seniority is low. And not all pilots enjoy international flying, even if it pays better.

Many pilots are based—or to use an ugly-sounding airline word, domiciled—in cities other than those in which they live, and will "commute," as we call it, back and forth. More than 50 percent of crewmembers commute, pilots and flight attendants alike. I'm one of them. I'm based out of New York, but I live in Boston. Although commuting is a privilege that allows crews to live where they please, it can also be practical. If you're a regional airline pilot making $30,000 and trying to support a family, living in an expensive metropolitan area like San Francisco or New York City would be very difficult. Also, aircraft and base assignments change frequently. The opportunity to commute keeps employees from having to uproot and move with every new bid posting.

Commuting can be stressful. Employees ride standby, and company rules require us to allow for backup flights in case of delays. This can mean having to leave home several hours before sign-in, or in many cases, a full day prior. Crewmembers commonly rent a part-time residency called a crash pad, where they'll stay, if needed, on either end of a commute. (The décor and sanitary standards of the average crash pad are a topic for another time.) Others, when it's affordable, rent hotel rooms.

One way to cut down on commutes is to bid international trips. Overseas rotations tend to be longer, with some lasting ten days or more, and you don't fly as many of them. An international category pilot might commute in only two or three times each month, while a pilot on domestic runs does it five or six times.

My own commute, with barely forty minutes of flying time, is as painless as they come. Multihour commutes through two or more time zones, however, are not the least bit uncommon. I've met pilots who commute to New York from Alaska, the Virgin Islands, and France. Legend has it there was once an Eastern Airlines captain who was domiciled in Atlanta but lived in New Zealand.

We hear a lot these days about pilot fatigue. Is exhaustion really a concern, and what can be done about it?

Crew fatigue has long been a serious issue. It has been cited as a contributing cause in several accidents, including the 1999 crash of American Airlines flight 1420, at Little Rock, Arkansas, and that of Colgan Air flight 3407 in 2009. The airlines and FAA have been very resistant to the tightening of flight and duty time regulations, with even small changes facing opposition by carriers and their lobbyists. It wasn't until December 2011 that the FAA finally got around to unveiling a comprehensive package of changes that, while imperfect, were a welcome and positive step.

In my opinion, too much of the agency's focus has been on long-haul flying. The circadian-scrambling effects of a twelve- or fourteen-hour nonstop are indeed of concern, but it's also true that long-haul fatigue is comparatively easy to manage. Long-haul pilots don't fly as often, and these flights carry augmented crews with comfortable onboard rest facilities. The more serious problem is at the other end of the spectrum: short-haul regional flying. Regional pilots fly punishing schedules, operating multiple legs in and out of busy airports, often in the worst weather, followed by short layovers at dodgy motels. I'll take a twelve-hour red-eye ocean crossing followed by seventy-two hours at the Marriott any day over having to wake up at 4:00 a.m. and fly six legs in a turboprop, with eight hours of supposed rest at the Holiday Inn Express.

And it isn't cockpit time per se that presents the toughest challenges. The real menaces are long stretches of duty time and the often-short layovers between them. On a given workday, a pilot might log only two hours on the flight deck. Sounds like an easy assignment, except when those two hours come at either end of a twelve-hour duty stretch that began at 5:00 a.m., the bulk of which was spent waiting out delays and killing time in the terminal.

In FAA-speak, the layover buffers between assignments are called "rest periods." Until the changes unveiled in 2011, a rest period could be as brief as nine hours, and the very definition of "rest" itself had failed to account for things like travel time to and from hotels, the need for meals, and so on. If a crew signed off in Chicago at 9:00 p.m. and was scheduled to sign on again at 5:00 a.m., that constituted an eight-hour rest. But once you subtract the time spent waiting for the hotel van, driving to and from the airport, scrounging for food and so on, what existed on paper as an eight-hour layover was in reality only six or seven hours at the hotel.

Finally this has changed. Pilots will now receive a minimum ten-hour rest between assignments, with an opportunity for at least eight hours of uninterrupted sleep. This provision was long overdue, but nonetheless is one of the smartest things the FAA has ever done.

Meanwhile, I disagree with the contention that high-tech cockpit automation exacerbates fatigue. Pilots grow complacent and bored, we're told, to the point of shirking their duties and in some cases falling asleep, thanks to the low-workload environment in a modern cockpit. It's a persuasive argument, but my feeling is that boredom and automation have relatively little to do with one another. Or, more to the point, they haven't any more to do with one another than they've had in the past. Pilots are at times extremely busy; at other times there are long periods of quiet. Duties come and go, ebb and flow. It has always been that way. Boredom was a factor sixty years ago, when planes had rudimentary autopilots and propellers spun by pistons. It's going to be a factor in any profession where there are long stretches of reduced workload—such as when flying across oceans—and when a large percentage of tasks become repetitive and routine. I operate eight-, nine-, even twelve-hour nonstops all the time. There's a certain tedium that I expect and have to deal with. But it's hardly the fault of automation. Heck, if I had to have my hands on the wheel that whole time, expending full concentration, by the end of the trip I'd be five times as bored and ten times as exhausted.

There has been a good deal of controversy surrounding the experience levels of regional pilots. What concerns should passengers have?

When I was hired into my first regional cockpit job in 1990, I had accrued 1,500 total flight hours and possessed a freshly minted ATP certificate. Those were, at the time, average to below-average qualifications. How things change. Over the next two decades, as the regional sector grew and grew, thousands of new pilot jobs were created. To fill these slots, airlines sharply lowered their experience and flight time minimums for new hires. Suddenly, pilots were being taken on with as little as 350 hours of total time, assigned to the first officer's seat of sophisticated regional jets.

The short answer is no. Logbook totals aren't necessarily a good prognosticator of skill or performance under pressure. A given pilot's smarts are not so easily quantified, and as the accident annals will attest, low-time crews hardly own a monopoly on mistakes. All pilots undergo rigorous airline training programs before they're allowed to carry passengers, and the largest regionals have state-of-the-art training facilities on par with any major and have tailored their curricula with low-time new-hires in mind.

The long answer is more complicated. I remember myself as a

young, five-hundred-hour pilot and imagine being assigned to a regional jet. Would I be qualified to the letter of the law? Sure. But am I the best and safest candidate for the job? No. The reality is, there are valuable intangibles that a pilot that green simply does not possess. Therefore, I suppose it is fair to say that regional airlines have become, on some level, less safe. Mind you, we're wrangling with statistical minutiae: less safe is not the same as *unsafe*, and this is by no means an admonition against flying aboard RJs. Nevertheless it warrants our attention.

Regulators agree, and the rules are getting tougher. The Airline Safety and Pilot Training Improvement Act, passed by the U.S. House of Representatives in 2009, brings important changes to training and hiring protocols. The law requires that pilots possess an ATP to be eligible for any airline cockpit job. Requirements for an ATP include a minimum of 1,500 hours of flight time (broken down over various categories) and satisfactory completion of written and in-flight examinations. Additionally the law will redefine the ATP certificate itself, emphasizing the operational environments of commercial air carriers and requiring specialized training in things like cockpit resource management (CRM), crew coordination, and so on.

These changes will make it easier to weed out pilots who lack the acumen for airline operations. For those who progress, it will allow an easier transition from general aviation into the high-demand training environment at a regional. It will lower their training costs and, ultimately, make for safer cockpits. And theoretically at least, it should encourage the regionals to begin offering better wages and benefits, since, for a would-be pilot, obtaining an ATP will entail a financial investment on the order of six figures.

As mentioned in an earlier chapter, most regional airlines, even those that are wholly owned, are entirely separate entities from whichever major they're sharing a paint job and flight number with. They are contractors, with their own employee groups, training departments, and so on. For crews, there is no automatic advancement from a regional to its big-league partner. A young pilot (or flight attendant) might get a thrill from flying an aircraft that says

United or Delta on the side, but it's the small print—Connection, Express—that counts. A pilot for United Express is no more a pilot for United Airlines than the cashier at the concourse newsstand. If he wants to fly a 777 for United, he submits his résumé and hopes for the best, just like anybody else. There are partial exceptions to this, such as at American Eagle and Compass Airlines, whereby limited numbers of pilots are granted conditional flow-through rights to American and Delta, respectively.

What about discount airlines like Spirit or Ryanair? Should we be wary? And how about cargo pilots?

All airlines will brag that their employees are, in some indefinable way, better than everyone else's, but it wouldn't be fair, as a general rule, to say a certain caliber of pilot goes to a certain caliber of airline. The top airlines have a gigantic pool of more or less evenly qualified applicants to choose from. Even in the headiest boom times, there will be hundreds, if not thousands, of highly impressive résumés sitting on a recruiter's desk. One is not exiled to a budget carrier for lack of talent; where you end up is less about skill than it is about luck and timing. As for cargo, companies like FedEx and UPS provide industry-leading pay and benefits, and many pilots prefer the anonymity of the freight business, away from the crowds and hassles. There's a certain cachet when carrying humans versus boxes, but its value varies from ego to ego.

I seldom come across female airline pilots. How many are out there, and is there a culture within the airline industry that works against them?

There is nothing inherent to flying that should keep women away. As one female airline pilot puts it: "Piloting has nothing to do with physical strength, the only obvious advantage men have over women. Technical proficiency can be trained in anyone with the proper aptitude, and this isn't gender-defined." Fair enough, yet it's obvious to anybody who travels that the vast majority of pilots are men, and I'm unsure what discourages women from joining them in greater number. I assume they're the same things, fair or unfair, that discourage them from pursuing other traditionally male professions, and vice versa. Part of it may be the military culture that, for many decades, dominated pilot ranks.

Whatever the reasons, the field isn't as male-dominated as it used to be. By the mid-1990s, up to 3 percent of all cockpit crewmembers in the United States were women—a total of about 3,500, representing a thirty-fold increase since 1960. As of this writing, the number hovers near 5 percent, rising and falling with the hiring and furlough trends.

On-the-job harassment of woman pilots is exceptionally rare, and airline seniority lists, regimented strictly by date of hire, ensure equal pay and promotion. Several of my colleagues are women, and their presence on the flight deck has become so commonplace that, on that initial meeting in the briefing room, it hardly registers that I'm shaking hands with a woman.

If you're wondering, the Organization of Black Aerospace Professionals reports a maximum of 675 African Americans, including 14 women, currently working for U.S. airlines—less than 1 percent of the 70,000 or so airline pilots nationwide.

We are told that modern commercial airplanes can essentially fly themselves. How true is this, and is the concept of remotely operated, pilotless planes really viable?

Air travel has always been rich with conspiracy theories and urban legends. I've heard it all. Nothing, however, gets me sputtering more than the myths and exaggerations about cockpit automation—the idea that modern aircraft are flown by computer, with pilots on hand merely as a backup in case of trouble. In some not-too-distant future, we're told, pilots will be engineered out of the picture altogether.

For example, in a 2012 *Wired* magazine story on robotics, a reporter had this to say: "A computerized brain known as the autopilot can fly a 787 jet unaided, but irrationally we place human pilots in the cockpit to babysit the autopilot, just in case."

That's about the most reckless and grotesque characterization of an airline pilot's job I've ever heard. To say that a 787, or any other airliner, can fly "unaided" and that pilots are on hand to "babysit the autopilot" isn't just hyperbole or a poetic stretch of the facts. It isn't just *a little bit* false. It's totally false. And that a highly respected technology magazine wouldn't know better and would allow such a statement to be published shows you just how pervasive this mythology is. Such assertions appear in the media all the time, to the point where they are taken for granted.

One thing you'll notice is that purveyors of this claptrap tend to be journalists or academics—professors, researchers, etc.—rather than pilots. Many of these people, however intelligent they are and however valuable their work might be, are highly unfamiliar with the day-to-day realities of commercial flying. Pilots too are occasionally part of the problem. "Aw, heck, this plane practically flies itself," one of us might say. We're often our own worst enemies, enamored of gadgetry and, in our attempts to explain complicated procedures to the layperson, given to dumbing down. We wind up painting a caricature of what flying is really like—in the process undercutting the value of our profession.

Essentially, high-tech cockpit equipment assists pilots in the way that high-tech medical equipment assists physicians and surgeons. It has vastly improved their capabilities, but it by no means diminishes the experience and skill required to perform at that level and has not come remotely close to rendering them redundant. A plane is able to fly itself about as much as the modern operating room can perform an operation by itself. "Talk about medical progress, and people think about technology," wrote the surgeon and author Atul Gawande in a 2011 issue of *The New Yorker*. "But the capabilities of doctors matter every bit as much as the technology. This is true of all professions. What ultimately makes the difference is how well people use technology." That about nails it.

And what do terms like "automatic" and "autopilot" mean anyway?

The autopilot is a tool, along with many other tools available to the crew. You still need to tell it what to do, when to do it, and how to do it. I prefer the term *autoflight system*. It's a collection of several different functions controlling speed, thrust, and horizontal and vertical navigation, together or separately—all of it requiring regular crew inputs to work properly. On the Boeing I fly, I can set up an automatic climb or descent in any of about seven different ways, depending on what's needed. The media will quote supposed experts saying things like "pilots fly manually for only about ninety seconds of every flight." Not only is this untrue, but it also neglects to impart any meaningful understanding of the differences between manual and automatic, as if the latter were as simple as pressing a button and folding your arms.

One evening I was sitting in economy class when our jet came in for an unusually smooth landing. "Nice job, autopilot!" yelled a guy behind me. Amusing, maybe, but wrong. It was a fully manual touchdown, as the vast majority of touchdowns are. Yes, it's true that most jetliners are certified for automatic landings—called "autolands" in pilot-speak. But in practice they are rare. Fewer than 1 percent of landings are performed automatically, and the fine print of setting up and managing one of these landings is something I could spend pages trying to explain. If it were as easy as pressing a button, I wouldn't need to practice them twice a year in the simulator or periodically review those highlighted tabs in my manuals. In a lot of respects, automatic landings are more work-intensive than those performed by hand.

A flight is a very organic thing—complex, fluid, always changing—in which decision-making is constant and critical. For all of its scripted protocols, checklists, and procedures, hundreds if not thousands of subjective inputs are made by the crew, from deviating around a cumulus buildup to troubleshooting a mechanical issue. I'm talking about the run-of-the-mill situations that arise every single day, on every single flight, often to the point of task saturation. You'd be surprised how busy the cockpit can become even in perfectly ordinary circumstances—with the autopilot *on*.

Another thing we hear again and again is how the automated

cockpit has made flying "easier" than it was in years past. On the contrary, it's probably more demanding than it's ever been. Once you account for all of the operational aspects of modern aviation, from flight-planning to navigating to communicating, the volume of requisite knowledge is far greater than it used to be. The emphasis is on a somewhat different skill set, but it's wrong to suggest that one set is necessarily more important than another.

But, you're bound to point out, what about the proliferation of remotely piloted military drones and unmanned aerial vehicles (UAVs)? Are they not a harbinger of things to come? It's tempting to see it that way. These machines are very sophisticated and have proven themselves reliable—to a point. A drone is not a commercial jet carrying hundreds of people. It has an entirely different mission and operates in a wholly different environment—with far less at stake should something go wrong. You can't simply take the drone concept, scale it up, build in a few redundancies, and off you go.

I'd like to see a remotely operated drone perform a high-speed takeoff abort after an engine failure, followed by a brake fire and the evacuation of 250 passengers. I would like to see one troubleshoot a pneumatic problem requiring a diversion over mountainous terrain. I'd like to see it thread through a storm front over the middle of the ocean. Hell, even the simplest things. On any given flight, there are innumerable contingencies, large and small, requiring the attention and *visceral* appraisal of the crew. I can't imagine trying to handle these issues from the ground, thousands of miles away.

And adapting the UAV model to the commercial realm would require tremendously expensive changes to our civil aviation infrastructure, from designing and testing a whole new generation of aircraft to rebuilding the air traffic control system. We still haven't perfected the idea of unmanned cars, trains, or ships; the leap to commercial aircraft would be harder and more expensive by orders of magnitude. And after all of that, you'd still need human beings to operate these planes remotely.

I'm not saying it's beyond our capabilities. We *could* be flying around in unmanned airliners, just as we *could* be living in cities on the moon or at the bottom of the ocean. Ultimately, this isn't a technological challenge so much as one of cost and practicality. It's a long way off—if it ever happens at all.

I know how this sounds to some of you. Here's this Luddite trying to defend his profession against the encroachment of technology and an inevitable obsolescence; it's precisely *because* I'm an airline pilot that my argument isn't to be trusted. You can believe that if you want to, but I assure you I'm being neither naïve nor dishonest. And by no means am I opposed to the advance of technology. What I'm opposed to are foolish extrapolations of technology, and starkly distorted depictions of what my colleagues and I actually do for a living.

Earlier you told us landings are sometimes purposely crooked or firm, and the smoothness of a landing is not a legitimate way for passengers to gauge a pilot's skill. What, then, is an accurate yardstick?

Regardless of whether a touchdown is intentionally or accidentally firm, a flight should be judged no more by its landing than the success of organ transplant surgery is judged by the alignment of the sutures. As for an accurate yardstick, I suggest there isn't one. Levels of skill, technique, and knowledge are not the kind of thing a passenger in row 14 can pick up on. Within an airline, all pilots are taught the same methods and will fly the same procedures at roughly the same angles, rates, and speeds. A particular angle of bank might seem capriciously steep, or a landing might be clumsy, but any number of factors could be at fault. The severity of a maneuver, whether perceived or actual, is not always a crewmember's whim or lack of finesse.

What are your thoughts on the alleged heroics of Captain "Sully" Sullenberger and the so-called Miracle on the Hudson?

Chesley "Sully" Sullenberger was the US Airways captain who guided his suddenly engineless Airbus into the Hudson River on January

15, 2009, after striking a flock of Canada geese. Together with the majority of my colleagues, I have the utmost respect for Captain Sullenberger. But that's just it: respect. It's not adoration or a false, media-fattened misunderstanding of what he and his crew faced that day. As the public has come to understand it, Sully saved the lives of everybody on board through nerves of steel and superhuman flying skills. The truth isn't quite so romantic.

I was getting a haircut (what's left of it) one day not long after the accident when Nick the barber asked what I did for a living. As is too often the case, any talk of piloting at some point turns to the saga of Sully-upon-Hudson, and this was no exception. Nick grew starry-eyed. "Man, that was something," he said. "How did the guy ever land that plane on the water like that?" Nick wasn t looking for a literal answer, but I gave him one anyway. "Pretty much the same way he's landed 12,000 other times in his career" was my response. There was silence after that, which I took to mean that Nick was either silently impressed or thinking "what an asshole."

I was exaggerating but eager to make a point: that the nuts and bolts of gliding into water aren't especially difficult. The common sense of water landings is one of the reasons pilots don't even train for them in simulators. Another reason is that having to land in water will always be the byproduct of something inherently more serious—a fire, multiple engine failures, or some other catastrophic malfunction. *That* is the crux of the emergency, not the resultant landing.

And nowhere in the public discussion has the role of luck been adequately acknowledged. Specifically, the time and place where things went wrong. As it happened, it was daylight and the weather was reasonably good; there off Sullenberger's left side was a 12-mile runway of smoothly flowing river, within swimming distance of the country's largest city and its flotilla of rescue craft. Had the bird-strike occurred over a different part of the city, at a lower altitude (beyond gliding distance to the Hudson), or under more inclement weather conditions, the result was going to be an all-out catastrophe, and no amount of talent or skill was going to matter.

Sullenberger, to his credit, has been duly humble, acknowledging the points I make above. People pooh-pooh this as false modesty or self-effacing charm, when really he's just being honest. He has also highlighted the unsung role played by his first officer, Jeffrey Skiles. There were two pilots on board, and *both* needed to rise to the occasion.

Nothing they did was easy, and a successful outcome was by no means guaranteed. But they did what they *had to do*, what they were trained to do, and what, presumably, any other crew would have done in that same situation. And let's not forget the flight attendants, whose actions were no less commendable. Thus the passengers owe their survival not to miracles or heroics, but to less glamorous forces. They are, in descending order (pardon the pun): luck, professionalism, skill, and technology.

There's little harm in celebrating the unlikely survival of 155 people, but terms like "hero" and "miracle" shouldn't be thrown around lightly. A miracle describes an outcome that cannot be rationally explained. Everything that happened on the river that day can be rationally explained. And a hero, to me, describes a person who accepts a great personal sacrifice, up to and including injury or death, for the benefit of somebody else. I didn't see heroics; I saw professional execution in the throes of an emergency.

And if we're going to lavish praise on men like Sullenberger, who did not perish, what of the others like him whose stories you've likely never heard, mainly because their planes didn't come splashing down alongside the world's media capital? I give you Captain Brian Witcher and his crew aboard United Airlines flight 854, a 767 flying from Buenos Aires to Miami in April 2004. They never made headlines, but what they had to deal with was almost unthinkable: a complete electrical failure over the Andes at three o'clock in the morning. Under darkness, with their cockpit instruments dead or dying fast, including all radios and navigational equipment, they managed a successful emergency landing in mountain-ringed Bogotá, Colombia.

Or consider the predicament facing American Eagle Captain Barry Gottshall and first officer Wesley Greene three months earlier. Moments after takeoff from Bangor, Maine, their Embraer regional jet suffered a freak system failure resulting in full and irreversible deflection of the plane's rudder. Struggling to maintain control, they returned to Bangor under deteriorating weather. Visibility had fallen to a mile, and as the thirty-seven-seater approached the threshold, Gottshall had to maintain full aileron deflection—that is, the control wheel turned to the stops and held there—to keep from yawing into the woods.

If you need a couple of heroes, take Gotshall and Greene, whose emergency must have been incredibly harrowing. Theirs was pure seat-of-the-pants improv. A fully deflected rudder? There are no checklists for that one.

We occasionally hear of pilots failing alcohol tests while on duty. Should the flying public be worried?

Few things irk me more than wisecracks about inebriated pilots. The remarks always come in that slightly nervous, joke-but-not-really-a-joke style: "Hey, how about those drunk pilots we keep hearing about? I mean, I know you guys aren't half-cocked up there, but...well, are you?"

Yes, it has happened. Over the years, a small number of pilots have been arrested after failing a breathalyzer or blood-alcohol test. Most infamous, in March 1990, an entire Northwest Airlines cockpit crew of three was arrested after arriving in Minneapolis. All three, who had spent the previous evening's layover at a bar in Fargo, North Dakota, downing as many as nineteen rum and Cokes, were found to have blood-alcohol levels far beyond the legal limit. Incidents like this have kept alive a lingering stereotype of the airline pilot: the hard-drinking, renegade divorcee, with crows' feet flanking his eyes and a whiskey-tempered drawl, a flask tucked into his flight case. And it's easy to jump to conclusions. For every pilot nabbed, there must be ten others over the legal limit, right?

No. Believe me, this isn't something pilots play fast and loose with. Why would they, with their careers hanging in the balance? Violators are subject to immediate, emergency revocation of their pilot certificates and possibly prison time as well. My personal observations aren't a scientific sample, but I have been flying commercially since 1990 and I have never once been in a cockpit with a pilot I knew or suspected of being intoxicated. I understand and expect that passengers worry about all sorts of things, rational and otherwise. But as a rule, this should not be one of them.

The FAA blood-alcohol limit for airline pilots is .04 percent, and we are banned from consuming alcohol within eight hours of reporting for duty. Pilots must also comply with their employer's in-house policies, which tend to be tougher. Above and beyond that, we're subject to random, unannounced testing for drugs and alcohol. Overseas, the regulations are even tighter. In Britain, the legal limit is set at 20 milligrams of alcohol per 100 milliliters of blood. That's four times lower than the British limit for drunk driving and equates to about .02 percent blood-alcohol level.

Having said all of that, it should go without saying that alcoholism exists in aviation just as it exists in every other profession. To their credit, air carriers and pilot unions like the Air Line Pilots Association (ALPA) have been very successful with proactive counseling programs that encourage pilots to seek treatment. Not long ago, I flew with a colleague who participated in the HIMS program, an intervention and treatment system put together several years ago by ALPA and the FAA. HIMS (the name is from a 1970s research project known as the Human Intervention Motivation Study) has treated more than four thousand pilots, with only 10 to 12 percent of participants suffering relapse. It has kept alcohol out of the cockpit and has helped prevent the issue from being driven underground, where it's more likely to be a safety issue.

Can a pilot grounded for drinking ever fly again? Among the most inspirational stories out there is that of Northwest captain Lyle Prouse, one of the trio arrested that morning in Minnesota in 1990. Prouse, an alcoholic whose parents had died of the disease, became a poster pilot for punishment and redemption. He was given sixteen months in federal prison and then, in a remarkable and improbable sequence of events, was able to return to the cockpit on his sixtieth birthday and retire as a 747 captain. Once out of jail, Prouse was forced to requalify for every one of his FAA licenses and ratings. Broke, he relied on a friend to lend him stick time in a single-engine trainer. Northwest's then-CEO, John Dasburg, who himself had grown up in an alcoholic family, took personal interest in Prouse's struggle and lobbied publicly for his return. You'll see Prouse in interviews from time to time, and inevitably you'll be struck by how forthrightly he takes responsibility, without resorting to the sobby self-flagellation of most public apologies. Always one is left, unexpectedly, to conclude that this convicted felon deserved his second chance. In 2001, he was among those granted presidential pardons by Bill Clinton.

What is the purpose of those complicated watches I always see pilots wearing? And what do you carry around in those heavy black briefcases?

The purpose of the watches is to tell us what time it is. Watches are required as backups to the ship's clocks, but nothing more elaborate than a sweep hand is needed. If a pilot prefers something fancy or expensive, that's his or her business. My fifteen-year-old Swiss Army watch does the job wonderfully.

Inside those black leather bags is a library of leather-bound navigational binders containing several hundred pages of maps, charts, approach procedures, airport diagrams, and other technical arcana. Additional books are the Aircraft Operating Manual (AOM) and General Operations Manual (GOM). You'll also find a headset, spare checklists, quick-reference cards, a flashlight, and various personal sundries (mine include Post-it pads, pens, earplugs, and a big batch of wet-nap packets to wipe away the dust, crumbs, and grime from the radio panels and other cockpit surfaces, which are routinely filthy).

You'll be seeing fewer and fewer of these bags, as airlines turn to digital versions of those bulky manuals. The "paperless cockpit," it's called, and it's already here. jetBlue's pilots have been relying on laptops for several years, while United, Delta, and Southwest are moving to tablet-based platforms. Depending on the carrier's needs and preferences, an iPad or other device can be issued to each pilot, or a pair of them can be mounted and wired into the cockpit itself. The cockpit will never be entirely paper-free, but the more cumbersome hard-copy material will be more quickly and easily accessible in digitized form.

And quickly and easily *revised*. The switch to electronic manuals is the best idea I've heard in years, if for no other reason than it frees the average pilot from the savagery and tedium of having to update and revise his books, which under normal circumstances are subject to hundreds of revisions every month. The tiniest addendum to any approach or departure procedure, and bang, eighteen different pages needed to be swapped out. A particularly hefty set of revisions can take two hours or more to complete. Common side effects include dizziness, repetitive motion injuries, and suicide.

Much of the problem here is that airlines and regulators insist on supersaturating crews with data and information. What should be a relatively thin volume of useful information becomes thousands of pages of fluffery. It'll still be there, but at least we won't need to lug it around with us anymore. United says that its move to iPads will save 16 million sheets of paper annually. I can believe it. It will also save time, fuel, and visits to the chiropractor.

What happens if the first officer topples a Coke Zero all over his new iPad or drops it on the floor? Not to panic: these are reference materials, not do-or-die sets of instructions. There will always be at least two devices on board, and anything truly critical will also remain in hard copy.

How are flights catered for the crew? Do pilots sometimes bring their own food from home?

It varies from carrier to carrier, but you can assume pilots and flight attendants are provided with food on any flight longer than about five hours. Some stations will stock a designated crew meal, but normally the cockpit crew gets the same food that is served in first or business class (yes, all the courses, including soup, salads, and desserts). At my airline we are handed a menu—the same one given to the passengers—prior to departure, and we write down our preferences. Passengers have priority on the entrees; we get what's left over. With the possibility of food poisoning in mind, pilots are encouraged to eat different entrees, but this is not a hard and fast rule. In practice, it comes down to your preferences and what's available.

Shorter-haul domestic and regional pilots are on their own. It's pretzels, peanuts, the food court, or whatever you carry with you.

And later that night…it's ramen time! If you fail to grasp why ramen noodles would be a must-carry item as important as clean socks and underwear, you've never been a very hungry pilot checking into a motel at midnight for an eight-hour layover. There are healthier and tastier things to eat, but ramen is cheap, never goes bad, and cooks fast. Give me a packet of Trader Joe's finest art noodles and an in-room coffeemaker, and I'll show you a feast:

Directions: (1) Rinse out coffeemaker filter basket; (2) Crush noodle brick into the carafe; (3) Fill coffeemaker with water and switch on; (4) Once carafe is full, wait three minutes, then add flavor packet and enjoy. Don't overfill, and always be sure the filter basket is clean, as coffee-flavored ramen is even worse than Creamy Chicken. Remember to carry a plastic fork to replace the metal one stolen by TSA, or you'll be forced to eat with your hands or by holding two pencils in the shape of chopsticks. For a touch of the exotic—that is, marginally less pathetic—spice up your snack with Guyanese hot sauce.

The late Mamofuku Ando developed ramen noodles during food shortages in postwar Japan. The company he founded, Nissin Food Products, once developed a special, vacuum-packed ramen for the benefit of Japanese astronaut Soichi Noguchi on his trip aboard the U.S. Space Shuttle. No word on whether Nissin ever thought about targeting airline workers, but I can attest to the product's easy adaptability to a life aloft.

We've all heard the stories from aviation's more glamorous days about flight attendants and pilots partying and hopping from bed to bed with one another. With flight attendants looking more matronly and pilots attaining the same level of mystique as taxi drivers, it's difficult, if not painful, to imagine that there's much hanky-panky still going on. Is there?

If so, I have long been excluded from it. Beyond that, I don't know what to say. All in all, it's probably not much different from any other work environment, though things are maybe faster and looser, which is to say younger, at the regionals.

In 2003, two Southwest Airlines pilots were terminated for going *au naturel* in flight. I don't know exactly what happened and I should probably withhold judgment, as these sorts of things have a way of becoming distorted when stripped, if you will, of context. But for the record, no, I have never taken my clothes off during flight.

Well, except once. It was the summer of 1995, and a pavement-melting heat wave was sweeping across the Midwest. I was based in Chicago as a first officer on a sixty-four-seat ATR-72. The European-built ATR is a sophisticated plane, but in all that wiring and plumbing they forgot the air conditioning. Tiny eyeball vents blow out tepid wisps of air. On this particular day, a superheated haze had settled over O'Hare, pushing the temperature to 107 degrees. I was up front, finishing my preflight checks and waiting for the captain. I was so hot that I could hardly move. So I took my shirt and tie off. Pilot shirts, which are mostly polyester, are uncomfortable enough even in a perfect climate. Crank the heat and it's like wearing chain mail. I also removed my shoes.

The captain arrived—a large, slow-moving fellow in his fifties who I'd never met before. He stepped into the cockpit and discovered his first officer drenched in perspiration, dehydrated, wearing only his trousers and a Sony headset. He didn't speak at first. Then he sat down, turned to me, and asked calmly: "You *are* going to put your clothes back on, aren't you?"

I told him I'd get dressed again as soon as the inside temperature fell below 95 degrees, provided I was still conscious. I offered to put a T-shirt on, but the only one I could reach, from my hand luggage, was a Hüsker Dü *Metal Circus* tour shirt—an artifact from 1983, as greasy and discolored as the burning Chicago sky.

"Arright, fine," said the captain. "Just don't let anyone see you." And so I flew bare-chested, all the way to Lansing and back.

Word on the street says that pilots are privy to some pretty good travel benefits.

It's true. However, with the exception of a privilege that allows access to the auxiliary cockpit jumpseats, the perks extended to us are no different from those enjoyed by any other airline employee. Normally, all full-time workers and their immediate family members (nowadays this includes domestic partners) are entitled to complimentary, space-available transportation throughout their carrier's network, with upgrades to first or business class if empty seats permit. Sometimes there is a small per-segment charge and a yearly fee; it varies company to company.

In addition, reciprocal agreements between carriers allow employees of one airline, plus their eligible family members, to fly on another, subject to what are called "ZED fares." That's an acronym for Zonal Employee Discount—a new, simplified system that replaces the more complex ID fare arrangement that had been in place for decades. Again, all travel is standby only, and ZED fares do not permit upgrades. Still, it's a fantastic deal. If I want to fly from Bangkok to Seoul on Korean Air or Thai Airways, it'll cost around $70 one way, fees and taxes included. New York to Amsterdam on KLM, about $100.

If you're looking to bring a friend along, or you want to reward that babysitter who puts up with your bratty kids, most airlines grant a limited number of reduced-rate tickets each year, commonly called "buddy passes," that can be given out to friends, extended family, the woman whose cat you ran over, etc. Buddy passes are considerably more expensive than the passes used by employees themselves, but they're fully refundable and reservations can be changed without penalty.

Traveling on your benefits is generally referred to as "nonrevving." The root term, nonrev, is shorthand for nonrevenue, as the airline makes little or no income from your patronage. Nonrevs are often conspicuous at the boarding gate: they're the ones sweating, looking nervous, and occasionally weeping as they wait for their name to be called at the last minute. Seats are never guaranteed; careful planning, patience, and flexibility are a must. All employees have one or more nightmare tales of getting stuck somewhere. I could tell you about the three days I spent at Charles de Gaulle airport, trying and failing to reach Cairo, and the nonrefundable trip through Egypt that it cost me.

Contrary to what a lot of travelers think, first and business class seats are *never* awarded to employees ahead of eligible passengers. I'm sorry if the opportunity for you to upgrade wasn't available on a particular flight; the rules for mileage redemption and whatnot are Byzantine and they don't always seem to be fair. Please direct your complaint to the airline's pricing, marketing, or frequent flyer departments. All I can tell you for sure is that no premium seat is ever blocked for a freeloading employee. If one of us is riding there, that seat was not available for upgrade and would otherwise be empty. The one exception would be an occasion when an on-duty crewmember is being repositioned—deadheaded, as we say—on an international flight, when work rules may stipulate a seat in business or first.

Despite our generous benefits, it might surprise you to learn that pilots are not, on the whole, especially adventurous travelers. Not to badmouth my brethren, but the average pilot's lack of wanderlust has never ceased to depress me. Nowadays pilots are required to hold passports, but it wasn't always this way, and in the past I encountered many a coworker who possessed neither a passport nor any particular interest in leaving the country. I remember one pilot who, it was revealed during casual conversation about vacation plans, had no idea what the capital of Spain was. Other employees too: I recall a young flight attendant on a layover in Quebec—Canada!—who would not leave her hotel room for fear of, as she put it, "culture shock."

You can find this attitude in any line of work, I suppose, but it's especially frustrating to find it in the airline business. Travel is what we do. Our customers spend years saving up for once-in-a-lifetime adventures, yet here are airline workers, whose benefits allow them to reach far corners of the world at little or no cost, who scorn the very notion of global travel.

Though maybe we shouldn't be shocked. After all, this is a mindset shared by millions of Americans. I am well aware that most citizens lack the time and money to go zipping around the planet, but the truth remains that too many Americans are shamefully, even willfully, disinterested in the world beyond their borders and have, at best, a superficial awareness of geography. One *National Geographic* survey revealed that 85 percent of Americans between ages eighteen and twenty-four were unable to locate either Afghanistan or Iraq on a map. Sixty-nine percent couldn't find Great Britain, and 33 percent of young Americans believed the U.S. population to be between 1 and 2 billion.

Is it healthy for the citizens of a nation that wields so much power, economically and militarily, to be so oblivious, if not xenophobic? Are global influence and global ignorance not, in the end, mutually exclusive? Do we ignore the rest of the world at our peril?

Traveling abroad, I'm often struck by the lack of American tourists compared to those from other nations. Several times I have been on group tours—in Botswana, Mali, Egypt—and out of ten or fifteen people, I was the only American. The Brits, Dutch, Australians, Germans, Israelis, and Japanese, on the other hand, are everywhere, joined by growing numbers from China and India. Nations like Australia, Denmark, Sweden, and the Netherlands have relatively tiny populations, yet per capita they travel far more widely than Americans. Granted, foreigners tend to receive a lot more vacation time than we do, and our country's geography, bookended by a pair of large oceans, makes long-distance travel difficult. At heart, however, this is less about practicality than a peculiar American inertia.

If it were up to me, every American student, in exchange for financial aid, ought to be conscripted into a semester or more of overseas service. And certain international travel, like the purchase of a hybrid car, should be tax-deductible.

All of that being said, I don't wish to idealize or romanticize the act of travel. There is plenty of beauty and splendor in the world to behold, it's true. But there is a greater amount of despair, poverty, pollution, and corruption. Travel can be relaxing, educational, and all the good things in between. And it can also be demoralizing and soul-crushing. Visit any number of places and you will see, right there in front of you, how the world is falling to pieces; how the planet has been ravaged, how life is cheap, and how there is little that you, with or without your good conscience, can do about it. It's enough to make you rush straight home and flush your passport down the toilet.

There are those who say the world is righting itself. We are, the thinking goes, on the cusp of some great, inexorable push toward social and ecological justice. We are moving this way because, with our backs against a wall of human-engineered oblivion, we have to. Well, I'm not sure I agree with that. My eyes have shown me too much of a world that is filthy, overcrowded, and desperate.

The downside of travel: a firsthand view of the planet's more unfortunate realities. This is a matter of perspective, of course, and one can easily argue that experiencing the world at its worst is in fact *more* valuable than savoring its grander, friendlier aspects. Perhaps if a critical mass of people took the time to see and confront these stark realities, things would be different.

The first step, in any case, is *getting out there*. I have, figuratively speaking, fished my passport out of the toilet more than once. I'll keep going, and you should too.

Accommodations: On the Road with Patrick Smith

Layovers for international crews are usually at four- or five-star properties in the heart of the city. I have fond memories of multiday layovers in places like Cairo, Amman, Cape Town, and Budapest. At the JW Marriott in Mexico City, the guestrooms have exposed beams, Aztec ceramics, and floor-to-ceiling views of the mountains. The right room, the right city, and the right amount of time, and your layover becomes a miniature paid vacation.

In Brussels, Belgium, back in my cargo-flying days, I logged over a hundred nights in the Hilton on Boulevard de Waterloo, where the facecloths are folded like lotus flowers and the man who comes to fix your toilet is wearing a suit. We got the executive floor, up on 23, with marble walk-in showers and a vista of the imposing, if perpetually scaffold-enshrouded, Palace of Justice. Once, after an especially late arrival and with our normal rooms occupied, I was given a deluxe apartment suite with a six-person hot tub and an eight-place dining table. The walls in that room, I'm sure, could have told stories of celebrities and NATO gener-als. And then, each morning, the gardenside buffet: a full American breakfast with omelets cooked to order.

In the Brussels Hilton, at last, I began to feel like, well, an *airline pilot*, in that '60s movie, Pan Am captain sort of way. Even on a sixty-hour layover I felt bad leaving the room. Why bother sightseeing when I could lounge around in my Hilton bathrobe, watching the BBC and slipping out to the lounge at cocktail hour?

But what a squander that would be. Brussels is an ideal jumping-off point for day trips. And so, after polishing off my omelet, I'd force myself out of the Hilton and onward to Antwerp, Paris, Luxembourg, or Liege. Antwerp's sumptu-ous railway station is itself worthy of a trip. Other excur-sions were up to moody Ghent (St. Bavo's Cathedral and the famous van Eyck triptych), tourist-choked Brugge, or the three-hour ride to Amsterdam.

Belgium's weather is perpetually gray, and one of my late-night customs in Brussels was taking long walks in the pre-dawn fog—past the Royal Palace and along the park; cutting left to the spectacular Grand-Place, with its gables and filigreed rooftops; up toward the Botanical Gardens and seedy Gare du Nord; then down the length of Waterloo. I abandoned these red-eye constitutionals after the night I had my arm smashed by a drunken vagrant. My elbow still aches from the contusion, having fallen backward against the curb while dodging the man as he slashed at me with a ballpoint pen. The stressful part wasn't the fall, or even the pre-dawn police car ride to a Belgian hospital, but having to call in sick for the trip home, a predicament that cost my airline untold thousands of dollars. The flight was delayed a full day in wait for my replacement, who had to be flown in from the States and legally rested. I spent two days recovering in my room, watching movies with my arm wrapped in gauze and dripping with orange anaesthetizing gel. In the days after my injury, fancifully embellished rumors of the assault began to circulate among my colleagues. Versions of the story included one where I was knocked unconscious by a gang of marauding Moroccans, and another where I was chased and beaten by a pimp. I denied nothing.

So the dazzle (and danger) of commercial flying isn't totally buffed away; you just need to know where to find it.

And chances are it won't be at a HoJo's in Pensacola. Things are a lot less swanky on the domestic front. Relaxing layovers in a downtown Hilton or Westin aren't uncommon, but neither are nine-hour overnights at a cookie-cutter motel next to the runway. Even the shorter stays are in decent places, but they're the kind of generic, fast-food hotel you find everywhere; you've seen their office park contours and over-fertilized lawns all over the country: Fairfield, Courtyard, Hampton. I know these places well, mostly from my regional pilot years. My ballpoint pen collection is like a drive down I-95 or a loop around O'Hare, and I possess an unsettling ability to tell a Holiday Inn Express from a La Quinta blindfolded, by the smell of the lobby.

Rest and recovery, not local attractions, are the focus when time is limited. Thus, in the minds of pilots and flight attendants, some destinations are perceived not as cities at all, but as rooms, beds, and amenities. I have been known to bid my trips in strict deference to three things: the tastefulness of wallpaper, the firmness of a mattress, and access to food. In most people's minds, forty-eight hours in New York City are a lot more fun than eleven hours in Dallas. That is, until you've spent back-to-back nights at the Five Towns Motor Inn near Kennedy airport. When the Hyatt in San Francisco airport stopped allowing crews into their lounge for complimentary hors d'oeuvres, I began bidding Miami instead, where the free breakfast at the AmeriSuites included pancakes and fresh fruit.

All of us love the guilty pleasure indulgences of a five-star high-rise, but there are a lot of things to dislike about even the nicest and most expensive hotel rooms: temperamental air conditioning, toe-breaking doorjambs, ergonomically hellish "work spaces." And here's another one: cardboard brochures. Nowadays, each and every hotel amenity, from room service to Wi-Fi, is hawked through one or more annoying advertisements displayed throughout the room. Cards, signs, menus, and assorted promotional materials— they're everywhere: on the dresser, in the closet, on the pillows, in the bathroom. I wouldn't mind if this laminated litter was placed unobtrusively, but it tends to be exactly in the way, and I resent having to spend five minutes after an exhausting red-eye gathering up these diabolical doo-dads and heaving them into a corner where they belong. One's first moments in a hotel room ought to feel welcoming, not confrontational.

Food and room service are another topic entirely. Be careful never to dine at the Pullman Hotel in Dakar, Senegal, where the surly poolside waitress might, eventually, bring you the pizza you ordered ninety minutes ago, and where the in-room menu offers such delectables as

- Chief Salad
- Roasted Beef Joint on Crusty Polenta
- The Cash of the Day
- Paving Stone of Thiof and Aromatic Virgin Sauce

That last one sounds like a chapter from a fantasy novel. Head instead to La Layal, a great little Lebanese place up the street, where, once you get past the Testicles with Garlic and the Homos with Chopped Meat, the menu is both coherent and tasty.

I shouldn't complain, seeing that most of my rooms are paid for. Yes, airlines cover the cost of all crewmember accommodations while on assignment. We are responsible only for incidentals. An hourly per-diem is also added to the employee's paycheck to cover meals. If you see a pilot or flight attendant paying for a room, chances are that he or she is off duty and on the front or back end of a personal commute. If an assignment begins early in the day or finishes late, leaving insufficient time to fly in or out, we're on the hook. Some crewmembers buddy up in crash pads; others will rent a room close to the airport (*see commuting and crash pads, page 113*).

Pilots spend a third or more of their lives on the road, sleeping in hotel rooms. It's a disorienting, at times depressing way to live. But for those who enjoy traveling, it can also be exciting and enlightening—even a touch glamorous.

5 EN ROUTE

Life in the Cabin

NORTH LATITUDE: FEAR AND LOATHING ON THE HIGH ATLANTIC

Brussels, Belgium, 1998

At midnight at the Brussels airport, three men in olive uniforms stand next to me at a checkpoint. They are straight and tall with skin like cinnamon—that distinct, horn-of-Africa brown. Their suits are crisp and spotless, with gold hash marks and sharply crested hats. The captain looks at his watch, and you can almost hear his sleeve, stiff as aluminum, snapping taut like a sheet.

I am tired and sweaty and the wheels of my luggage need oil. The three men nod without smiling. They are pilots, but the impression they make is closer to one of soldiers, of an elite military unit protecting some corrupt head of state. Surreptitiously I read the tags affixed to their cases, and I learn they are a crew from Ethiopian Airlines. Minutes earlier I'd spotted their jet parked on the mist-shrouded tarmac, its old-fashioned livery a throwback to an earlier, more prestigious time: three colored stripes twisting sharply into a lightning bolt, bisected by the figure of the Nubian lion. High on the tail, the letters EAL fill three diagonal flashes of red, yellow, and green.

I feel my pulse quicken. "Nice flight?" I ask the captain.

In perfect English, he answers. "Yes, not too bad, thank you."

"Where did you come in from?"

"Addis," he says. And of course he is referring to Addis Ababa, that mysterious Ethiopian capital. "By way of Bahrain," he adds. He speaks quietly, flatly, but his voice is dark and full of command. He's well over six feet, and it feels like he's looking down at me from a great distance, sizing me up with the same grievous scrutiny he'd give a bank of approach lights appearing out of the Addis fog.

I look at the first officer, and it strikes me that he's probably no older than twenty-five, a fact obscured by the seriousness of his uniform. I remember myself at that age, and I'm unable to decide in what amounts his presence mocks or impresses me. Here's this young man who somehow rose from the rugged, war-torn highlands of East Africa to unprecedented dignity, carrying his nation's flag to places like Rome and Moscow and Beijing. In his passenger cabin, Ethiopian traders, Russian bankers, and Eritrean warriors fling themselves to impossible corners of the world.

And the next time somebody asks why I chose to become an airline pilot, I'll stammer and stare off, wishing I could just spit out the image of these three men in the doorway. I already know that later I will try to write this down, and when I do it will be impossible to find the right words.

☆ ☆ ☆

But first is the matter of the Monster, which needs to be preflighted and prepared for the eight-hour crossing to New York.

From the van I catch sight of its ink-dark silhouette, out on the cargo pad, looming out of the murky Zaventem night. "Monster" is my affectionate nickname for the Douglas DC-8. Or not so affectionate, really, as I assume the lumbering hulk of metal is destined, one way or another, to kill me. Sure, it's my first jet. And sure, it's big. But it's also ancient. The real airlines gave up flying these things nearly two decades ago, and the cockpit looks like something from a World War II Soviet submarine. Hell, the DC-7, its immediate and piston-powered predecessor, had a rudder covered not with aluminum or high-tech composite, but with *fabric*.

I'm the second officer—the flight engineer—and the preflight is all mine. I work at my own pace. Most guys can, even for an international run, get the DC-8 ready in less than an hour. I stretch it to a meditative ninety minutes. To me, there is, or there should be, something Zen about the act of preflighting.

It begins in the cockpit with a flip through the aircraft logbook, making sure the signoffs are there and taking note of items that have recently been deferred. This is followed by an intense, top-to-bottom panel check. Every radio, instrument, light bulb, and electronic box is given the once-over. Then I take a seat at the engineer's panel—my office, as it were—highlighter in one hand and coffee cup in the other, running through the twenty-page flight plan, marking up the important parts: flight time, route, weather, alternates, fuel planning.

When all that's done, I stock and set up the galley. Third in command on this trawler means preparing the food and emptying the trash. I don't mind. The cooking duties are a welcome break from the headier duties up front.

Next is the exterior check, or the "walk-around," as we call it. I circle the plane clockwise, eyeing the various lights, sensors, doors, and control surfaces. It's a leisurely, almost peaceful stroll—except for the landing gear bays.

A look into the gear bay of a jetliner is, if nothing else, sobering—the prowess of human engineering starkly unmasked. We take for granted the ease and safety of howling through the air at 600 miles per hour, but a glimpse into the bays shows you just how complex and difficult it all is. An airplane is such a smooth, streamlined thing from afar. Down here, it's an apocalyptic collection of cables, pumps, and ducts. I'm ostensibly checking the tires, inspecting the brakes, scanning for any wayward hydraulics. I'm also looking up at hideous nests of wires, impossible snarls of tubing, and struts thicker than tree trunks, shaking my head, wondering who in the name of heaven ever conceived of such a terrifying assemblage of machinery, and who would be stupid enough to trust it all.

Returning to the cockpit, my duties include monitoring and supervising the intake of fuel. This morning we'll be needing 121,000 pounds of the stuff. That equates to 18,000 gallons, to be divided among eight tanks inside the wings and belly. En route, maintaining proper balance and engine feed requires periodic shifting. The tank valves are opened and shut by a row of eight hand-operated vertical levers that run across the lower portion of the second officer's workstation. Trimming up the tanks, I look like a madman trying to play a pipe organ.

Working with lots of fuel means working with lots of numbers. They don't require anything too elaborate—I'll add them, subtract them, portion them in half or a quarter—but they are big, six-digit affairs that are constantly changing. That's bad news for me because I'm terrible at math. It's funny, because I often hear from aspiring pilots-to-be worried that below-average mathematics skills might keep them grounded. There's a lingering assumption that airline pilots are required to demonstrate some sort of Newtonian genius before every takeoff—a vestige, maybe, from the days when airmen carried slide rules and practiced celestial navigation. "Dear Patrick, I'm a high school junior who hopes to become a pilot, but my B-minus in honors level pre-calculus has me worried. What should I do?"

What these people don't realize is that I would have killed for a B-minus in elementary algebra. My final report card from St. John's Prep, class of 1984, read something like this: B, B, B, A, D. That's math at the end. I can only vaguely define what precalculus might be, and I frequently struggle to make change for a dollar or add up my Boggle scores without electronic assistance. Not to fear: I never graded lower than 97 percent on any FAA written exam, and my logbook records no math-related mishaps.

The basics are what pilots encounter. Routine arrival assignments demand some quickie mental arithmetic. Modern flight management systems will hash out descent profiles automatically, but on older planes you have to run the data in your brain: "Okay, if we need to be at 14,000 feet in 60 miles, assuming a 2,000 foot-per-minute descent and 320 knots groundspeed, at what point should we start down? It's a sort of high-altitude SAT question, with ATC and the rest of your crew assuming you know the answer.

Thus, the most indispensable gauge in the DC-8 was *not* furnished by the designers at Douglas, who conceived this hideous ark back in the mid-1950s, when men were men and could fly and do long division at the same time. I'm referring to my $6.95 calculator from CVS—the one flight-bag accessory more indispensable than an emergency checklist, aircraft deicing guide, or bag of ramen noodles. Mine is marked with a Day-Glo orange sticker, affixed in mortal fear that I might otherwise leave it behind.

Fueling takes half an hour. And now, from outside, comes the diesel roar of a pallet-lifter. Out on the apron sits a disordered array of boxed and shrink-wrapped cargo, tonight about 50 tons of it, waiting to be packed on board. When it's empty, a glance into the freight deck is like peering through a long, empty highway tunnel. I walk back there sometimes, imagining what that space must have looked like twenty or thirty years ago, when the plane carried passengers for Air Canada. In 1982, I flew to Jamaica with my family on an Air Canada DC-8. This very one, possibly.

Time for some noodles and one of those dreadful cucumber sandwiches from the snack tray. Just me and the Monster. These pre-departure routines have a way of enhancing our love/hate relationship. The DC-8 speaks to me. I will kill you, it says, if you don't take proper care of me.

So, I take proper care.

☆ ☆ ☆

In a drizzly predawn darkness, we lift off.

It's eight-plus hours to New York. That's nothing by modern standards, but still it's a long time. We're somewhere south of Iceland. I've got my shoes off. Foil trays of half-eaten chicken sit on the floor, and a trash bag is bursting with discarded cups and cans of Coke Light.

Transoceanic flying induces a unique feeling of loneliness. Out here, you are on your own; there is no radar coverage or conventional air traffic control. Flights are spaced apart by time and speed, sequenced along paths of latitude and longitude. We report our positions to monitoring stations hundreds, even thousands of miles away, silently via satellite link—or, in the case of the old DC-8, over high frequency radio. There's something in the crackle and echo of an HF transmission that intensifies a sense of distance and isolation.

"Gander, Gander," calls the captain. "DHL zero one one, position. Five eight north, three zero west at zero five zero four. Flight level three six zero. Estimate five eight north, four zero west at zero five four six. Next: five six north, five zero west. Mach decimal eight five. Fuel seven two decimal six, over?" That's our current location, ETA for the next reporting fix, speed, altitude, and remaining fuel. A moment or two later comes the acknowledgment from a controller in far-off Newfoundland, his voice so faint he may as well be on the moon.

For the second officer, the cruise phase is pretty relaxed. There's not much to do, and thoughts will wander—sometimes in the wrong direction, resulting in a distinctly maudlin karmic brew:

In an interview years ago, the novelist Kurt Vonnegut was asked how he'd choose to die. "In a plane crash on Mount Kilimanjaro," was Vonnegut's answer. And if you think about it, there's something poetic, almost romantic about that—a jet getting lost in the fog, smacking into the side of that big Tanzanian mountain.

Granted, you'd be hard pressed to find people who think of airplane crashes as anything but the cold hard triumph of gravity over some hulking contraption, but for those of us in love with air travel there can be something almost mystical about them. It's not the Hollywood stuff—the explosions, the fireballs, and all that. It's a deeper thing that requires a context and the passage of time—the disaster as a nugget of history, spiced with drama and mystery. And not every crash can lay claim to this special aura. Lockerbie and Tenerife had it (*see Tenerife story, page 229*); ValuJet in the Everglades did not. Sometimes there's mystique, and sometimes there's nothing but the sorrow of a violent death.

This is what I'm pondering, midflight across the Atlantic Ocean. And it's that latter category, I figure—that most mystique-less and prosaic of crashes—that awaits us, should we plummet to a sudden and watery doom. Three guys in a cargo plane? We'd be lucky to get a mention in the paper. Depressing.

A pilot's worst nightmare, other than his airline going bankrupt or the caterers forgetting the meals, is an onboard fire. This old jet has two identical fire detector systems for its 150-foot-long upper cargo deck. These are rotary dial things with yellow annunciator bulbs at the bottom. The bulbs say: CARGO SMOKE. Of course, this is an airplane laid out when Eisenhower still had a combover, so guess what? Thanks for the heads-up, but there's nothing to actually put the fire out with once it has been detected. (DC-8s are all but extinct and were taken out of the passenger-carrying business a long time ago, so don't worry.) There are bigger, brighter lights in this cockpit, but it's those square, innocuous-looking yellow lights that I do not ever want to see come on, particularly when the closest spot of land, two hours away, is the glaciered coast of Greenland.

I'm also aware, however, that in the compartment behind us are 20,000 pounds of fresh-cut flowers from Belgium and the Netherlands headed to America. The scent of the flowers has made the cockpit smell like baby powder. And it happens that when thousands of pounds of flowers are piled together, they tend to give off clouds of microscopic dust—tiny bits that fill the air like a fragrant cloud of powder. Meanwhile, the DC-8's old-fashioned detectors are designed to detect not flames or heat, but smoke particles, and are very susceptible to false alarms triggered by dust or powder.

So I'm staring at the warning lights, waiting for them to tell me we're on fire over the middle of the ocean. Or is it only dust? And I think about how, after planes crash at sea, they go out on a boat and toss flowers into the waves, and how if something happened and we found ourselves in a watery grave, we'd save everyone the trouble by spreading a veritable slick of tulips halfway to Labrador.

Making matters worse, the captain takes out a chart and starts playing with the GPS. "Ha!" he shouts. Bored and curious, he has plotted the exact latitude and longitude of the wreck of the *Titanic*, which is 40,000 feet below us (28,000 of air and 12,000 of salt water), just a short ride south of our course.

"Oh come on," I say. "Don't be doing stuff like that."

I sit in front of my instrument panel—a wall of dials and switches, all arranged in a perfect working sequence, with a collective purpose nothing short of mechanical infallibility. Green lights, red lights, blue lights, circular windows with quivering white needles. In modern planes it's all LED or liquid crystal, but these are the old-style analog gauges, which give the cockpit that U-Boat look. Old, and dizzyingly complex for just that reason. I slide back my seat and consider it all, with the criticism and respect an artist might give to his canvas.

In that moment I am a maestro of ordered technology. But if only you could see what lurks *behind* that console. The maintenance people sometimes take the panels off, and there's pandemonium back there: wildly knotted bundles of wires and cables, like a spaghetti factory has exploded. Most people have never seen the guts of an airplane—those vast and complex blocks of machinery conspiring to fool gravity. When you look at the eyes of a pretty girl—that superficial beauty of an iris in the sunlight, do you consider the tangle of optic nerve behind it? And in that brain of hers, what is she *thinking?* Like a fire secretly smoldering behind me, amid all those flowers. And when it's finally too late: CARGO SMOKE.

No, not this time. And a few hours later we're safe at Kennedy.

And doesn't it always end this way? Amazing that it all works, all those wires and pumps and moving parts—almost infallibly and every time. But it does, and that's the point about these spooky ruminations. It's our imagination, not our technology, that is prone to failure.

The other lesson here is that we're all afraid of flying on some level and that it's perfectly healthy to be that way. Particularly if you're a pilot. Our job, in essence, is the management of *contingency*. Passengers will ask pilots if we're ever frightened; do we consider the possibility that the next flight could be our last? This always has struck me as both a profound and asinine question. "Yes," I'll answer. "Of course I am scared. I am *always* scared." You can take that with the wink it deserves, but nonetheless, it contains a nugget of truth. Fires, explosions, physics gone bad—all the nasty scenarios the simulator instructors love—it's all there, coiled behind the instrument panel, waiting to spring in a game of comfortable, though never perfect odds. And the pilot's role is to spring right back. Do pilots worry about crashing? Of course they do. As a matter of practicality, they have to. It's their job. It's in their best interest, and yours as well. ✈

Why the annoying rules pertaining to window shades, seat backs, tray tables, and cabin lights during takeoffs and landings?

Your tray has to be latched so that, in the event of an impact or sudden deceleration, you don't impale yourself on it. Plus it allows a clear path to the aisle during an evacuation. The restriction on seat recline provides easier access to the aisles and also keeps your body in the safest position. It lessens whiplash-style injuries and prevents you from "submarining," as it's called, under the seat belt. Keep your belts low and tight. Nothing is more aggravating than hearing a passenger voice the theory that should a crash occur they are guaranteed to perish, so what's the point? Most crashes do have survivors, and something as simple as a properly buckled belt could mean the difference between serious and minor injury.

Raising your window shade makes it easier for the flight attendants to assess any exterior hazards—fire, debris—that might interfere with an emergency evacuation. It also helps *you* remain oriented if there's a sudden impact—rolling, tumbling, etc. Dimming the lights is part of the same strategy. Burning brightly, the glare would make it impossible to see outside. And by pre-adjusting your eyes, you won't be suddenly blinded while dashing for the doors in darkness or smoke.

On Airbus planes, it's common to hear a loud whirring sound emanating from the floorboards during taxi or at the gate. Sometimes it's a high-pitched whine; other times it's a staccato *WOOF, WOOF, WOOF*, like the barking of a very agitated dog. What's going on down there?

This pertains to twin-engine Airbus models: the A320 series (includes the subvariants A319 and A321) and the larger A330. In the United

States, the largest operators of these types are Delta, United, jetBlue, and US Airways. Almost every frequent flyer has encountered this sound at one time or another. Crews rarely make efforts to explain it, leaving passengers befuddled and sometimes worried. Because the noise is akin to a motor repeatedly trying—and failing—to start, there's often the assumption that something is malfunctioning.

What you hear is a device called the power transfer unit, or PTU, which is designed to ensure adequate hydraulic pressures during single-engine operations. To conserve fuel, it's fairly routine for two-engine planes to taxi with an engine shut down. Each engine normally pressurizes its own hydraulic system, but with a motor not running, that leaves one system without a power source. That's where the PTU comes in, helping left power the right, or right power the left. Since it is activated only when the pressure falls below a certain level, the PTU cycles on and off, on and off, on and off. Due to pressure fluctuations, the noise will sometimes continue even after both engines are up and running. It also does a self-test when the starboard engine is started, so you'll hear it then as well. Some Boeing aircraft also employ a PTU, but the operation is slightly different and it doesn't bark like a dog.

Another noise peculiar to Airbus models is a shrill, prolonged whine heard at the gate prior to departure and again after landing. This is an electric hydraulic pump used to open and close the cargo doors.

Could you clear the air, as it were, regarding one of the most common water cooler topics pertaining to flying: the quality of cabin air. We hear lots of anecdotal talk about how filthy and germ-laden it is.

Filthy, germ-laden, rotten, disgusting, wretched, skanky, rancid, putrid, fetid, and fart-filled are just a few of the adjectives used to describe cabin air, and legion are the accounts of flyers allegedly made ill by microscopic pathogens circulating throughout a plane. In reality, the air is very clean.

On all modern aircraft, passengers and crew breathe a mixture of fresh and recirculated air. Using this combination rather than fresh air only makes it easier to regulate temperature and helps maintain a bit of humidity (more on the humidity in a moment). The supply is bled from the compressor sections of the engines. Compressed air is very hot, but the compressors only compress; there is no contact with fuel, oil, or combustion gasses. From there it is plumbed into air conditioning units for cooling. It's then ducted into the cabin through louvers, vents, and the eyeball vents above your seat. (The AC units are known to pilots as "packs." That's an acronym for pneumatic air cycle kit. Usually there are two per plane.)

The air circulates until eventually it is drawn into the lower fuselage, where about half of it is vented overboard—sucked out by the pressurization outflow valve. The remaining portion is remixed with a fresh supply from the engines and run through filters, and the cycle begins again.

Studies have shown that a crowded airplane is no more germ-laden than other enclosed spaces—and usually less. Those underfloor filters are described by manufacturers as being of hospital quality. I needn't be reminded that hospitals are notorious viral incubators, but Boeing says that between 94 and 99.9 percent of airborne microbes are captured, and there's a total changeover of air every two or three minutes—far more frequently than occurs in offices, movie theaters, or classrooms.

One persistent urban myth holds that pilots routinely cut back on the volume of airflow as a means of saving fuel. It's especially regrettable when even our most august and reliable news sources parrot this baseless assertion. Case in point: the following is from a 2009 issue of *The Economist*: "Typically an airline will strike a balance by using a 50:50 mixture of fresh and recirculated air," says the magazine. "Although pilots can reduce the amount of fresh air to save fuel. Some are thought to cut it back to only 20 percent." My mouth dropped open when I read this. I love that sentence, "Some are thought to cut it back to only 20 percent," with its oily overtones of conspiracy

To start with, pilots cannot tinker with a plane's air-conditioning systems to modify the ratio of fresh to recirculated air. This ratio is predetermined by the manufacturer and is not adjustable from the cockpit. On the Boeings I fly, we have direct and accurate control over temperature, but only indirect control over flow. If you asked me to please "cut it back to 20 percent," I would politely inform you that this is impossible. The switches are set to automatic mode prior to flight, and the packs more or less take care of themselves. So long as both engines are turning and everything is operating normally, the flow is perfectly adequate. Only when there's a malfunction are the settings changed.

I am not as familiar with Airbus models, but let's talk to somebody who is.

"Airbus series aircraft, from the A320 through the much larger A380, do provide a way for pilots to vary airflow," says Dave English, an A320 captain and aviation writer. "But not in the way characterized by *The Economist.*"

English explains that the Airbus controllers have three positions, labeled HI, NORM, and LO. "Almost all the time you're in the NORM position, and flow control is automatic. The HI position is used when you need a rapid change in temperature. The LO position does as the name implies. It reduces flow and provides some fuel savings, but they are minimal and this isn't used very often. Company guidance is to use LO whenever the passenger load is below a hundred. It's not a big change. Sitting in the cabin, it's almost impossible to notice the difference."

You'll occasionally notice a strong odor when the plane is on the ground—a pungent smell similar to the exhaust from an old car or bus that fills the cabin shortly after pushback. Usually this happens when exhaust gases are drawn into the air conditioning packs during engine start. The wind is often to blame, causing air to backflow or blowing fumes through the pack inlets. It normally lasts only a minute or so, until the engine is running and stabilized. It's unpleasant but little different from the fumes you occasionally breathe in your car while stuck in traffic.

If passengers have one very legitimate gripe, it's about dryness. Indeed, the typical cabin is exceptionally dry and dehydrating. At around 12 percent humidity, it is drier than you will find in most deserts. This is chiefly a by-product of cruising at high-altitudes, where moisture content is somewhere between low and nonexistent. Humidifying a cabin would seem a simple and sensible solution, but it's avoided for different reasons: First, to amply humidify a jetliner would take large quantities of water, which is heavy and therefore expensive to carry. Humidifying systems would need to recapture and recirculate as much water as possible, making them expensive and complicated. They do exist: one sells for more than $100,000 per unit and increases humidity only by a small margin. There's also the important issue of corrosion. Dampness and condensation leeching into the guts of an airframe can be damaging.

The Boeing 787 has the healthiest air of any commercial plane, thanks to filters with an efficiency of 99.97 percent. Humidity too is substantially higher. The plane's all-composite structure is less susceptible to condensation, and a unique circulation system pumps dry air through the lining between the cabin walls and exterior skin.

None of this is disputing that people don't occasionally become unwell from flying. While the air is clean, the dryness is bad for sinuses and can break down mucous barriers, making it easier to catch what bugs might be present. Usually, though, it's not what passengers are breathing that makes them sick, but what they are *touching*— lavatory door handles, contaminated trays and armrests, etc. A little hand sanitizer is probably a better safeguard than the masks I occasionally see passengers wearing.

Neither am I disputing that the airplane isn't a potentially exquisite vector for the spread of certain diseases. The benefits of high-speed, long-range air travel are obvious—and so are its dangers. Once after arriving on a flight from Africa, I noticed a lone mosquito in the cockpit. How easy it would be, I thought, for that tiny stowaway to escape into the terminal and bite somebody. Imagine an unsuspecting airport worker or passenger who has never before left the country, and suddenly he's in the throes of some exotic tropical malady. Actually, it's been happening for years. Cases of "airport malaria" have been documented in Europe, resulting in several deaths after faulty or delayed diagnosis. It's just a matter of time before this happens in America, if it hasn't already. It is instructive, fascinating, and frankly a little scary to see just how efficiently global air travel can spread pathogens from continent to continent.

Is it true that pilots reduce oxygen levels to keep passengers docile?

This is one of flying's most enduring fallacies, similar to the one just covered about reducing airflow to save fuel. Not only is it patently false, but it also would have a rather undesirable effect on a plane's occupants: shortage of oxygen brings on a condition known as hypoxia. Although hypoxia can, at first, make a person feel giddy and relaxed, it also induces confusion, nausea, and migraine-strength headaches. A pilot would have to be pretty sadistic to provoke that kind of mass agony. I remember the multiday hypoxia headache I endured some years ago in Cuzco, Peru—an experience I wouldn't wish on my worst enemy, let alone a planeload of customers.

Oxygen levels are determined by pressurization, and almost never are the pressurization controls tinkered with during cruise unless there's a malfunction. Crews set up the system before departure; the rest happens automatically. While en route, the cabin is held at the equivalent of somewhere between 5,000 and 8,000 feet above sea level, depending on aircraft type and cruising altitude (*see pressurization, page 40*).

And pilots are breathing the same air as everybody else. An aircraft fuselage does not contain separate compartments with different pressure settings. The entire vessel is pressurized equally from front to back. This includes the cabin, cockpit, and lower-deck cargo holds.

What about the lack of air conditioning when parked at the terminal? How about some sympathy for those of us waiting out a delay in an overheated cabin?

At the gate, planes are cooled or heated one of two ways. The first is through an external air supply plumbed into the cabin through a valve in the lower fuselage. This is the heavy yellow hose that you sometimes see running between the airplane and the jet bridge. The second way is via the plane's auxiliary power unit (*see APU, page 9*). This small turbine engine supplies air and electricity when the main engines aren't running. Although the APU tends to be more effective, the general rule is to rely on external air, if available, because it's cheaper. Pretty much all carriers, however, have a policy that allows crews to start the APU if conditions become uncomfortable. Despite the emphasis on saving fuel, no captain would be penalized for using the APU to cool down an overheated cabin (or warming up a cold one).

So why do passengers find themselves sweating in a crowded cabin? The culprit might be an inoperative APU or an insufficient or malfunctioning ground source. If things get bad enough, speak up. It is well within your rights to complain to a flight attendant. They, in turn, can request we turn on the APU or check out the ground connection. Although we have cabin temperature readouts in the cockpit, we often rely on the cabin crew to let us know when temps are becoming extreme.

One small but effective way of keeping a plane cooler is to close the window shades between flights. Flight attendants will sometimes ask passengers to lower their shades as they disembark.

Departing Tokyo on a jam-packed 747, the air conditioning was turned off just before takeoff. It quickly became very warm and stuffy. A few minutes later, once we were airborne, it was turned back on. What was this all about?

That's called a packs-off takeoff. The air-conditioning packs run on bleed air from the engines and, in the process, rob some of their power. Therefore, certain heavyweight takeoffs require that one or more packs not be used until safely airborne. It depends on weight, runway length, and temperature. The predeparture performance data—a printout of all relevant speeds, power, and flap settings—tells the crew if this is necessary. The packs will be switched off just prior to the roll, then turned on again during the early portion of climb—usually around the time of the first scheduled power reduction, at a thousand feet or so (*see climbout cutback, page 73*).

Could some crazy or ill-intentioned person open one of the doors during flight?

It seems that a week can't go by without hearing or reading a story about a passenger who went cuckoo and tried to yank open an emergency exit, only to be tackled and restrained by those around him, who thought they were on the verge of being ejected into the troposphere. While the news never fails to report these events, it seldom mentions the most important fact: You cannot—I repeat, *cannot*—open the doors or emergency hatches of an airplane in flight. You can't open them for the simple reason that cabin pressure won't allow it. Think of an aircraft door as a drain plug, fixed in place by the interior pressure. Almost all aircraft exits open inward. Some retract upward into the ceiling; others swing outward; but they open inward *first*, and not even the most musclebound human will overcome the force holding them shut. At a typical cruising altitude, up to eight pounds of pressure are pushing against every square inch of interior fuselage. That's over 1,100 pounds against each square foot of door. Even at low altitudes, where cabin pressure levels are much less, a meager 2 psi differential is still more than anyone can displace—even after six cups of coffee and the aggravation that comes with sitting behind a shrieking baby. The doors are further held secure by a series of electrical and/or mechanical latches.

So, while I wouldn't recommend it, and unless you enjoy being pummeled and placed in a choke-hold by panicked passengers, you could, conceivably, sit there all day tugging on a handle to your heart's content. The door is not going to open (though you might get a red light flashing in the cockpit, causing me to spill my Coke Zero). You would need a hydraulic jack, and TSA doesn't allow those.

On the nineteen-passenger turboprop I used to fly, the main cabin door had an inflatable seal around its inner sill. During flight the seal would inflate, helping to lock in cabin pressure while blocking out the racket from the engines. Every now and then the seal would suffer a leak or puncture and begin to deflate, sometimes rapidly. The resultant loss of pressurization was easily addressed and ultimately harmless, but the sudden noise—a great, hundred-decibel sucking sound together with the throb of two 1,100-horsepower engines only a few feet away—would startle the hell out of everybody on the plane, including me.

On the ground, the situation changes—as one would hope, with the possibility of an evacuation in mind. During taxi, you *will* get the door to open. You will also activate the door's emergency escape slide. As an aircraft approaches the gate, you will sometimes hear the cabin crew calling out "doors to manual" or "disarm doors." This has to do with overriding the automatic deployment function of the slides. Those slides can unfurl with enough force to kill a person, and you don't want them billowing onto the jet bridge or into a catering truck.

Why are the cabin windows so small? Why not bigger windows for a better view?

Cabin windows need to be small—and round—to better withstand and disperse the forces of pressurization. This size and shape also helps assimilate the bending and flexing of a fuselage that results from aerodynamic forces and temperature changes. For these same reasons, it's beneficial to place the windows along the flattest portion of a fuselage, which is why they're sometimes aligned in a less-than-optimum viewing position.

The Caravelle, a French-built jetliner of the 1960s, had triangular cabin windows—rounded at the corners, but distinctly three-sided. The Douglas DC-8 was another exception. Not only were its windows squared-off, they were uniquely oversized, with almost twice the glass of today's Boeings or Airbuses. (And one of my favorite tidbits: Look closely at an Air India jet and you'll see that each cabin window is meticulously outlined with a little Taj Mahal motif that makes each jet reminiscent of a Rajasthani palace.)

But what about cockpit windows? Aren't they much larger, and square-ish? That's true, but they also are made of multilayered glass thicker than a bank teller's and bolstered by high-strength frames—unbelievably resilient against pressure differentials, hail, and oncoming birds. I once saw a video of maintenance workers attempting—and failing—to shatter a discarded cockpit windscreen with a sledgehammer. Swapping out a single pane of cockpit glass can run into the hundreds of thousands of dollars.

Despite the many Hollywood depictions to the contrary, I am not aware of a passenger ever being sucked through a ruptured cabin window. I can, however, vouch for the story of a British Airways captain who was partially ejected through a blown-out cockpit pane. He survived with minor injuries.

Looking out the window, I often notice a circular halo across the surface of the cloudbank below, moving with the aircraft almost like its shadow. It sometimes has concentric colored rings, like a lens flare.

Special thanks to Gregory Dicum's enjoyable book *Window Seat* for help with this one. The phenomenon described is called a "glory," or a "pilot halo." They're common under the right conditions of cloud cover and sunlight angle. The aura of colored bands is caused by sunlight diffracted and reflected by water droplets inside the cloud. Sometimes you do see the airplane's shadow directly in the halo's center; other times only the rings are visible.

How are pets treated below deck? I've heard they are kept in unheated, unpressurized sections of the plane.

At 35,000 feet the outside air temperature is about 60 degrees below zero and there is not enough oxygen to breathe. That's worse even than economy, and transporting animals in these conditions would not please most pet owners. So, yes, the underfloor holds are always

pressurized and heated. Usually there is one zone designated specifically for pets. This tends to be the zone in which temperature is most
easily regulated. Maintaining a safe temperature is straightforward
during flight—there's not a lot to it, and controls are set the same
way, pets or no pets—but it can be tricky on the ground during hot
weather. For this reason, some airlines embargo pets for the summer
months. The flight crew is always told when live animals are below.
Passengers are known to send handwritten notes to the cockpit asking
that we take special care. This isn't really necessary, and there's only
so much we can do, but go ahead if it makes you more comfortable.

What is the lowdown on cell phones and portable electronic devices? Are they really dangerous to flight?

Few rules are more confounding to airline passengers than those
regarding the use of cell phones and portable electronic devices. Are
these gadgets really hazardous to flight? People want a simple, fits-all
answer. Unfortunately, there isn't one. It depends on the gadget and
how and when that gadget is used.

Let's take laptops first. In theory, an old or poorly shielded
computer *can* emit harmful energy. However, the main reasons laptops need to be put away for takeoff and landing is to prevent them
from becoming high-speed projectiles during a sudden deceleration
or impact and to help keep the passageways clear if there's an evacuation. Your computer is a piece of luggage, and luggage needs to be
stowed so it doesn't kill somebody or get in the way. This is why,
after landing, flight attendants make an announcement permitting
the use of phones but not computers. There's still the possibility,
remote as it might be, of an emergency evacuation, and you don't
want people tripping over their MacBooks as they make for the exits.

Next, we have tablet devices like Kindles, Nooks, and iPads.
From an interference perspective, it's tough to take a prohibition
seriously now that many pilots are using tablets in the cockpit (*see
page 129*). The projectile argument would appear similarly spe-
cious: nobody wants an iPad whizzing into his or her forehead at

180 miles per hour, but hardback books are just as heavy, if not heavier. If we're going to ban tablets during takeoffs and landings, why should books be exempt? The FAA is mulling this over as we speak. It's possible that by the time you're reading this, the tablet rules will have been relaxed.

And finally the big one: cellular phones. Can cellular communications *really* disrupt cockpit equipment? The answer is potentially yes, but in all likelihood no, and airlines and the FAA are merely erring on the better-safe-than-sorry side. You want something meatier, I know, but that's about as accurate an answer as exists.

Aircraft electronics are designed and shielded with interference in mind. This *should* mitigate any ill effects, and to date there are no proven cases of a phone adversely affecting the outcome of a flight. But you never know. If the plane's shielding is old or faulty, for example, there's a greater potential for trouble.

Even if it is not actively engaged with a call, a cell phone's power-on mode dispatches bursts of potentially harmful energy. For this reason, they must be placed in the proverbial off position prior to taxiing, as requested during the never-tedious pre-takeoff safety briefing (*see briefing babble, page 164*). The policy is clearly stated but obviously unenforced, and we assume the risks are minimal or else airline personnel would collect or inspect phones visually rather than rely on the honor system. I'd venture to guess at least half of all phones, whether inadvertently or out of laziness, are left on during flight. That's about a million phones a day in the United States. If indeed this was a recipe for disaster, I think we'd have more evidence by now.

That said, cell phones may have had a role in at least two serious incidents. The key word here is "may," as interference can be impossible to trace or prove. Some blame a phone for the unsolved crash of a Crossair regional plane in Switzerland in 2000, claiming that spurious transmissions confused the plane's autopilot. Interference was cited as a likely contributing factor in a fatal RJ crash in New Zealand in 2003. In another case, a regional jet was forced to make an emergency landing after a fire alarm was allegedly triggered by a ringing phone in the luggage compartment.

Those are extremes. What would interference normally look like? You imagine a hapless passenger hitting the SEND button and suddenly the plane flips over. In reality, it's liable to be subtle and transient. The electronic architecture of a modern jetliner is vast to say the least, and most irregularities aren't exactly heart-stoppers: a warning flag that flickers for a moment and then goes away; a course line that briefly goes askew. Or something unseen. I'm occasionally asked if I have ever personally witnessed cellular interference in a cockpit. Not to my knowledge, but I can't say for sure. Planes are large and complicated; minor, fleeting malfunctions of this or that component aren't uncommon, and their causes are often impossible to determine.

It's possible that airlines are using the mere possibility of technical complications as a means of avoiding the *social* implications of allowing cellular conversations on planes. The minute it can be proven beyond reasonable doubt that phones are safe, a percentage of flyers will demand the right to use them, pitting one angry group of travelers against another, with carriers stuck in the middle. If indeed airlines are playing this game, count me among those sympathetic who hope the prohibition stays in place—not out of technical concerns, but for the sake of human decency and some bloody peace and quiet. The sensory bombardment inside airports is overwhelming enough. The airplane cabin is a last refuge of relative silence (so long as there isn't a baby wailing). Let's keep it that way.

On every flight, we hear a series of dings or chimes. What do these signals mean?

The chimes you hear are one of two kinds. The first kind is basically just a phone call. The flight attendant stations and cockpit share an intercom system through which any station is able to call another. When a call is made, the recipient's phone will "ding."

Chimes also are used by pilots as a signaling device for the cabin crew. On the plane I fly, we create this sound by cycling the seat-belt sign an appropriate number of times. Airlines have their own rules for how many chimes mean what and when they're given, but the basics are the same: ordinarily, those after takeoff indicate the plane has passed through 10,000 feet, at which point passengers can use approved electronic devices and flight attendants may contact the cockpit without fear of interrupting a critical phase of flight. During descent, it's equivalent to, "We'll be landing soon, so please get the cabin ready."

None of the signals, by the way, has anything to do with landing clearance. Often, after the second round of descent dings, you'll hear a flight attendant announce, "Ladies and gentlemen, we have been cleared to land, so please put away…" I don't know when this habit got started, but in reality the flight attendants have no idea when the plane is cleared to land. They're using the term for convenience. Actual landing clearance, assigned by air traffic control, usually comes much later, sometimes only seconds prior to touchdown, and it is *not* something communicated between pilots and cabin crew.

For the record, it is not true that a runway must be vacant before a flight is cleared to land on it. Flights are cleared to land all the time with other arriving or departing planes still on the strip. It simply means that you may go ahead and land without further communications with the control tower. If the runway is not vacant in time, ATC will cancel the clearance and have you go around.

On some flights the audio system has a channel through which I can hear communications between pilots and controllers. I always find this enthralling, but often it's switched off.

At United Airlines, one of the few purveyors of this oddly intriguing form of entertainment, this is called Channel 9 in honor of its position in your audio panel. It's either fascinating or tediously indecipherable, depending on your infatuation with flight. It is sometimes unavailable, at the crew's discretion, because of the unfriendly letters people send and the litigation they threaten when it's perceived the pilots have made some "mistake." Also, passengers not familiar with the vernacular may misinterpret a transmission and assume nonexistent or exaggerated troubles. Let's say a controller asks, "United 537, um, do you think you can make it?" This is a common query pertaining to whether a plane can hit a specific altitude or navigational fix at a specific time or speed. Depending on the controller's intonation—or the pilot's reply, "No, we can't make it"—such innocuous exchanges might have a passenger bursting into tears and picturing his wife and children.

If you're tuned in, listen up for some of the more colorful airline call-signs. While private aircraft use their registration numbers for radio identification, commercial flights use a call sign and flight number. Usually that call sign is simply the airline's name. "Delta 202, descend and maintain eight thousand feet." Many, though, have adopted idiosyncratic handles, Pan Am's "Clipper" being the most famous example. "Clipper 605, you are cleared for takeoff." One you'll hear quite a bit is "Cactus." Originally the call sign of America West, it was later taken up by US Airways after the merger of those two companies and remains in use. Aer Lingus uses the classic "Shamrock," while at China Airlines it's "Dynasty." A "Springbok" is an antelope and also the handle of South African Airways. British Airways' "Speedbird" refers to the nickname of an old corporate logo—a delta-winged bird of sorts—originally used by Imperial Airways, one of BA's predecessors, as far back as 1932. Others from the past are New York Air's "Apple," Air Florida's "Palm," and ValuJet's unfortunate choice of "Critter."

In the late 1970s, riders on American Airlines's DC-10s were entertained by a live-action video feed from the cockpit during takeoff and landing, projected onto the movie screen. Nowadays various airlines show the view from a nose, tail, or belly-mounted camera. Passengers can switch between shots using their seat-back video controls. On Emirates you can choose between a forward view and one that points straight down, showing what the plane is passing over. (The latter resulted in a rather silly controversy in Britain when nude backyard sunbathers worried that overflying passengers were getting a free peepshow.) Some Airbus A340s have a tail-mounted camera showing an aft-facing view—a fun, if dizzying, perspective that lets you watch the runway falling away on takeoff.

What's with those flight attendant briefings? Nobody is listening in the first place, so why are they so long?

In America, commercial flying is governed by a vast tome known as the Federal Aviation Regulations, or FARs—an enormous, frequently unintelligible volume that personifies aviation's boundless tendency to take the simplest ideas and present them in language as tangled and convoluted as possible. Of its crown jewels, none is a more glittering example than the safety briefing—twenty-five seconds of useful information hammered into six minutes of rigmarole so weighed down with extraneous language that the crew may as well be talking Urdu or speaking in tongues.

Whether prerecorded and shown over the entertainment system or presented live the old-fashioned way, the safety demo is a form of camp—a performance art adaptation of legal fine print overflowing with redundant airline-ese. "At this time we do ask that you please return your seat backs to their full and upright positions." Why not "Please raise your seat backs?" Or, my favorite: "Federal law prohibits tampering with, disabling, or destroying any lavatory smoke detector." Excuse me, but are those not the same bloody things? Doesn't "tampering with" pretty much cover it?

With a pair of shears and common sense, the average briefing could be trimmed to a maximum of half its length, resulting in a lucid oration that people might actually listen to. All that's really needed is a short tutorial on the basics of exits, seat belts, flotation equipment, and oxygen masks. This shouldn't take more than a minute.

Once upon a time, when riding along as a passenger, I would shoot dirty looks at those who ignored the demo and even made a point of paying undue attention just to help the cabin staff feel useful. After a while, realizing that neither the FAA nor the airlines has much interest in cleaning up this ornamental gibberish, I stopped caring. Note: this does not excuse those passengers who insist on carrying on conversations over the announcements, effectively doubling the volume. Whether we need to hear a flight attendant explain the operation of a seat belt is disputable, but we definitely do *not* need to hear the guy in row 25 talking about his favorite seafood restaurant in Baltimore.

Reach into the seat pocket, and you'll discover a pictorial version of the same fatty babble: the always popular fold-out safety card. These too are a pedantic nod to the FARs. The talent levels of the artists speak for themselves; the drawings appear to be a debased incarnation of Egyptian hieroglyphs. Still worse are the cards spelling out the emergency exit row seating requirements. The rules covering who can or can't sit adjacent to the doors and hatches were a controversy for some time, and one result was a new standard in FAR superfluity—an excruciating litany set to cardboard and packed with enough regulatory technobabble to set anyone's head spinning. Exit row passengers are asked to review this information before takeoff, which is a bit like asking them to learn Japanese in twelve minutes.

As for announcements made by pilots, there are company guidelines for acceptable tone and content. You'll find stipulations against discussions of politics, religion, and anything derogatory. Sayeth your General Operations Manual, chapter five, verse 12: Jokes, off-color innuendo or slurs of any kind are forbidden. Thou shalt maintain only nonconfrontational rapport, lest the Chief Pilot summon and smite thee. Rules might also restrict—and not without good intentions— the use of potentially frightening language or alarming buzzwords. One airline I worked for had a policy banning any announcement that began with the words, "Your attention please." I strongly advocate the recitation of college football scores be added to the list of prohibitions, but that's just me.

"Your attention please. Southeastern Central Nebraska Tech has just kicked a last-minute field goal to pull ahead of North Southwestern Methodist State, 31–28."

We should also be careful not to overburden people with information they can't use. Take the weather. Does anybody care that the wind is blowing from the southwest at 14 knots or what the dew point is? They want to know if it's sunny, cloudy, rainy, or snowy and what the temperature is.

Another no-no is, or should be, launching into complicated, jargon-rich explanations. "Yeah, uh, ladies and gentlemen, looks like 31L at Kennedy just fell to less than an eighth. It's under six hundred right now on all three RVR. They're calling it Cat III, and we're only

Cat II up here, so, um, we're gonna do a few turns over the VOR, then spin around and shoot the ILS to 22L. They've got a three-hundred and a half over there."

Thanks.

First, business, economy... Where the hell am I sitting, and what's the difference?

To a degree, each of these is open to interpretation, but there are four standard cabins: first class, business class, economy class, and Ryanair. Or, okay, there are three: first, business, and economy. The latter is often called coach or tourist, and you might hear first and business referred to collectively as the "premium" cabins.

An airline may configure a plane with all three classes, two of them, or just one. The number of cabins, as well as the seating styles and amenities within, will differ from plane to plane and market to market. The premium cabins on longer-haul flights tend to be markedly more luxurious—with private sleeper pods, widescreen video, and so forth—than those found on shorter hauls. As a general rule, first class is more luxurious (and more expensive) than business, but it's relative. Long-haul business class is usually fancier than domestic U.S. or intra-Europe first class.

Several airlines blur the distinctions through gimmicky branding techniques. Virgin Atlantic has only one premium cabin, which it calls "Upper Class." China Airlines has "Dynasty Class," while Alitalia's premium passengers relax in "Magnifica Class." To sweeten the implications of "economy," Air France sells tickets for "Voyageur" class. British Airways offers three different economy classes and three different business classes, all with different names, depending on the route. If that's not confusing enough, Continental Airlines (now part of United) came up with something called, in all possible obfuscation, "BusinessFirst." Somewhere in the fine print, and in the price, you can figure out which of the traditional subdivisions they're talking about.

On many intra-European flights, classes are partitioned on short notice according to demand. The seats themselves don't change, but the dividing bulkheads and curtains are slid along tracks. On Air France, economy becomes business by virtue of blocking out the middle seat of a three-abreast block. Another popular trend is dividing economy into two sections, one with extra legroom and, in some cases, a fancier seat. "Economy Plus" or "Economy Comfort" are among the branding terms, though technically it's still, well, coach.

While people will never stop complaining about the discomforts of economy class, it happens that premium class, be it first or business, has never been more extravagant than it is right now. Not since travelers slept in private berths in the 1940s have things been so swanky up front—though definitely in a sleeker, twenty-first century flavor. Not long ago, a fat leather seat and a doting flight attendant were the hallmarks of inflight luxury. Today, competition and technology have brought us all kinds of eccentric goodies. On outré-chic carriers like Singapore Airlines, Virgin Atlantic, Emirates, and Qatar Airways, one finds a stand-up cocktail lounge and even an inflight beauty therapist. Passengers doze in individual mini-suites with 6-foot seat-beds, down-filled duvets, and electric privacy barriers. Cabin staff perform turndown service while you slip into designer pajamas, and there's sometimes a pull-up ottoman if you'd like company during dinner. Circadian-friendly phases of ceiling lighting are adjusted by the crew, including constellations projected onto the overhead bins during nighttime hours. On its transatlantic flights, Turkish Airlines brings along a business class chef.

It goes without saying, of course, that most folks aren't riding around on expense accounts and haven't got $9,000 to drop on a seat to Hong Kong. If it's any consolation, economy class has its modern-day frills as well. Live TV, on-demand movies, and inflight Wi-Fi are among the common amenities. Some Asian and European carriers have switched to shell-style seats that, when reclined, slide forward rather than tip rearward, preserving space for the person behind you. And although complimentary meals are increasingly rare on shorter flights, buy-onboard options are affordable and often tasty.

People are under the impression that airlines continue to cram ever more seats into their economy sections. This is mostly untrue.

Airlines cannot simply shove in as many seats as they want; commercial planes are certified for a maximum occupancy based on, among other things, the number of emergency exits. Actually, economy class layouts have hardly changed since jets first became popular in the 1960s. In the early days, carriers flirted with five abreast seating on narrow-body planes instead of the standard six, or nine-abreast on a 747 instead of the ten used today, but these were short-lived schemes. The cross-sections of airliners as you see them today are basically unchanged from forty years ago. If anything, they are slightly roomier. The Airbus A380 has the same ten-abreast floor plan as the 747 but is wider by approximately a foot, while six-abreast aircraft such as the popular A320 have a few more inches of head and elbow room than the 707s and 727s of old.

It's legroom, though, not elbow space, that flyers gripe about most. The distance between rows is called "pitch," and here too, historically, things have been better *and* worse. It's true that carriers have been tightening up the rearmost rows to accommodate those roomier (and more expensive) "Economy Plus" sections up front, but anyone who flew the old PeoplExpress remembers how pitiless and pitchless a cabin can be laid out. Or Laker Airways, whose "SkyTrain" service ran between the United States and London in the 1970s. Sir Freddie Laker, the airline's flamboyant founder, configured his DC-10s with a bone-crushing 345 seats—about a hundred more than most DC-10s at the time (the plane had eight full-size exits that helped keep this legal, and there was no first or business class).

If you ask me, what makes economy uncomfortable is only partly to do with legroom. It's more about the shapes of the seats themselves and the dreadful ergonomics of the surrounding space. Each time I settle into an economy chair, I silently wonder what malformed extraterrestrial it was designed for. "Settle in" is the wrong term; you don't attempt to relax so much as balance yourself in place. The pressure points are all wrong, your legs are unsupported, there's no place for your arms, and lumbar support is nil. The tray tables and armrests are the wrong shape and in the wrong location.

The most obvious way to make economy more pleasant would be to have fewer seats in the first place, but until people are willing to pay substantially higher fares, this a nonstarter. Engineers are also faced with the challenge of designing a frame that is lightweight and extremely strong, able to withstand several times the force of gravity. Nevertheless, there's no excuse for the poorly designed seats we're accustomed to. Through the use of high-tech materials and a bit of imagination, a chair can be safe, lightweight, sturdy, and comfortable all at once. Indeed, ergonomically sculpted seats from innovative manufacturers like Recaro and Thompson Solutions have been on the market for years. If only more carriers would buy them.

In addition to a seat that actually conforms to the shape of a human body, below are six things that ought to be standard in any economy class:

1. Lumbar support. Existing seats lack any kind of lower-back cushioning. There is only a vacant space into which your lower back sinks, dragging down and contorting the rest of you.
2. Inflight Wi-Fi and on-demand, in-seat video with a personal screen of at least nine inches. I'm lumping these together because they both capitalize on the strategy of *distraction*, and that's what keeping passengers happy is all about. Browsing the Web or watching a movie are ideal time-killers. Five or ten dollars for Internet isn't unreasonable, but it should be free in first or business.
3. An adjustable headrest. Not the half-assed kind that allows your head to loll around, but one that fits snugly.
4. A tray table that extends to reach the body, so a passenger needn't hunch over to eat or work. Ideally, the tray should have a curved leading edge to better fit your torso and should be the sort that unfolds from the armrest, not from the seat in front. This solves the hunch-over problem *and* avoids the hazard of having your computer crushed when the person in front of you suddenly reclines, pinching your screen between the table and the upper cushion. "Assault recliners" is my name for those passengers who come hauling back all at once, leaving you but a split-second to save your laptop from this deadly nutcracker. Tray tables also need a raised edge to keep food and beverages from spilling into your lap during climb or in rough air.

Some have recessed cup holders, but many are perfectly flat and smooth, so that your coffee comes skating backward whenever the plane is nose-high. A quarter-inch ridge would prevent this. One assumes that aircraft interior designers are more or less familiar with the concept of gravity; there's no reason for such a tweak not to be universal. It wouldn't cost more than a few pennies per tray, if anything at all. And while we're at it, give us one of those ring-style cup holders that fold out from the seat back. (They're common in Europe, but I've never seen one on a U.S. carrier.) They help prevent spills and free up space on your tray.

5. Power ports. If a full AC outlet is asking too much, at least give us a USB connection. They're increasingly common on long-haul jets, but at some point, every plane ought to have them.

Whether or not you're comfortable back there, remember to get up and stretch at periodic intervals. With long-haul flying times now surpassing the gestation periods of many small mammals, there are growing concerns about an affliction known as deep vein thrombosis, or DVT, brought on by the immobilizing confines of an airplane seat. Also called "economy class syndrome," it's a condition where potentially lethal blood clots form in the legs and can spread through the body. Those with preexisting conditions (obesity, smoking) are at higher risk, but all passengers should avoid remaining sedentary for extended periods. Stand, stretch, take a walk up the aisle. Ultra-long-range jets are often outfitted with inflight buffet zones and lounges—socializing areas laid out with drinks and snacks. More than just a perk, the idea is to entice people to move around at regular intervals. For those who wander in barefoot after sleeping, the buffet zone on the A340-500 has a heated floor.

The boarding process has become a nightmare. What could airlines—and passengers—do to make it better?

None of us enjoys the tedium of boarding and disembarking. Bottlenecks in the aisles and the throat of the jet bridge can be eternal, and it takes several minutes just to get from the doorway to your seat, or vice versa.

If you want to make things slightly easier on your fellow travelers, here's a simple recommendation: when boarding, please do not place your carry-on bags in the first empty bin that you come to. Use a bin as close to your seat as possible. It drives me crazy when I see a guy shoving his 26-inch Tumi into a bin above row 5, then continuing on to his assigned seat in row 52. I know it's tempting, but this causes the forward bins to fill up quickly. Those seated in the front must now travel backward to stow their belongings, then return upstream, against the flow of traffic, slowing everybody down. Then, after landing, these same people have to fight their way rearward again while everybody else is trying to exit. Am I wrong to suggest that assigned bins might be a good idea? There are a lot more seats than bins, you can argue, and not everybody carries the same sized carry-ons, but I'm convinced there's a way to make it work. If nothing else, airlines should make a gate-side announcement requesting that passengers please use compartments at or near their seats.

The traditional method of filling a plane from back to front has been part of the problem. A lot of airlines now board by "zone" or "group" instead. One element of these techniques is to board window and center seats first, followed by the aisles, so that fewer people have to squeeze around one another. Another option is to board rows out-of-sequence, in staggered sets rather than consecutively. You call every second or third row, allow people to stow their bags, then repeat. According to one study, you can load a plane up to ten times faster this way.

Not that it makes a whole lot of difference, as many people hate getting on a plane early and will wait as long as possible, ignoring the boarding calls. These last-minute boarders cause at least as many holdups as the bin-hoggers.

Another recommendation: families with kids in strollers should be boarded first, and upon arrival they should be asked to stay in their seats until everybody else has exited. How many total hours are wasted each day waiting for parents to assemble their strollers and gather up the approximately 90 pounds of travel gear that is apparently required by every child younger than five?

Using multiple doors also speeds things up. We don't see them much in the United States, but boarding bridges that attach to both the forward and center doors (on those planes that have them) are common in Europe and Asia. A number of gates at Amsterdam's Schiphol airport have unusual bridges with access to the *rear* doors as well, passing over the plane's left wing. (Boarding and disembarking almost always takes place on the left side of the plane. The right side is used for cargo and baggage loading, servicing, and catering.)

Meanwhile, I'm sure you're wondering about those situations, of which there are far too many, when a plane stops short of the terminal, accompanied by the embarrassed crew announcing that "our gate is currently occupied" or that the marshaling personnel aren't yet in place. Yes, the arrival station is kept abreast of every flight's ETA, so why, why, why, is the gate not ready on time? I'm afraid I haven't got a good answer. There can be more to these situations that meets the eye—a plane's assigned parking spot is based on arrival and departure times, passenger loads, customs and immigration issues—but I suspect that understaffing has a lot to do with it. Pilots find this as frustrating as the rest of you.

I'm old enough to remember when passengers used to applaud on every landing. Does this ever happen anymore?

Clapping upon landing was still widespread as recently as the late '70s and early '80s. No surprise that it scarcely happens anymore. The number of Americans who fly at least twice a year has more than quadrupled in the past quarter century. The familiarity of the routine, and the hassles that come with it, have rubbed away whatever sense of excitement or novelty was still there. It remains somewhat common overseas, however, where passengers aren't (yet) as jaded. In the past few years, on trips I've taken to Asia, Africa, and the Middle East, cheers and applause could be heard on roughly a quarter of the landings.

Do crews feel offended or insulted? Not in the least. It isn't a critique of the landing or a judgment on the pilots' skills. Neither is it an outburst of relief at having cheated gravity and lived to tell about it. Even the most nervous flyers are more optimistic than that. I wouldn't deconstruct it too much. It pretty much speaks for itself and needn't be taken too seriously. It's just having fun, and to me it lends a folksy, humane touch to the end of a flight.

And you'll notice, when it does happen, it's a strictly economy class phenomenon. People in first or business never clap. You'll be apt to look for a socioeconomic meaning to this, and maybe there is one, but the dynamics of economy class—more people sitting closer together—lend itself to the occasion. There's a certain communal spirit, especially after a long-haul flight, when you've spent several hours in a relatively intimate space with hundreds of people. In a way, the applause acts like a big collective handshake.

Another thing you don't see much anymore are passenger visits to the cockpit. People seem to think that security rules prohibit such visits, but that's not so. It can't be done in the air, of course, but you're more than welcome to drop by when the plane is parked at the gate, before or after a flight (just be sure to ask a flight attendant first). Kids will sometimes come up, often with their parents in tow, to look around and maybe get their picture taken in the captain's seat, but adults almost never stop by on their own. Which is too bad. Meeting the crew can be helpful for nervous flyers, and most pilots are flattered by somebody taking interest in our odd little workspace.

Looking Out: Memorable Views from Aloft

On a typical 747 with four hundred passengers, a mere quarter of them will be lucky enough, if that's the correct word, to be stationed at a window. In a ten-abreast block, only two of those seats come with a view. If flying has lost the ability to touch our hearts and minds, perhaps that's part of the reason there's nothing to *see* anymore.

There's something instinctively comforting about sitting at the window—a desire for orientation. Which way am I going? Has the sun risen or set yet? For lovers of air travel, of course, it's more than that. To this day, the window is always my preference, even on the longest and most crowded flight. What I observe through the glass is no less a sensory moment, potentially, than what I'll experience sightseeing later on. Traveling to Istanbul, for instance, I remember the sight of the ship-clogged Bosporus from 10,000 feet as vividly as I remember standing before the Süleymaniye Mosque or the Hagia Sofia.

For pilots, obviously, there isn't much choice. We spend hours in what is essentially a small room walled with glass. Cockpit windows are surprisingly large, and although there's often little to see except fuzzy gray cirrus or pitch-blackness, the panorama they provide is occasionally spectacular:

- New York City. The arrival patterns into LaGuardia will sometimes take you along the Hudson River at low altitude, skirting the western edge of Manhattan and offering a breathtaking vista of the New York skyline— that "quartz porcupine," as Vonnegut termed it.

- Shooting stars (especially during the annual, late-summer Perseids meteor shower). Most impressive are the ones that linger on the horizon for several seconds, changing color as they burrow into the atmosphere. I've seen shooting stars so bright they were visible even in daylight.

- The Northern Lights. At its most vivid, the aurora borealis has to be seen to be believed. And you needn't traipse to the Yukon or Siberia; the most dazzling display I've ever witnessed was on a flight between Detroit and New York. The heavens had become an immense, quivering, horizon-wide curtain of fluorescence, like God's laundry flapping in the night sky.

- Flying into Africa. I love the way the Cap Vert penin-
  sula and the city of Dakar appear on the radar screen,
  perfectly contoured like some great rocky fishhook—
  the westernmost tip of the continent, and the sense
  of arrival and discovery it evokes. There it is, Africa!
  And further inland, the topography of Mali and Niger.
  From 30,000 feet, the scrubby Sahel looks exactly like
  40-grade sandpaper, sprayed lightly green and spat-
  tered with villages—each a tiny star with red clay roads
  radiating outward.

- The eerie, flickering orange glow of the Venezuelan oil
  fields—an apocalyptic vista that makes you feel like a
  B-17 pilot in 1945.

- Similar, but more depressing, are the thousands of
  slash-and-burn fires you'll see burning throughout the
  Amazon. Some of the fire fronts are miles long—walls
  of red flame chewing through the forests.

- Compensating for the above are the vast, for-now
  untouched forests of Northeastern South America.
  Over Guyana in particular the view is like nothing else
  in the world—an expanse of primeval green as far as the
  eye can see. No towns, no roads, no clear-cutting or
  fires. For now.

- Climbing out over the "tablecloth"—the cloud deck
  that routinely drapes itself over Table Mountain in
  Cape Town, South Africa.

- The frozen, midwinter oblivion of Northeastern Canada.
  I love passing over the jaggedy, end-of-the-world
  remoteness of Newfoundland, Labrador, and Northern
  Quebec in midwinter—a gale-thrashed nether-region
  of boulders, forests, and frozen black rivers.

- The majestic, primordial nothingness of Greenland. The great circle routes between the United States and Europe will sometimes take you over Greenland. It might be just a brush of the southern tip, but other times it's forty-five minutes across the meatier vistas of the interior. If you've got a window seat, do *not* miss the opportunity to steal a peek, even if it means splashing your fast-asleep seatmate with sunshine.

Other views aren't spectacle so much as just peculiar...

One afternoon we were coasting in from Europe, about 200 miles east of Halifax, Nova Scotia. "Gander Center," I called in. "Got time for a question?"

"Yeah, go ahead."

"Do you have any idea what the name of that strange little island is that we just passed over?"

"Sure do," said the man in Gander. "That's Sable Island."

Sable Island is one of the oddest places I've ever seen from aloft. The oceans are full of remote islands, but Sable's precarious isolation makes it especially peculiar. It's a tiny, ribbony crescent of sand, almost Bahamian in shape and texture, all alone against the relentless North Atlantic. It's like a fragment of a submerged archipelago—a miniature island that has lost its friends.

"Island," maybe, is being generous. Sable is really nothing more than a sand bar, a sinewy splinter of dunes and grass— 26 miles long and only a mile wide—lashed and scraped by surf and wind. How staggeringly vulnerable it appears from 38,000 feet.

I'd flown over Sable many times and had been meaning to ask about it. Only later did I learn that the place has been "the subject of extensive scientific research," according to one website, "and of numerous documentary films, books, and magazine articles." Most famously, it's the home of 250 or so wild horses. Horses have been on Sable since the late eighteenth century, surviving on grass and fresh water ponds. Transient visitors include grey seals and up to 300 species of birds. Human access is tightly restricted. The only permanent dwelling is a scientific research station staffed by a handful of people.

But all right, okay, enough with the terrestrial stuff. I know that some of you are wondering about UFOs. This is something I'm asked about all the time. For the record, I have never seen one, and I have never met another pilot who claims to have seen one. Honestly, the topic is one that almost never comes up, even during those long, dark flights across the ocean. Musings about the vastness of the universe are one thing, but I cannot recall ever having had a conversation with a colleague about UFOs specifically. Neither have I seen the topic discussed in any industry journal or trade publication.

I once received an email asking me about a supposed "tacit agreement" between pilots that says we will not openly discuss UFO sightings out of fear of embarrassment and, as the emailer put it, "possible career suicide." I had to laugh at the notion of there being a tacit agreement among pilots over *anything*, let alone flying saucers. And although plenty of things in aviation are tantamount to career suicide, withholding information about UFOs isn't one of them.

6 ...MUST COME DOWN

Disasters, Mishaps, and Fatuous Flights of Fancy

TERMINAL MADNESS: WHAT IS AIRPORT SECURITY?

In America and across much of the world, the security enhancements put in place following the catastrophe of September 11, 2001, have been drastic and of two kinds: those practical and effective, and those irrational and pointless.

The first variety have taken place almost entirely behind the scenes. Comprehensive explosives scanning for checked luggage, for instance, was long overdue and is perhaps the most welcome addition. It's the second variety, unfortunately that has come to dominate the air travel experience. I'm talking about the frisking, x-raying, body scanning, and confiscating that goes on at thousands of concourse checkpoints across the globe. These procedures waste our time, waste our money, and humiliate millions of us on a daily basis.

There are two fundamental flaws in our approach:

The first is a strategy that looks upon every single person who flies—old and young, fit and infirm, domestic and foreign, pilot and passenger—as a potential terrorist. That is to say, we're searching for weapons rather than people who might actually use weapons. This is an impossible, unsustainable task in a system of such tremendous volume. As many as 2 million people fly each and every day in the United States alone. Tough-as-nails prison guards cannot keep knives out of maximum security cell blocks, never mind the idea of guards trying to root out every conceivable weapon at an overcrowded terminal.

The second flaw is our lingering preoccupation with the tactics used by the terrorists on September 11—the huge and tragic irony being that the success of the 2001 attacks had almost nothing to do with airport security in the first place. As conventional wisdom has it, the 9/11 terrorists exploited a weakness in airport security by smuggling aboard box cutters. But conventional wisdom is wrong. It was not a failure of airport security that allowed those men to hatch their takeover scheme. It was, instead, a failure of *national* security—a breakdown of communication and oversight at the FBI and CIA levels. What the men actually exploited was a weakness in our mindset—a set of presumptions based on the decades-long track record of hijackings and how they were expected to unfold. In years past, a hijacking meant a diversion to Beirut or Havana, with hostage negotiations and standoffs; crews were accordingly trained in the concept of passive resistance. The presence of box cutters was merely incidental. They could have used anything—onboard silverware, knives fashioned from plastic, a broken bottle wrapped in tape—particularly when coupled with the bluff of having a bomb. The weapon that mattered was the intangible one: the element of surprise. And so long as they didn't chicken out, they were all but guaranteed to succeed.

For a number of reasons, just the opposite is true today. The hijack paradigm was changed forever even before the first of the Twin Towers had fallen to the ground, when the passengers of United 93 realized what was happening and began to fight back. The element of surprise was no longer a useful tool. Hijackers today would face not only an armored cockpit, but also a planeload of people convinced they're about to die. It's hard to imagine a hijacker, be it with a box cutter or a bomb, making it two steps up the aisle without being pummeled. It's equally hard to imagine that organized terrorists would be willing to expend valuable resources on a scheme with such a high likelihood of failure.

In spite of this reality, we are apparently content spending billions of taxpayer dollars and untold hours of labor in a delusional attempt to thwart an attack that has already happened and cannot happen again—guards pawing through our luggage in a hunt for what are effectively harmless items: hobby knives, scissors, screwdrivers. Not to mention even a child knows that a deadly weapon can be crafted out of virtually anything, from a ballpoint pen to a shattered first class dinner plate.

The folly is much the same with respect to the restrictions on liquids and gels, put in place following the breakup in 2006 of a London-based cabal planning to blow up jetliners using liquid explosives. The threat of liquid explosives does exist. We recall Ramzi Yousef's detonation of a nitroglycerine bomb aboard a Philippine Airlines flight in 1994—a test run for the so-called Project Bojinka, the long-forgotten al-Qaeda scheme to simultaneously destroy eleven widebody airliners over the Pacific Ocean. But such explosives are not easily concocted, and the idea that confiscating snow globes and ice cream cones makes us safer is, let's admit it, more than a little ridiculous.

But of all the half-baked measures we've grown accustomed to, few are sillier than the policy decreeing that pilots and flight attendants undergo the same x-ray and metal detector screening as passengers. As this book goes to press, a program is finally under testing in the United States that will soon allow on-duty pilots to bypass the normal checkpoint. It's a simple enough process that confirms a pilot's identity by matching up airline and government-issue credentials with information stored in a database. That it took twelve years for this to happen, however, is a national embarrassment when you consider that tens of thousands of U.S. airport ground workers, from baggage loaders to cabin cleaners and mechanics, have been exempt from screening all along. Many of these individuals have full, unescorted access to aircraft, inside and out. Some are airline employees, though a large percentage are contract staff belonging to outside companies. An airline pilot who once flew bombers armed with nuclear weapons is not to be trusted and is marched through the metal detectors. But those who cater the galleys, sling the suitcases, and sweep out the aisles have been able to saunter onto the tarmac unmolested for years. If there has been a more ringing, let-me-get-this-straight scenario anywhere in the realm of airport security, I'd like to hear it. Although nobody is implying that the hardworking caterers, baggage handlers, and the rest of the exempted employees out there are terrorists-in-waiting, this is nevertheless a double standard so staggeringly audacious that it can hardly be believed.

The Transportation Security Administration (TSA) will point out how the privileges granted to tarmac workers are contingent upon fingerprinting, a ten-year criminal background investigation, and crosschecking against terror watch lists and that ground employees are additionally subject to random physical checks. All right, but the background checks for pilots are no less thorough. And as for those random spot checks, one apron worker told me that he hadn't been stopped or patted down in over three years. "All I need is my ID, which I swipe through a turnstile. The only TSA presence we notice is when the blue-shirts come down to the cafeteria to get food."

Here's a true story:

I'm at the TSA checkpoint at a major U.S. airport. I'm on duty, in my full uniform, and have all of my gear with me. I hoist my luggage onto the x-ray belt, then pass through the metal detector. Once on the other side, I'm waiting for my stuff to reappear when the belt suddenly groans to a stop.

"Bag check!" shouts the guard behind the monitor. Two of the most exasperating words in air travel, those are.

The bag in question turns out to be my roll-aboard. The guard has spotted something inside. The seconds tick by as she waits to confer with her colleague. One minute passes. Then two. Then three. All the while, the line behind me grows longer.

"Bag check!"

At last, another guard ambles over. There's a conference. For some reason, these situations require a sort of football huddle, with lots of whispering and pointing, before the belt can be switched on again. Why an offending piece of luggage can't simply be pulled from the machine and screened separately is a topic for another time, but let us ponder, for a moment, how much time is wasted each day by these checks.

Finally the second guard, the intensity of whose scowl is exceeded only by the weight of the chip on her shoulder, lifts my roll-aboard from the machine and walks toward me. "Is this yours?" she wants to know.

"Yes, it's mine."

"You got a knife in here?"

"A knife?"

"A knife," she barks. "Some silverware?"

Yes, I do. I always do. Inside my suitcase I carry a spare set of airline-sized cutlery—a spoon, a fork, and a knife. Along with packets of noodles and small snacks, this is part of my hotel survival kit, useful in the event of short layovers when food isn't available. It's identical to the cutlery that accompanies your meal on a long-haul flight. The pieces are stainless steel and about five inches long. The knife has a rounded end and a short row of teeth—I would call them serrations, but that's too strong a word. For all intents and purposes, it's a miniature butter knife.

"Yes," I tell the guard. "There's a metal knife in there—a butter knife."

She opens the compartment and takes out a small vinyl case containing the three pieces. After removing the knife, she holds it upward between with two fingers and stares at me coldly. Her pose is like that of an angry schoolteacher about to berate a child for bringing chewing gum to class.

"You ain't taking this through," she says. "No knifes [*sic*]. You can't bring a knife through here."

It takes a moment for me to realize that she's serious. 'I'm... but...it's...'

She throws it into a bin and starts to walk away.

"Wait a minute," I say. "That's airline silverware."

"Doesn't matter what it is. You can't bring knifes [*sic*] through here."

"Ma'am, that's an airline knife. It's the knife they give you on the plane."

"Have a good afternoon, sir."

"You can't be serious," I say.

With that, she grabs the knife out of the bin and walks over to one of her colleagues seated at the end of the checkpoint in a folding chair. I follow her over.

"This guy wants to bring this through."

The man in the chair looks up lazily. "Is it serrated?"

She hands it to him. He looks at it quickly, then addresses me.

"No, this is no good. You can't take this."

"Why not?"

"It's serrated." He is talking about the little row of teeth along the edge. Truth be told, the knife in question, which I've had for years, is actually smaller and duller than most of the knives handed out by airlines to their first and business class customers. You'd be hard pressed to cut a slice of toast with it.

"Oh, come on."

"What do you call these?" He runs his finger along the minuscule serrations.

"Those… but… they… it…"

"No serrated knives. You can't take this."

"But, sir, how can it not be allowed when it's the same knife they *give you on the plane?*"

"Those are the rules."

"That's impossible. Can I please speak to a supervisor?"

"I am the supervisor."

There are those moments in life when time stands still and the air around you seems to solidify. You stand there in an amber of absurdity, waiting for the crowd to burst out laughing and the *Candid Camera* guy to appear from around the corner.

Except the supervisor is dead serious.

Realizing that I'm not getting my knife back, I try for the consolation prize, which is getting the man to admit that, if nothing else, the rule makes no sense. "Come on," I argue. "The purpose of confiscating knives is to keep people from bringing them onto planes, right? But the passengers are *given* these knives with their meals. At least admit that it's a dumb rule. "

"It's not a dumb rule."

"Yes, it is."

"No, it isn't."

And so on, until he asks me to leave.

This was wrong on so many levels that it's hard to keep them straight. Just for starters, do I really need to point out that an airline pilot at the controls of his plane would hardly need a butter knife if he desired to inflict damage?

I know this comes across as a self-serving complaint, but at heart this isn't about pilots. It's about how diseased our approach to security is overall. Like most airline crewmembers, I'd have no problem going through screening if it were done fairly, logically, and rationally. In a way, TSA is going about this backward. They're working to come up with a system that exempts pilots, when what they ought to be doing is improving the rules for *everybody*.

Thousands of travelers, meanwhile, have their own versions of stories like mine: the girl who had her purse confiscated because it was embroidered with beads in the shape of a handgun; the woman whose cupcake was taken away; the pilot in San Francisco whose infant daughter's baby rattle was taken because it had liquid inside. And this gets me thinking. Why can't TSA exhibit common sense now and then? If we're to believe that TSA screeners are well-trained professionals, as the agency maintains, why can they not handle the responsibility of an occasional judgment call? Why can't they be *empowered* to allow some on-the-spot decision-making? If a screener is shown a 6-ounce tube of toothpaste that is obviously only half full, does it really need to be taken and flipped into the waste bin, as currently happens 90 percent of the time?

"Our screeners are allowed to exercise leeway in some cases," a TSA spokesperson told me. "They have the training, and the obligation, to exercise discretion." Maybe, but I'm not seeing much leeway and discretion. I'm seeing a draconian obsession with the exactness of container volumes and the dimensions of objects, up to and including whether a pilot's tiny knife has serrations on its blade, as if they alone could be the difference between unsafe and safe. Enforcement of this kind transcends mere tedium and becomes downright unsafe. Maybe you've heard the story about a test in which TSA screeners are presented with a suitcase containing a mock explosive device with a water bottle nestled next to it? They ferret out the water, of course, while the bomb goes sailing through.

Notice too the uniforms adopted by TSA. Screeners are now

called "officers," and they wear blue shirts and silver badges. Not by accident, the shirts and badges look exactly like the kind worn by police. Mission-creep, this is called. In fact, TSA workers do not hold law enforcement power as such—much as they have done a good job of fooling people into believing otherwise. TSA holds the authority, legitimately, to inspect your belongings and prevent you from passing through a checkpoint. It does *not* have the authority to detain you, interrogate you, arrest you, force you to recite the Pledge of Allegiance, or otherwise compromise your rights. Both TSA and the traveling public need to remember this.

In 2010, following the failed bombing of a Northwest Airlines flight from Amsterdam to Detroit, things were taken to the next level with the introduction of full-body scanners. This has been one of the more controversial—and disheartening—developments in our long war on the abstract noun called terrorism. The first-generation machines, the scanned images which left little to the imagination, are being replaced by those showing only a generic contour of the body. While this somewhat settles the privacy debate, it doesn't solve their tactical shortcomings.

The scanners have been promoted as a key component of airport security, yet some airports have them while others don't. There's a scanner at one checkpoint, but no scanner at the one right next to it; scanners at some terminals, but not at others. Are terrorists that stupid? And if somebody is going to attempt to sneak a bomb through a checkpoint, it is much more likely to happen someplace in Europe, Asia, Africa, or the Middle East than it is in Peoria, Wichita, or Cleveland. But domestically is where most of the machines have been installed; overseas, they are rare.

It's easy to be cynical. Was development of the body scanner really in the interest of keeping passengers safe, or was it for the interests of the corporations who stand to make billions in their design and deployment? It's questionable whether they're making us safer, but rest assured they're making somebody wealthy. But here it has come to pass, and our reaction, aside from one or two muffled complaints, has been a sheeplike acquiescence.

No less frustrating is the strained notion that, beginning with the events of September 11, air travel suddenly entered a new age of danger and threat. The grandiosity of the 2001 attacks, with their Hollywood thriller plotline and operatic fireballs, has gummed up our memories. We talk of the "post-9/11 era," whereas politically motivated violence against civil aviation has been with us for decades. In fact, we see it a lot less often than we used to. The 1970s through the 1990s were a sort of Golden Age of Air Crimes, rife with hijackings and bombings. In the five-year span between 1985 and 1989, there were no fewer than six major terrorist attacks against commercial planes or airports, including the Libyan-sponsored bombings of Pan Am 103 and UTA 772; the bombing of an Air India 747 that killed 329 people; and the saga of TWA flight 847. Flight 847, headed from Athens to Rome in June 1985, was hijacked by Shiite militiamen armed with grenades and pistols. The purloined 727 then embarked on a remarkable, seventeen-day odyssey to Lebanon, Algeria, and back again. At one point passengers were removed, split into groups, and held captive in downtown Beirut. The photograph of TWA Captain John Testrake, his head out the cockpit window, collared by a gun-wielding terrorist, was broadcast worldwide and became an unforgettable icon of the siege.

I say "unforgettable," but that's just the thing. How many Americans remember flight 847? It's astonishing how short our memories are. And partly because they're so short, we are easily frightened and manipulated. Imagine TWA 847 happening tomorrow. Imagine six successful terror attacks against planes in a five-year span. The airline industry would be decimated, the populace frozen in fear. It would be a catastrophe of epic proportion—of wall-to-wall coverage and, dare I suggest, the summary surrender of important civil liberties. What is it about us, as a society, that has made us so unable to remember and unable to cope?

But all right, enough of what we shouldn't be doing. What about things we *should* be doing? If I'm going to spend all this time complaining, it's only fair that I offer up some solutions, no?

Well, airport security overall ought to be scaled back into a leaner but more focused operation. I wouldn't say that we have too much security, necessarily, but we certainly have too much in the wrong places, out of synch with the hierarchy of threat. First up, every dime currently being spent looking for pointy objects, double-checking people's IDs, and confiscating innocuous liquids needs to be reallocated.

The primary threat to commercial aviation is, was, and shall remain bombs. Therefore, every piece of luggage, both checked and carry-on, as well as cargo, ought to be scrutinized for explosives. This already happens, officially, though I reckon we could be doing a more thorough job of it, with a stronger emphasis on airports outside the United States. The likeliest point of entry for a bomb is not Omaha or Tucson, and I'd suggest shifting a good 35 percent of TSA resources to locations overseas. If that should require some touchy negotiations with foreign airport authorities, so be it.

And like it or not, the time has come to put greater emphasis on passenger profiling. Profiling is a dirty word to some, but it needn't be a one-dimensional preoccupation with skin color or national origin. Indeed, as security specialists will tell you, racial or ethnic profiling doesn't work. Routine is weakness, and the more predictable our methods, the easier they are to foil. Effective profiling uses a multipoint approach that takes in a wide range of characteristics, both tangible and behavioral. TSA has been training staff in the finer points of behavioral pattern recognition. That's good, though for the time being, screeners are a lot more adept at picking out scissors and shampoo bottles than picking out terrorists.

The International Air Transport Association (IATA) has proposed a plan in which passengers would be categorized into one of three risk groups and then screened accordingly. Biometric proof of identity, such as a fingerprint or encoded passport, will be checked against a stored profile containing various personal data and against watch lists. This, together with flight booking data, will determine which of three lines a traveler is assigned to. Those in the first line would receive little more than a cursory bag check. Those in the second line get a slightly closer look, while those in the third would face an enhanced inspection similar to the current TSA procedures. This wouldn't be perfect—and like many people, I get a little nervous when I hear the words "biometric" and "profile containing various personal data"—but it's maybe the best idea yet when it comes to restoring sanity to airport security. IATA says that an early version of the three-tiered system could be up and running in under three years.

That is, if governments cooperate. IATA is making sense, but I'm afraid it lacks the clout of the U.S. Department of Homeland Security, the federal branch under whose auspices TSA operates. Enacting serious change would take, more than anything else, the political will and courage of our leaders in Congress. We have thus far seen little political opposition, bipartisan or otherwise, to TSA's squandering of our time and money. While I hate to sound like a conspiracy theorist, our leaders talk and act as if they enjoy the status quo, unwilling to disenfranchise any facet of what has become a vast and profitable security-industrial complex.

To be fair, there are plenty of bright and resourceful people at the TSA who know a lot more about the challenges of airport security than I ever will. And they openly admit that a philosophical change is needed—a shift toward focusing on passengers themselves rather than on their belongings. This, they understand, is the only viable strategy for the future. But TSA is, in the end, a bureaucracy. No doubt it sees the IATA proposal, and others like it, as a threat to its funding and authority. This was an agency created in haste and granted considerable powers and relatively little accountability. Any idea, however beneficial, faces an uphill battle against such a potent government entity, especially when aided and abetted by a lethargic populace and an irresponsible media.

What TSA has signed off on are third-party programs, run by outside contractors, in which passengers submit biometric and personal data in exchange for expedited screening—for a fee. Count me among those who find these programs objectionable. Rather than fixing the problem, citizens can pay money and cut to the front of the line. Your taxes will continue to support a dysfunctional system, and now you can pay even more to circumvent that system. This is progress?

It doesn't have to be this way. The solution is out there. Give us good intelligence-gathering and law enforcement, together with on-site random searches, thorough explosives scanning, and smartly managed profiling, and what have we got? A security strategy that is, frankly, pretty good.

As good as it can be, anyway. Somewhere beneath all of this rests the uncomfortable, seldom-acknowledged fact that no matter how hard we try, we're never going to make flying completely safe. Neither all the determination in the world nor the most sweeping regulations we dare codify will outsmart a cunning enough saboteur. Sound, competent security greatly improves our chances, whether against the concoctions of a single deranged individual or organized terror from the caves of Central Asia. But with every new technology and pledge of better safeguards, we correspondingly inspire the imaginations of those who wish to defeat us. There will always be a way to skirt the system.

This brings us to a third fundamental flaw in our approach, whereby we refuse to acknowledged that the *real* job of keeping terrorists away from planes is not the job of airport screeners in the first place. Rather, it's the job of government agencies and law enforcement. The grunt work of hunting down terrorists takes place far offstage, relying on the diligent work of cops, spies, and intelligence officers. Air crimes need to be stopped in the planning stages. By the time a terrorist gets to the airport, chances are it's too late. And the rage of angry radicals, dangerous as it may be, is a long-term anthropological mission to be dealt with separately; it is not an excuse to turn airports into fortresses and subvert freedoms.

In the end, I'm not sure which is more distressing, the inanity of the existing regulations or the average citizen's acceptance of them. There ought to be a tide of opposition rising up against this mania. Where is it? At its loudest, the voice of the traveling public is one of grumbly resignation. The op-ed pages are silent; the pundits have nothing to say.

The airlines, for their part, are in something of a bind. That carriers and industry advocates seem content with such high levels of aggravation among their customers suggests a business model that is almost surreally masochistic and self-destructive. On the other hand, imagine the outrage in certain circles should airlines be caught lobbying for what is perceived to be a dangerous abrogation of security and responsibility—even if it's not. Carriers caught plenty of flak, almost all of it unfair, in the aftermath of September 11. Understandably, they no longer want that liability.

How we got to this point is an interesting study in reactionary politics, fear mongering, and a disconcerting willingness of the public to accept almost anything, no matter how illogical, inconvenient, or unreasonable, in the name of security. Conned and frightened, what we get is not actual security, but security spectacle. The idea that this spectacle "helps travelers to feel better" is about its only excuse and is hardly enough justification to keep it funded and running. And although a high percentage of passengers, along with most security experts, would concur that it leaves us no safer, and perhaps even increases our risks, there has been little to no protest. In that regard, maybe, we've gotten exactly the system we deserve.

In Perspective:
The Golden Age of Air Crimes

1970: A Pan Am 747 bound for New York is skyjacked after take-off from Amsterdam. The flight is diverted to Cairo, where all of the 170 occupants are released. Radicals then blow up the plane.

1970: In what were known as the Black September hijackings, five jets, including planes belonging to TWA, Pan Am, and Israel's El Al, are commandeered over Europe during a three-day span by a group called the Popular Front for Liberation of Palestine (PFLP). After all passengers are freed, three of the five planes are diverted to a remote airstrip in Jordan, rigged with explosives, and blown up. A fourth is flown to Egypt and destroyed there.

1971: A man using the name D. B. Cooper skyjacks and threatens to blow up a Northwest Orient 727 flying from Portland, Oregon, to Seattle. Over southwestern Washington, he parachutes out the back of the plane with a hefty ransom and is never seen or heard from again.

1972: A JAT (Yugoslav Airlines) DC-9 en route from Copenhagen to Zagreb explodes at 33,000 feet. The Ustashe, aka Croatian National Movement, admits to the bombing.

1972: Explosion aboard a Cathay Pacific jet flying from Bangkok to Hong Kong kills eighty-one people. A Thai police lieutenant is accused of hiding the bomb to murder his fiancée.

1972: In the arrivals lounge of Lod Airport near Tel Aviv, three men from the Japanese Red Army, recruited by the Palestinian PLFP, open fire with machine guns and grenades, killing twenty-six people and injuring eighty.

1973: As passengers board a Pan Am 747 at the airport in Rome, terrorists spray the plane with gunfire and toss grenades into the cabin, killing thirty.

1973: Eighty-one perish as an Aeroflot jet explodes over Siberia during an attempted skyjacking.

1974: A TWA 707 flying from Athens to Rome falls into the sea near Greece, the result of an explosive device hidden in a cargo compartment.

1974: A man detonates two grenades aboard an Air Vietnam 727 when the crew refuses to fly him to Hanoi.

1976: A Cubana DC-8 crashes near Barbados, killing seventy-three. An anti-Castro exile and three alleged accomplices are put on trial but acquitted for lack of evidence.

1976: Air France Flight 139, bound from Tel Aviv to Athens to Paris, is hijacked by a combined force of PFLP and Revolutionäre Zellen (RZ). The plane is diverted first to Benghazi, Libya, before continuing to Entebbe, Uganda. At Entebbe, 105 hostages are held until the plane is raided by commandos from the Israel Defense Forces. During the raid, three passengers, seven hijackers, one Israeli, and approximately forty Ugandan soldiers are killed. (The dead Israeli, Yonatan Netanyahu, was the younger brother of Israeli Prime Minister Benjamin Netanyahu.)

1977: Both pilots of a Malaysian Airline System (today called Malaysia Airlines) 737 are shot by a skyjacker. The plane crashes into a swamp.

1985: The Abu Nidal group kills twenty people in a pair of coordinated ticket-counter assaults at airports in Vienna and Rome.

1985: Shiite militiamen hijack TWA Flight 847 from Athens to Rome, holding hostages for two weeks. The sole casualty is a U.S. Navy diver, who is shot and dumped on the tarmac. All remaining hostages are eventually released, but not before the Israeli government agrees to free more than seven hundred Shiite prisoners.

1985: An Air India 747 on a service between Toronto and Bombay is bombed over the North Atlantic by Sikh militants. The 329 fatalities remain history's worst single-plane act of terrorism. A second bomb, intended for another Air India 747, detonates prematurely in Tokyo before being loaded (*see ten worst crashes, page 203*).

1986: As TWA flight 840 descends through 10,000 feet toward Athens, a bomb goes off in the cabin. Four people are ejected through a tear in the 727's fuselage.

1986: At the airport in Karachi, Pakistan, a Pan Am 747 is preparing for departure when four heavily armed members of the Abu Nidal group seize the aircraft. When Pakistani forces storm the plane, the terrorists begin shooting and lobbing grenades. Twenty-two passengers are killed and 150 wounded. Although all four terrorists were captured and sent to prison in Pakistan, they were released in 2001.

1987: A Korean Air Lines 707 disappears over the Andaman Sea en route from Baghdad to Seoul. One of two Koreans suspected of hiding a bomb commits suicide before he's arrested. His accomplice, a young woman, confesses to leaving the device— fashioned from both plastic and liquid explosives—in an overhead rack before disembarking during an intermediate stop. Condemned to death, the woman is pardoned in 1990 by the president of South Korea.

1987: At Los Angeles International Airport, a recently fired ticket agent, David Burke, sneaks a loaded gun past security and boards a Pacific Southwest Airlines (PSA) jet on its way to San Francisco. During cruise, he breaks into the cockpit, shoots both pilots, then noses the airplane into the ground near Harmony, California, killing all forty-four on board. (Unbelievable as it might sound, the government's response to this crime was to implement checkpoint security screening not for ground personnel, but instead for pilots and flight attendants.)

1988: Pan Am flight 103 is carrying 259 people when it is destroyed by a bomb blast over the town of Lockerbie, Scotland. One of the most intensive criminal investigations in history brings two Libyan operatives, al-Amin Khalifa Fhimah and Abdel Baset Ali al-Megrahi, to trial in the Netherlands. Fhimah is acquitted. Al-Megrahi is found guilty and sentenced to life but is released by the British government in 2009. Until you-know-what, the bombing of flight 103 represents the worst-ever terrorist attack against a civilian U.S. target (*see ten worst crashes, page 203*).

1989: Libya will also be held responsible for the bombing of UTA flight 772 nine months after Lockerbie. Most Americans don't remember this incident, but it has never been forgotten in France. A hundred and seventy people from seventeen countries were killed when an explosive device went off in the forward luggage hold of the McDonnell Douglas DC-10 on a flight from Brazzaville, Congo, to Paris. The wreckage fell into the Tenere region of the Sahara, in northern Niger, one of the planet's most remote areas. A French court eventually convicted six Libyans in absentia for the murders, including Muammar Gaddafi's brother-in-law.

1989: In a plot to kill police informants, members of a cocaine cartel blow up Avianca Flight 203 bound from Bogotá to Cali. There are no survivors among 110 crew and passengers.

1990: A young man claiming to have explosives strapped to his body forces his way into the cockpit of a Xiamen Airlines 737 and demands to be flown to Taiwan. Running out of fuel, the crew attempts a landing at Canton (Guangzhou), when a struggle erupts. The plane veers off the runway and collides with two other aircraft.

1994: Riding along as an auxiliary crewmember, Auburn Calloway, an off-duty Federal Express pilot scheduled for termination, attacks the three-man crew of a DC-10 with a spear gun and a hammer, nearly killing all of them. His plan, before he's finally overtaken by the battered and bloodied pilots, is to crash the airliner into FedEx's Memphis headquarters.

1994: An Air France A300 is stormed by a foursome of extremist Muslims in Algeria. The plane is forced to Marseilles where seven people die when French troops rush aboard for a rescue. News footage shows an Air France pilot hurling himself out of a cockpit window while a stun grenade flashes behind him.

1996: An Ethiopian Airlines 767 is hijacked over the Indian Ocean. The jet runs out of fuel and heads for a ditching off the Comoros Islands. Hijackers wrestle with the pilots, and the plane breaks apart upon hitting the water, killing 125.

1999: An All Nippon Airways 747 lands safely after a deranged man forces his way onto the flight deck and stabs the captain to death with an eight-inch knife.

1999: Air Botswana captain Chris Phatswe steals an empty ATR commuter plane and slams it into two parked aircraft, killing himself and destroying virtually the entire fleet of his nation's tiny airline.

And not to forget what might have been, I'll remind you again of the near success of the 1994 Project Bojinka conspiracy to bomb eleven widebody jets simultaneously over the Pacific. Bojinka, or "big bang," was the brainchild of Ramzi Yousef, a master mixer of liquid explosives, and his uncle Khalid Sheikh Mohammed. The latter would go on to mastermind the September 11 attacks, while Yousef was, at the time, already a wanted man for his role in the 1993 World Trade Center prelude. The bombs, made from nitroglycerin, sulfuric acid, acetone, and other chemicals, would be hidden with the under-seat life jackets. In 1995, Yousef completed a successful, small-level test run on a Philippine Airlines 747, killing a Japanese businessman. The plot was broken up after authorities investigated a chemical fire in the Manila apartment of one of Yousef's accomplices. ✈

How about some encouragement, please, for those who are terrified of flying?

Can I cure *your* fear of flying? That depends more on the nature of your fears than my skills of explanation. I'm not a psychologist, and not everybody's fears are rational. In a high percentage of cases, what fearful flyers actually fear has little or nothing to do with flying itself and cannot be dispatched by explanations, statistics, or straight talk. They don't need a pilot; they need a counselor or a mental health professional.

A certain level of fear is normal, whether you're a first-time flyer or a seasoned crewmember. I can't be surprised that millions of reasonable people find it hard to reconcile the notion of traveling hundreds of miles per hour, far above the Earth, inside pressurized tubes weighing hundreds of thousands of pounds. Such an activity is not natural for human beings, and while it doesn't quite violate the laws of physics, it does seem to violate any and all common sense. Technology has made it work, but while airplane travel isn't statistically dangerous, *inherently* it's another story.

As for stats, Bill James, the baseball academic, likes to say, "Never use a number when you can avoid it." Normally he's right, and I don't enjoy dishing out numerical platitudes. We're so used to abstract validation of air safety that it no longer makes us *think*. A few statistics, however, are worth our time. For example, this one, which you can almost visualize: each day, in the United States alone, about 25,000 commercial flights take to the air. Globally, extrapolation yields about 50,000 daily trips. That's every day, every week, every month. The ten most popular airlines alone make close to six million flights per year. Of these, the number failing in their attempt to flout gravity can be totaled in astonishingly short shrift.

How short? Here in the United States, we are riding strong amid the safest-ever stretch in the history of commercial aviation. As this manuscript is being prepared in 2013, we have not seen a large-scale crash involving a major airline in more than eleven years. That's a record dating back to the advent of the jetliner itself. Our last catastrophe was that of American Airlines flight 587 near Kennedy airport in November 2001. Since then, the only major-carrier fatality was that of a young boy killed when a Southwest Airlines 737 overran a snowy runway in Chicago in 2004. The boy was in an automobile struck by the skidding plane. Granted, there have been several nonfatal incidents (Sully-upon-Hudson, to cite one) and a handful of tragedies involving regional planes, but even with these included, the nation's fatal accident rate has fallen 85 percent since 2000. From 2008 through 2012, the odds of being in a fatal accident were approximately one in 45 million.

This, despite the industry's unprecedented fiscal woes. The fallout from September 11 gave us thousands of layoffs and four major carrier bankruptcy filings, then came the 2007–08 fuel-spike crisis, followed by a terrible recession. Say what you want of customer service, but even though our largest airlines have been reeling financially, they've remained impeccably safe.

Here's more: In a 2003 study published by *American Scientist* magazine, University of Michigan researchers reevaluated the old flying-versus-driving contention. To be as conservative as possible, their technique calculated probabilities based not on kilometers covered, but on numbers of takeoffs and landings, when more than 90 percent of air crashes occur. And they considered highway data only from rural interstates—one of the *safest* driving environments. Their data showed that if a passenger chooses to drive rather than fly the distance of a typical flight segment, that person is sixty-five times more likely to be killed.

Elsewhere around the globe, the statistics are no less impressive. There are twice as many commercial aircraft worldwide, carrying twice as many passengers, as existed in 1980. Yet, per passenger-miles flown, flying is an estimated five times safer. Narrowing it to the past ten years, the number of people who fly annually has increased by roughly 20 percent, to just over two *billion*. Over that span, the number of fatal accidents has held steady at around twenty per year. According to the Aviation Safety Network, 2012 was the safest year globally since 1945.

Getting to this level wasn't easy. Mainly it's the result of better pilot training, improved cockpit technology, and the seldom-acknowledged collaborative efforts of the airline industry, regulators, pilot groups, and international organizations like ICAO. (ICAO—*Eye-kay-oh*, the International Civil Aviation Organization—is the aviation directorate of the United Nations and sets global protocols on a wide range of safety issues, from runway markings to approach procedures.) Not long ago, as air travel was beginning to expand rapidly in places like China, India, and Brazil, experts warned of a tipping point. Unless certain deficiencies were addressed, we were told, disasters would become epidemic, at a rate of up to one per week. Fortunately they *were* addressed, most notably in the area of crew training, and the end result is that we've effectively engineered away some of the most common causes of crashes.

Maintaining such high standards, however, is going to take some effort. And while I shouldn't have to say it, here goes: At some point our luck *will* run out. There *will* be another catastrophic accident. Affirming this today is a good way of reducing the shock later on. It's not to suggest that we let our guard down; it's to recognize the inevitable and acknowledge that no system, no matter how good, can ever be perfect. And when it happens, we should probably brace ourselves for the reaction. The amount of media attention given to minor mishaps, precautionary landings, and harmless malfunctions in recent years is a depressing precursor of what's to come when something legitimately serious happens. The worst thing about the next big crash will be the loss of life. The second worst thing will be the overreaction and hype.

Most of us acknowledge the safety of commercial flying. We get it. Nevertheless, what are some of the nightmare scenarios in the back of a pilot's mind? What emergencies do they dread most?

This is a tricky one. The mere suggestion that a pilot "dreads" a particular scenario is enough to convince the already-nervous flyer that it's about to happen. The last thing I want to do is scare the bejesus out of the person who has turned to this chapter for comfort. Just the same, it's a fair question and one that deserves an answer.

For the most part, pilots fear those things they cannot control. We are less afraid of committing a fatal error than of finding ourselves victimized by *somebody else's* error, or else at the mercy of those forces impervious to our skills or expertise. I'd put lithium battery fires, bird strikes that take out multiple engines, catastrophic mechanical malfunctions, and ground collisions at the top of my list. We talked about birds in chapter two (*see bird strikes, page 48*), and we'll get to collisions later in this chapter. "Catastrophic mechanical malfunction" is a catchall for things like flight control failure (loss of rudder, elevator, or aileron control), uncommanded reverser deployment, and other worst-case terrors that can render a plane unflyable. Improbable as these things are, all of them have happened once or twice.

As to battery fires, high-energy lithium power packs—both lithium-ion and the lithium-polymer types found in many laptop computers and other devices—are susceptible to a phenomenon called thermal runaway, a chemical chain-reaction causing them to rapidly and uncontrollably overheat. The danger isn't a small fire in the passenger cabin, where it can be readily put out with an extinguisher, but the possibility of a larger, unseen fire in a baggage or freight compartment. Frighteningly, tests have shown these fires to be resistant to the Halon-based cargo compartment extinguishing systems used on commercial aircraft.

The FAA has recorded more than seventy incidents involving lithium battery fires since the 1990s. The two most serious were the fatal crash of a UPS 747 near Dubai in 2010 and a nearly fatal fire aboard a UPS DC-8 in Philadelphia in 2006. Both blazes are believed to have been touched off by large shipments of lithium batteries. And in 2013, all Boeing 787s were temporarily grounded following a series of lithium battery fires in the planes' electronics bays.

The bulk shipment of lithium batteries is now prohibited aboard passenger planes, as is the carriage of loose (i.e. spare) batteries in checked baggage. The possibility always remains, however, of a shipment sneaking through. If a lithium fire strikes you as a very small possibility, you're right, it is. But it's healthy, I think, and in the best interest of safety overall, that as pilots we keep certain things in the back of our minds.

As a nervous traveler, I'm constantly trying to read the facial expressions of the crew. Is it general policy not to inform passengers of emergencies to avoid panic? Will I see it in the flight attendant's eyes?

That glazed look in the flight attendant's eyes is probably one of exhaustion, not fear. Nervous flyers are prone to envision some silently impending disaster, with distressed crewmembers pacing the aisles and whispering to each other in secret. In reality, passengers *will* be told about any emergency or serious malfunction.

And most nonserious ones too. If you're informed about a landing gear snafu, pressurization problem, engine trouble, or the need for a precautionary landing, do *not* construe this to be a life-or-death situation. It's virtually always something minor—though you'll be kept in the loop anyway. With even an outside chance of an evacuation in mind, you *have* to be kept in the loop.

On the other hand, a crew will not inform passengers of small malfunctions with no legitimate bearing on safety. Being blunt about every little problem invites unnecessary worry, not to mention embellishment. "Ladies and gentlemen, this is the captain. Just to let you know, we've received a failure indication for the backup loop of the smoke detection system in the aft cargo compartment." In this example, passengers come home with, "Oh my god, the plane was on fire." Not that people aren't bright enough to figure out what is or isn't dangerous, but we're dealing with jargon and terminology that begs to be misunderstood.

This topic brings to mind the unfortunate saga of jetBlue flight 292, an Airbus A320 that made an emergency landing in Los Angeles in 2005 because of a landing gear problem. Although only a minor incident from a technical point of view, the entire affair was caught on live television, engrossing millions of Americans and needlessly scaring the daylights out of everybody on the plane:

Moments after liftoff from Burbank, California, the pilots realized their forward landing gear had not properly retracted and was cocked at 90 degrees. Unable to realign it, they would have to make an emergency landing with the tires twisted sideways. The pilots and jetBlue's dispatch team agreed to a diversion to Los Angeles, primarily to take advantage of LAX's long runways. But first came the matter of the plane's gross weight, which was several thousand pounds above its maximum allowable heft for touchdown. The A320, like other smaller jetliners, does not have fuel dump capability (*see fuel jettison, page 45*). This meant three hours of leisure flying over the Pacific until the poundage was down to the appropriate amount.

Those three hours are what allowed this relative nonevent to be catapulted into a full-on network spectacle. The California news outlets, out and about in search of the usual car chases and traffic accidents, had only to tip their cameras upward to catch the Airbus as it circled. On board, 146 souls readied for what, according to the commentators, could very well be a devastating crash. Grown men were seen weeping. Others scribbled good-bye notes to loved ones. Words like "terrifying" and "harrowing" would later show up in interviews with those who "survived."

Those of us who knew better weren't nearly as alarmed. We saw a jetliner with a mildly threatening problem preparing for what would be a telegenic but perfectly manageable landing. And that's what we got. The plane touched down smoothly on its main tires, the nose gently falling as speed bled away until the wayward gear scraped sideways into the pavement, kicking up a rooster tail of sparks. There were no injuries.

As if the live-action saga hadn't been enough, the media spent the next three days choking on its own hype and melodrama, showing slow-motion replays, interviewing passengers, and generally giving jetBlue all the free advertising it could possibly hope for.

For those who'd been aboard, jetBlue's seat-back TV screens helped induce panic, beaming in reckless live coverage from the networks. What the passengers needed was a calm and accurate explanation of exactly what was going on, and what was likely to happen at touchdown. What they got was sensational commentary from people who had no idea what they were talking about. The whole thing set up a weird and distasteful voyeuristic triangle: the terrified and transfixed passengers assumed they were watching themselves, where in truth they were watching *us* watch *them*. And all along there were better things on TV.

But assuming such a high level of safety exists, why are the airlines so shy about it? You rarely hear carriers talking about safety. Why not use it to their advantage?

As a rule, airlines in America do not use safety as a marketing tool. All employ the word in a vague and general fashion, but seldom with regard to specific programs or innovations. To do so would be, on one hand, statistically manipulative, and on the other hand, a potential form of market suicide, undercutting the presumption of air safety in general. Not to mention the humiliation a given carrier would endure should a disaster transpire. For airline A to sell itself as safer than everyone else, there needs to be a presumption of danger aboard its competitors. This would entail some dubious statistical maneuvering. Since the terror attacks of 2001, American Airlines has had one fatal accident; the other network carriers none. For United or Delta to brag of having a better record than American would be, even if mathematically accurate, a little underhanded.

Few of us require a primer on the ruthlessness of corporate advertising, but in this case there's a risk factor that compels the airlines into a collective quiet. With casualties so rare, the statistical swing from a "safe" airline to a "dangerous" one hinges on select few events drawn from hundreds of thousands of departures. Reputations can be lost through a single act of folly or stroke of lousy luck. Quite understandably, airlines have no desire to put their competitive eggs in such a precarious basket.

Furthermore, the moment any airline dares put safety into the mix, the issue loses its statistical context and becomes a play on passenger emotions. All airlines will suffer if, in effect, passengers are encouraged to openly contemplate their mortality while surfing Travelocity. Flying is safe, and a majority of people, including most fearful flyers, assent to this reality with little or no fuss. That's good enough for the airlines.

Having said all that, there are ways to play the game slyly. An airline is never faulted for boasting that its crews receive the best training possible; the preflight demo rambles imperatively of seat belts and oxygen masks; the captain reminds you that nothing is more important than the well-being of everybody on board. But these are not mass-market pitches. Protocol permits any airline to call itself safe. Just not *safer*.

Just because an airline doesn't showboat its safety initiatives doesn't mean they don't exist. Cynics will be eager to cite a seeming trail of greed and negligence: airlines found culpable for certain crashes, fines for maintenance violations, and so on. But I hasten to remind you how much a carrier stands to lose should one of its planes go down. Liability can run into the billions, and a single disaster can destroy an airline outright. Hard as it might be for some of you to accept, to suggest the industry, along with its federal overseers, are playing fast and loose with the lives of the traveling public is a terrible distortion.

The Ten Deadliest Air Disasters of All Time

Even the most uptight flyers grow bored from monotonous reminders about the safety of flying. For those of you brave enough to indulge your morbid curiosities, I present the following catalog—tastefully and educationally, of course. As you'll see, I've left out the World Trade Center attacks. The planes-as-weapons phenomenon really bends the definition of "air disaster," and including the Twin Tower implosions would be a stretch. Would a Cessna detonating a bomb over a crowded city qualify as an air disaster? How about the overloaded Russian turboprop that plowed into a crowded market in Zaire in 1996, killing over three hundred people, only *two* of whom were on the plane? Where to draw the line is unclear. Perhaps the fairest method is to remove *all* on-the-ground casualties from crash totals? Until there's a formal consensus, here's the generally accepted list of history's worst crashes:

1. **March 27, 1977.** Two chartered Boeing 747s operated by KLM and Pan Am collide on a foggy runway at Tenerife, in Spain's Canary Islands, killing 583 people (61 people survive, all from Pan Am). Confused by instructions, KLM begins its takeoff sans permission and strikes the other jet as it taxies on the active runway. There are several contributing factors, including a blocked radio call that prevents the control tower from realizing KLM's error in time (*see Tenerife story, page 229*).

2. **August 12, 1985.** A Japan Air Lines 747 crashes near Mt. Fuji on a domestic flight, killing 520. The rupture of an aft pressure bulkhead, which had undergone improper repairs following a mishap seven years earlier, allows a rush of air to destroy the airplane's rudder and tail. A JAL maintenance supervisor later commits suicide. The airline's president resigns, accepting formal responsibility, and visits victims' families to offer a personal apology.

3. **November 12, 1996.** An Ilyushin IL-76 cargo jet from Kazakhstan collides in midair with a Saudia 747 near Delhi, India; all 349 aboard both planes are killed. The Kazakh crew disobeys instructions from ATC, and neither plane is equipped with now-standard collision avoidance technology.

4. **March 3, 1974.** A THY (Turkish Airlines) DC-10 goes down near Orly airport, killing 346. A faultily latched cargo door bursts from its frame, and the resulting decompression causes the cabin floor to collapse, impairing cables to the rudders and elevators. Out of control, the plane slams into the woods northeast of Paris. McDonnell Douglas, maker of the DC-10, is forced to redesign the cargo door system.

5. **June 23, 1985.** A bomb planted by a Sikh extremist blows up an Air India 747 on a service between Toronto and Bombay. The plane falls into the sea east of Ireland, killing 329. Canadian investigators cite shortcomings in baggage screening procedures and employee training.

6. **August 19, 1980.** A Saudia L-1011 bound for Karachi returns to Riyadh, Saudi Arabia, following an inflight fire just after departure. For reasons never understood, the plane rolls to the far end of the runway after a safe emergency landing and sits with engines running for more than three minutes. No evacuation is commenced. Before the inadequately equipped rescue workers can open any doors, all 301 passengers and crew die as a flash fire consumes the cabin.

7. **July 3, 1988.** An Airbus A300 operated by Iran Air is shot down over the Straits of Hormuz by the U.S. Navy cruiser *Vincennes*. The crew of the *Vincennes*, distracted by an ongoing gun battle, mistakes the A300 for a hostile aircraft and destroys it with two missiles. None of the 290 occupants survive.

8. **May 25, 1979.** As an American Airlines DC-10 lifts from the runway at Chicago's O'Hare airport, an engine detaches and seriously damages a wing. Before the crew can make sense of what's happening, the airplane rolls 90 degrees and disintegrates in a fireball. With 273 fatalities, this remains the worst-ever plane crash on U.S. soil. Both the engine pylon design and airline maintenance procedures are faulted, and all DC-10s are temporarily grounded.

9. **December 21, 1988.** Libyan agents are later held responsible for the bombing of Pan Am flight 103, which blows up in the evening sky over Lockerbie, Scotland, killing 270 people, including 11 on the ground. The largest section, a flaming heap of wing and fuselage, drops onto Lockerbie's Sherwood Crescent neighborhood, destroying twenty houses and ploughing a crater three stories deep. The concussion is so strong that Richter devices record a 1.6 magnitude tremor.

10. **September 1, 1983.** Korean Air Lines flight KL007, a 747 carrying 269 passengers and crew from New York

to Seoul (with a technical stop in Anchorage) is shot from the air near Sakhalin Island in the North Pacific by a Soviet fighter after drifting off course and into Soviet airspace. Investigators attribute the deviation to "a considerable degree of lack of alertness and attentiveness on the part of the flight crew."

Abstracting these ten events gets slithery. One could surmise that the 747 is the most dangerous plane in the sky, for instance, having been involved in seven of the top-ten disasters, neglecting its immense capacity. Still, we find some curious points, such as the lack of crew culpability, that is, pilot error, in all but three of the disasters. All together, these accidents involved twelve airplanes and ten airlines. Pan Am played a role in two of them, as did the lesser-known Saudia (now called Saudi Arabian Airlines). An interesting breakdown also includes

- Number that occurred in the United States: 1
- Number that occurred prior to 1974: 0
- Number that occurred during the 1970s or 1980s: 9
- Number in which pilot error was cited as a direct or contributing cause: 3
- Number resulting from terrorist sabotage: 2
- Number that were shot down mistakenly: 2
- Number that crashed as a result of mechanical failure or design flaw: 3
- Total fatalities: 3,530
- Total survivors: 65 (61 from Pan Am at Tenerife, and 4 from JAL)

Those 3,530 combined fatalities equals about a tenth of the number of people killed each year in automobile accidents in the United States.

We in the West occasionally hear of the dangers of flying aboard certain airlines overseas. Are such fears justified?

We should start by acknowledging that there is virtually no such thing as a "dangerous" airline, anywhere. Some are safer than others, but even the least safe airline is still very safe.

The region of the world with the worst reputation by far is sub-Saharan Africa, where scores of small companies operate without anywhere near the oversight or resources of airlines in the West. But even here the statistics can be misleading. It's important to make the distinction between mainline African carriers and lower-tier cargo and nonscheduled operators. Flying on South African Airways or Ethiopian Airlines, for example, which have perfectly respectable records, is not the same as flying aboard some ad-hoc Congolese cargo runner or a Guinean charter outfit. Africa's "dangerous" airlines are not even airlines as most people think of them.

"Americans have no reason to be afraid of foreign carriers," says Robert Booth of AvMan, an aviation consulting firm in Miami. "Plenty of these companies have cultures of safety that meet or exceed our own," he points out.

That's a sensible assessment, though some airlines have had a tough time shaking their bad reputations. Russia's Aeroflot, for example. Once upon a time, measured in raw crash totals, Aeroflot had a comparatively poor record. On the face of it, anyway. Several asterisks were required, not the least of which was that Aeroflot, in its heydays, was a gigantic entity roughly the size of all U.S. airlines *put together*, and it engaged in all manner of far-flung operations to outposts as remote as Antarctica. During the 1990s, Aeroflot was splintered into dozens of independent carriers, one of which—still the largest, but nowhere near the heft of the original—inherited the Aeroflot name and identity. Based in Moscow, the Aeroflot that exists today operates about 120 aircraft and transports 14 million passengers annually. Since 1994, it has had only two serious accidents, one of them at the hands of a subsidiary.

Korean Air is another. In 1999, Korean was put under FAA

sanction and had a code-sharing arrangement with Delta temporarily severed after an earlier string of fatal incidents. People still hold this against them, despite the Korean government's ambitious overhaul of its entire air system, and despite a sterling critique by ICAO in 2008. It ranked Korea's aviation safety standards, including its pilot training and maintenance, as the highest in the world, beating out more than a hundred other countries.

Frankly, in certain regions I'd be more comfortable with a local carrier that knows its territory and the quirks of flying there. One example I love to cite is Bolivia's LAB—Lloyd Aereo Boliviano—the former national airline of one of the poorest countries in South America. LAB is gone now, but from 1925 through 2008 it plied the treacherous peaks of the Andes in and out of La Paz, the planet's most highly situated commercial airport. Since 1969, LAB suffered only two fatal crashes on scheduled passenger runs, killing a total of 36 people. This was not a mainstay airline making thousands of daily flights, but two crashes in thirty-four years amid jagged mountains and the hazards of the high Altiplano was exemplary.

Or how about Ethiopian Airlines? Here is another impoverished country surrounded by rugged terrain. Yet the record of its national carrier, over seven decades of operations—three fatal events, one of them a hijacking—is exceptional. Ethiopian is one of the proudest and arguably one of the safest airlines in the world.

Following is a list of airlines that have gone fatality-free for at least the past thirty years. All qualifying airlines have been in existence since at least 1980:

- Aer Lingus
- Air Berlin
- Air Jamaica (now part of Caribbean Airlines)
- Air Malta
- Air Mauritius
- Air New Zealand
- Air Niugini (Papua New Guinea)
- Air Portugal
- Air Seychelles
- Air Tanzania
- All Nippon Airways
- Austrian Airlines
- Bahamasair
- Cathay Pacific
- Cayman Airways
- Finnair

- Hawaiian Airlines
- Icelandair
- Meridiana (Italy)
- Monarch Airlines (UK)
- Oman Air
- Qantas
- Royal Brunei

- Royal Jordanian
- Syrianair
- Thomsonfly (formerly Britannia Airways)
- Tunisair
- Tyrolean Airways (Austria)

I chose 1980 to best account for the changeover period from older, first-generation jets and propliners to what most would consider modern fleets. Most of the companies listed have perfect records pre-dating that year. Several, including Air Jamaica, Oman Air, and Tunisair, have *never* recorded a fatality. Allowing for *one* fatal mishap since 1980 takes in, just for starters, Royal Air Maroc, TACA, and Yemenia. Even the much-maligned Air Afrique, a West African collective that went bust in 2001, listed but a single accident in over three-plus decades of flying. Ghana Airways, another African star until its demise in 2004, had an even cleaner record, marred by a single fatality in 1969.

Whether the fortunes of some of these carriers attest to exemplary levels of oversight and professionalism or merely to luck is somewhat open to argument. Royal Brunei Airways, to pick one from the list above, is a tiny outfit with only a handful of aircraft. Compare to American Airlines, with hundreds of planes and thousands of daily departures. American has outcrashed Royal Brunei 5–0 since 1980, but plainly the comparison is lopsided. Nonetheless, any unblemished legacy lasting thirty years is impressive on its own accord, particularly when the setting is an underdeveloped nation with substandard facilities and infrastructure.

In America, the FAA, whose penchant for safety is outdone only by a fondness for annoying acronyms, has come up with the International Aviation Safety Assessment (IASA) program to judge standards of other countries, using criteria based on ICAO guidelines. Classifications are awarded to nations themselves and not to individual airlines. Category 1 status goes to those who meet the mark, and Category 2 to those who do not "provide safety oversight of air carrier operators in accordance with the minimum safety standards." Because the categories pertain to countries and not specific companies, and because the restrictions apply unilaterally, IASA has its critics. Category 2 airlines can still operate to and from the United States, but may not add capacity. Yet reciprocal service is unaffected. Robert Booth finds the program's logic flawed. "If a country's oversight is supposedly inadequate, how come our airlines can fly there without penalty, but theirs can't fly here?" Booth recommends a bilateral capacity freeze to level the field and encourage governments to meet better standards.

In 2005, the European Union began compiling its own airline blacklist. Renewed every three months, it bans select airlines from various countries, as well as all carriers from some of them, such as Congo, Benin, Equatorial Guinea, Liberia, and Gabon. But importantly, the vast majority of the forbidden operators are airlines that a typical traveler wouldn't ever fly on in the first place. They consist mainly of marginal cargo outfits, most of them based in West and Central Africa. To give you some idea, the *highest* profile names on the blacklist have belonged to Indonesia's national carrier Garuda, North Korea's Air Koryo, and Afghanistan's Ariana. The latter is a company with a storied history going back more than fifty years, but for obvious reasons, it lacks the resources to currently meet European standards.

Isn't it true that Qantas, the Australian airline, has never suffered a fatal accident?

That's the myth, perpetuated far and wide—and which, no surprise, Qantas doesn't exactly rush to dispel. Let the record show, however, that the history of Qantas is scarred by at least seven fatal incidents. All of these, to be fair, took place prior to 1951, and the carrier has been perfect ever since. So while the details aren't quite right, the gist of the Qantas legend stands: its record is an outstanding one.

Qantas stands as a kind of anti-Aeroflot. Whereas many people's perceptions of Aeroflot are based on silly caricature—vodka-swilling pilots at the controls of patched-together Cold War rust buckets, with brutish babushkas shouting at passengers—an even greater number have fallen for the myth of the Immaculate Qantas. This false history was even immortalized by Hollywood, through an exchange between Tom Cruise and Dustin Hoffman in the 1988 movie *Rain Man.*

"All airlines have crashed at one time or another," Cruise says to Hoffman. "That doesn't mean that they are not safe."

"Qantas," responds Hoffman. "Qantas never crashed."

I love that exchange because it's Cruise's character, not Hoffman's, who makes the more accurate and valuable point.

So, if Qantas isn't the safest airline, which is?

I'm hit with this question all the time. I do not have an answer because there isn't one. Considering just how rare crashes are, such comparisons are little more than an academic exercise. The nervous flyer's tendency is to make distinctions in an abstract, purely statistical sense rather than a practical one. But these distinctions aren't particularly meaningful when a small handful of incidents is spread over thousands or even millions of departures. Sites like Airsafe.com happily serve up airline-versus-airline safety data, but why drive yourself crazy poring over the fractions of a percentage that differentiate one carrier's fatality rates from another? Really, is airline A, with one crash in twenty years, a safer bet than airline B, with two crashes over that same span? If you feel more comfortable picking United over Aeroflot, or Lufthansa over China Airlines, go for it. Will you actually *be* safer? Maybe, when hashed out to the third decimal place, but for all *reasonable* intents and purposes, they're the same. Price, schedule, and service are the only criteria you really need to bother with.

This same line of reasoning extends to the equally popular aircraft-versus-aircraft debate. Which are more trustworthy, 737s or A320s? Answer: take your pick. Virtually every established airline, and every certificated commercial plane, is safe by any useful definition.

What about the safety of budget carriers?

See above. And what is a budget carrier, exactly? Southwest would probably fit that bill by most folks' definition, yet its only fatality in forty-plus years of flying was a runway overrun incident in Chicago that killed a boy in a car. There is longstanding suspicion that young, competitively aggressive airlines are apt to cut corners. It's an assertion that, while it *feels* like it makes sense, isn't bolstered by the record. In the United States, a twenty-five-year lookback, encompassing every upstart carrier since the industry was deregulated in 1979, from PeoplExpress to jetBlue, reveals only a handful of fatal crashes and an overall accident rate in proportion to market share.

There are, and always have been, newer and smaller airlines that run highly professional, button-down operations up to the highest possible standards. Others have run looser ships and paid the price. At the same time, some of the world's eldest and most respected carriers have, on occasion, been guilty of deadly malpractice.

What happens to pilots involved in mishaps? Do they get rewarded for saving a plane from disaster? And what of surviving pilots deemed at fault for something? What happens to their careers?

Commendations typically come in the form of flattering letters from your bosses, handshakes at a banquet, and maybe a plaque. The Air Line Pilots Association (ALPA), the industry's largest pilots union, gives out awards each year for outstanding airmanship. Not that there's anything wrong with a nice shiny plaque and a free buffet, to say nothing of the personal and professional satisfaction that comes from having performed well under pressure, but no, you don't get a promotion or extra pay. You might earn some congratulatory time off, but nothing, not even saving the lives of hundreds of people, trumps the seniority system.

It's the other kind of time off a pilot hopes to avoid. Minor infractions that do not cause damage or injury—accidental deviations from a clearance, for instance—rarely result in a harsh penalty, but in cases of serious negligence the sanctions range from mandatory remedial training to suspension to being fired.

FAA "certificate action" is independent of punishment levied by the airline. The agency issues letters of warning or correction—pilots call these "violations"—or your license can be suspended or revoked. You might get to keep your existing job, but any administrative action on a pilot's record can be a huge, even fatal hindrance if seeking employment later on.

In the United States, airlines and the FAA have partnered in a program called the Aviation Safety Action Program (ASAP), which permits crews to self-report small-scale deviations or inadvertent procedural breaches in exchange for immunity. ASAP protects pilots from punitive action and allows airline training departments and regulators to collect and monitor important data. Rather than looking to blame and punish somebody for every infraction, the idea is to spot unsafe trends and deal with them proactively. It's a well-received program with benefits to all vested parties, including passengers, and the concept has spread to other industries, such as medicine and nuclear power.

I don't know of any cases in the United States where pilots have faced civil action, as when a doctor is sued for malpractice (attorneys realize it's the airlines and manufacturers with the deep pockets, not employees), but in many other countries pilots have been arrested and put on criminal trial for their professional mistakes. One prominent case involved manslaughter charges brought against the captain of a turboprop that crashed in New Zealand in 1995. In 2000, three pilots of a Singapore Airlines 747 were taken into police custody in Taiwan after a crash at Taipei's Chiang Kai Shek airport. They were forced to remain in Taiwan for two months, facing up to five years in prison on charges of "professional negligence." Pilots in Brazil, Italy, and Greece have dealt with similar situations. In 2001, a Japanese crew was interrogated by law enforcement after taking evasive action to avoid an inflight collision with another aircraft. Several people were injured during the maneuver, and police officers were sent to the cockpit after landing.

"Fortunately, in the United States and many other nations, the emphasis is on getting to the root causes of accidents and fixing the problem," says an ALPA representative. "It doesn't work that way in all countries, and that includes industrialized democracies where you'd think they'd know better. Pilots, controllers, and even company officials can do hard time for an inadvertent error that doesn't come close to a reasonable definition of criminal negligence. You can imagine what a chilling effect that has on the accident investigation process."

Watching planes land, it strikes me that their tires must endure a lot of stress. Are blowouts common?

They're not common, but they happen once in a while. Blowouts of a plane's forward nose gear tires are by nature pretty innocuous. Those involving main-gear tires beneath the wings and fuselage are a little different and potentially more serious.

The most probable time for a tire failure is during or shortly after any sort of high-speed braking event such as a takeoff abort or a sudden stop after landing. Heavy braking generates tremendous amounts of energy and heat, some of which is transferred to the tires themselves. Although airplane tires are filled with inert nitrogen and affixed with fuse plugs that cause them to automatically deflate rather than burst, failure of a main-gear tire at high runway speed can still induce all sorts of unpleasantness, from reduced braking capabilities to fire. Making things worse is the possibility of a single failed tire propagating the failure of those around it. A runway abort with multiple expired tires can be a dicey operation, and should a burst occur anywhere near takeoff speed the smartest course of action is to *continue* the takeoff and deal with the problem once airborne.

In 1986, a Mexicana 727 went down after takeoff from Mexico City, killing 167 people. An overheated brake caused one of the plane's four main tires to burst, with shrapnel severing fuel, hydraulic, and electrical lines. It had been erroneously serviced with air instead of nitrogen. Inflation pressure too is important; a too-low tire can generate intense temperatures. In 1991, a Canadian-registered DC-8 crashed in Saudi Arabia, killing 261 people. A single, underinflated tire transferred energy to a second one, and both came apart during takeoff. Bits of material then began to burn after gear retraction, spreading fire through the cabin as the plane circled back. And the fiery crash of an Air France Concorde in 2000 was linked to a fuel tank puncture brought on by a burst tire.

Though, to be clear, the vast majority of blowouts, even at high speeds, turn out to be harmless. Modern airliners are protected by highly effective anti-skid systems, brake temperature readouts in their cockpits, and wheel-well fire suppression systems in the gear bays. The catastrophes above involved models now obsolete.

One of them was a DC-8, a plane that I'm all too familiar with, having worked aboard a freighter version for the better part of four years (*see "North Latitude," page 141*). Late one night in 1998, we were prepping for takeoff out of Brussels, Belgium, at our highest allowable tonnage when the ground controllers gave us a long, circuitous route to runway 25R. Rolling along the apron in predawn darkness, we suddenly heard a bang and felt a shudder. A small pothole, we concluded, and kept going, as otherwise the aircraft felt normal. Just as we turned onto the runway and were cleared for takeoff, we heard a second bang, followed rapidly by a third, and then a fourth. And with that, the airplane—all 355,000 pounds of it—seized and wouldn't move.

The first noise we'd heard was one of the DC-8's eight underwing tires violently giving up the ghost. At max weight and after several sharp turns along the taxiways, it was only a matter of time before the adjacent one met a similar fate. With two gone, stress on the remaining two sent them popping as well. We were glad things happened when they did, and not at 150 knots. The runway was closed until the plane could be unloaded, de-fueled, and towed away for repairs.

What are the chances of a nonpilot safely landing a jetliner? If the entire cockpit crew became incapacitated, could a person with no formal training somehow get the plane on the ground?

There's a ladder to this. Do you mean somebody who knows nothing at all about flying? How about a private pilot who has flown four-seaters, or a desktop simulator buff who has studied a jetliner's systems and controls? The outcome in all cases is liable to be a catastrophe, but some would fare better than others. It depends too on the meaning of "land." Do you mean from just a few hundred feet over the ground, in ideal weather, with the plane stabilized and pointed toward the runway, with someone talking you through it? Or do you mean the whole, full-blown arrival, from cruising altitude to touchdown?

Even a rube has a fighting chance with the former. The touchdown will be rough at best, but with a little luck you won't become a cartwheeling fireball. In 2007, the Discovery Channel show *Mythbusters* set things up in a NASA simulator stripped down to represent a "generic commercial airliner." Hosts Adam Savage and Jamie Hyneman took the controls, while a seasoned pilot, stationed in an imaginary control tower, carefully instructed them via radio. On the first try, they crashed. The second time, they made it.

But all they really did was land a make-believe airplane from a starting point already close to the runway. The scenario most people envision is the one where, droning along at cruise altitude, the crew suddenly falls ill, and only a brave passenger can save the day. He'll strap himself in, and with the smooth coaching of an unseen voice over the radio, try to bring her down. For somebody without any knowledge or training, the chance of success in this scenario is zero. This person would have to be talked from 35,000 feet all the way to the point where an automatic approach could commence, complete with any number of turns, descents, decelerations, and configuration changes (appropriately setting the flaps, slats, and landing gear). I reckon that would be about as easy as dictating organ-transplant surgery over the telephone to somebody who has never held a scalpel.

It'd be tough even for a private pilot or the most obsessive desktop sim hobbyist. Our would-be hero would have a hard enough time finding the microphone switch and correctly configuring the radio panel, let alone the maneuvering, programming, navigating, and configuring it would take to land safely.

A few of you might remember the film *Airport '75*. A 747 is struck near the flight deck in midair by a small propeller plane, and all three pilots are taken out. I almost hate to say it, but dangling Charlton Heston from a helicopter and dropping him through the hole in the fuselage wasn't as far-fetched a solution as it might sound. It was about the only way that jumbo jet was getting back to earth in fewer than a billion pieces. The scene where Karen Black, playing a flight attendant, coaxes the crippled jumbo over a mountain range was, if less than technically accurate, useful in demonstrating the difficulty any civilian would have of pulling off even the simplest maneuver.

A few years ago, here in New England, after the lone pilot of a Cape Air commuter plane became ill, a passenger took over and performed a safe landing. The TV news had a field day with that one, though the passenger was a licensed private pilot and the aircraft was only a ten-seat Cessna. Otherwise, there has never been a case where a passenger needed to be drafted for cockpit duty. I guess that means either it never will happen, or it is destined to happen soon, depending how cynical you are about statistics.

All right, but what of the hijacker pilots on September 11, 2001? Doesn't their success at steering Boeing 757 and 767 jets into their targets contradict what I've just said and demonstrate that not only can a nonpilot fly, but fly well?

No, not really. The hijacker pilots, including Mohammad Atta, were licensed private pilots, and he and at least one other member of the cabal had purchased several hours of jet simulator training. Additionally they had obtained manuals and instructional videos for the 757 and 767 (the planes used in the attacks), openly available from aviation supply shops. In any case, they neither needed nor demonstrated any in-depth technical knowledge or skill. The intent was nothing more than to steer an already airborne jetliner, in perfect weather, into the side of a building. And their flying, along the way, based on radar tracks and telephone calls from passengers, was violent and unstable.

Hijacker pilot Hani Hanjour, at the controls of American flight 77, was a notoriously untalented flyer who never piloted anything larger than a four-seater. Yet, according to some, he is said to have pulled off a remarkable series of aerobatic maneuvers before slamming into the Pentagon. But when you really look at it, his flying was exceptional only in its recklessness. If anything, his erratic loops and spirals above the nation's capital revealed him to be exactly the shitty pilot he by all accounts was. To hit the building squarely he needed a bit of luck, and he got it. Striking a stationary object, even a large one with five beckoning sides, at high speed and at a steep descent angle, is very difficult. To make the job easier, he came in obliquely, tearing down light poles as he roared across the Pentagon's lawn. If he'd flown the same profile ten times, seven of them he'd probably have tumbled short of the target or overflown it entirely.

Maybe this is a crazy question, but why don't commercial planes carry parachutes for each passenger? Granted a novice skydiver would be risking life and limb, but it's a better option than hitting the ground at 400 miles per hour.

Ignoring for a moment the issues of cost and weight and the likelihood of killing yourself as you leap from a plane with no prior experience, consider the nature of aviation disasters. They tend to occur with little warning, and usually during takeoff or landing, meaning that chutes would seldom be helpful. Normal skydiving takes place under tightly controlled parameters. To even entertain the idea of jumpers making it safely to the ground from a passenger jet, the plane would need to be in very stable flight and at a low-enough speed and altitude—yet high enough for a chute to properly deploy. How many times, in the history of civil aviation, has a crew known for certain that a serious crash was imminent, yet still had enough time and control to prepare for a coordinated mass evacuation? One that comes to mind, maybe, is the 1985 Japan Air Lines catastrophe (*see worst disasters, page 203*). After a bulkhead rupture and rudder failure, the Boeing 747 floundered about for several minutes before going down near Mt. Fuji. Had chutes been aboard, we can speculate that *some* of the passengers *may* have survived.

A few single-engine private planes have built-in parachutes for use in certain emergencies, such as an engine failure over rough terrain. I know what you're thinking: imagine that crippled JAL 747 floating to the ground under a giant chute. But that type of accident was highly atypical, and the size and weight of jetliners would make any commercial application extraordinarily difficult.

With the skies as crowded as they are, how grave is the danger of a midair collision?

Airplanes do, on occasion, breach the confines of one another's space. Usually this is a brief, tangential transgression. Almost always the mistake is caught, and safeguards are in place to minimize any hazard. Pilots are required to read back all assigned headings and altitudes, for example.

As a backup, airliners today carry onboard anticollision technology. Linked into the cockpit transponder, Traffic Collision Avoidance System (TCAS, pronounced *Tea-Cass*), gives pilots a graphic, on-screen representation of nearby aircraft. If certain thresholds of distance and altitudes are crossed, TCAS will issue progressively ominous oral and visual commands. If two aircraft continue flying toward each other, their units work together, vocalizing a loudly imperative "CLIMB!" instruction to one and "DESCEND!" to the other.

In 1978, a Pacific Southwest Airlines 727 collided with a Cessna while preparing to land at San Diego. In 1986, an Aeromexico DC-9 plunged into a Los Angeles suburb after hitting a Piper that had strayed, sans permission, into restricted airspace. Ten years later, a Saudi Arabian 747 was struck by a Kazakh cargo jet over India. Tragedies all, but these accidents occurred when TCAS was not yet standard equipment and when ATC protocols were not as sharp as they are today. Through technology and training, the threat of midair collisions has been greatly reduced.

But, for everything to work as it should requires the cooperation of both human and technological elements, bringing to mind the 2002 collision between a DHL freighter and a Bashkirian Airlines Tu-154 over the border between Switzerland and Germany. An ATC error had put the two planes on a conflicting course. A Swiss controller eventually noticed the conflict and issued a command for the Bashkirian crew to descend. At the same time, both airliners' TCAS systems correctly interpreted the hazard, issuing their own instructions in the final seconds. TCAS told DHL to descend, and Bashkirian to climb. DHL did as instructed and began to lose altitude. The Bashkirian crew, however, disregarded the TCAS order to climb and chose instead to descend, in compliance with the controller's original request. This was a mistake. Standard procedure is that TCAS, being the last word on an impending collision, override previous ATC instructions. Had the TCAS alarm been obeyed, the jets would have been sent on safely divergent vectors. Instead, they descended directly into one another, killing 71 people.

An even worse catastrophe happened over the Amazon in 2006. A Boeing 737 collided with an Embraer executive jet. The latter managed a safe emergency landing, but the Boeing plunged into the forest, killing everybody on the plane. The investigation revealed a chain of procedural mistakes made by Brazilian controllers, compounded by evidence that the executive jet's TCAS system may have been switched off inadvertently.

But what of dangers here in the United States, home to the world's most crowded airspace? Isn't our air traffic control system outmoded and much of its equipment obsolete? Aren't improvements badly needed? To some extent, yes, and with more planes in the air than ever before, the terminal area—airspace in and around airports, where collisions are most likely to occur—has never been busier. At the same time, a need for ATC improvements does not imply that the system is rickety and rife with collision hazards. Measured year to year, the rate of airspace incursions in the United States occasionally spikes. While this can sound scary, only the rarest incursion is the sort of close call that should make people nervous. Overall our record is an excellent one, and a testament to the reliability of our ATC system, clunky and maligned as it is.

What about collision hazards on the ground?

Chances are you've come across one or more recent stories about the rise in so-called runway incursions at airports across America. That's a euphemism for when a plane or other vehicle erroneously enters or crosses a runway without permission from air traffic control, setting up a collision hazard. The vast majority of incursions are minor transgressions, but the numbers are going up and a handful of incidents have resulted in genuine near misses.

The problem isn't the volume of planes per se, but the congested environments in which many of them operate. La Guardia, Boston, and JFK are among airports that were laid out decades ago for a fraction of today's capacity. Their crisscrossing runways and lacework taxiways are inherently more hazardous than the parallel and staggered layouts seen at newer airports. That does not imply that these locations are unsafe, but they present challenges both for crews and air traffic controllers, particularly during spells of low visibility.

The FAA has been working fast and furious on new programs and technologies to reduce the number of mistakes and/or mitigate the consequences when they occur. These include an upgrade of tarmac markings and mandatory anti-incursion training programs for pilots and controllers. Under testing are improved runway and taxiway lighting systems and an emerging, satellite-based technology known as Cockpit Display of Traffic Information (CDTI) that will provide pilots with a detailed view of surrounding traffic both aloft and during ground operations. And a growing number of airports are outfitted with sophisticated radar that tracks not only planes in the air, but those on runways and taxiways.

Those are all good ideas, but the FAA has a habit of over-engineering complicated fixes to simple problems. There will be no magic technological bullet. At heart this is a human factors issue.

The FAA's most valuable contribution to the problem might be something they've already done: stirred up awareness. When it comes right down to it, the best way to prevent collisions is for pilots and controllers to always be conscious of their possibility.

Meanwhile, not to close on a morbid note, but I'll remind you that aviation's worst-ever catastrophe, at Tenerife in 1977, involved two 747s that never left the ground (*see Tenerife story, page 229*).

What were your experiences on September 11, and how, from a pilot's take, has flying changed since then?

Among my vivid memories of that morning is that of the enormous black cockroach I saw crawling across the platform of the Government Center subway station at 7:00 a.m. while waiting for the train that would take me to Logan Airport. Once on the train, I would chat briefly with a United Airlines flight attendant, whose name I never got and, who knows, may have been headed for flight 175. I was on my way to Florida, where I'd be picking up a work assignment later that day. My airplane took off only seconds after American's flight 11. I had watched it back away from gate 25 at Logan's terminal B and begin to taxi.

About halfway to Florida, we started descending. Because of a "security issue," our captain told us, we, along with many other airplanes, would be diverting immediately. Pilots are polished pros when it comes to dishing out euphemisms, and this little gem would be the most laughable understatement I've ever heard a comrade utter. Our new destination was Charleston, South Carolina.

I figured a bomb threat had been called in. My worry was not of war and smoldering devastation. My worry was being late for work. It wasn't until I joined a crowd of passengers in Charleston clustered around a TV in a concourse restaurant that I learned what was going on.

I'm watching the video of the second airplane, shot from the ground in a kind of twenty-first century Zapruder film. The picture swings left and picks up the United 767 moving swiftly. The plane rocks, lifts its nose, and, like a charging, very angry bull making a run at a fear-frozen matador, drives itself into the very center of the south tower. The airplane vanishes. For a fraction of a second there is no falling debris, no smoke, no fire, no movement. Then, from within, you see the white-hot explosion and spewing expulsion of fire and matter.

To me, had the airplanes crashed, blown up, and reduced the upper halves of those buildings to burned-out hulks, the whole event would nonetheless have clung to the realm of believability. Had the towers not actually fallen, I suspect our September 11 hangover, which rages to this day, might not have been so prolonged. It was *the collapse*—the groaning implosions and the pyroclastic tornadoes whipping through the canyons of lower Manhattan—that catapulted the event from ordinary disaster to historical infamy. As I stand awestruck in this shithole airport restaurant in South Carolina, the television shows the towers of the World Trade Center. They are not just afire, not just shedding debris and pouring out oil-black smoke. They are *falling down*. The sight of those ugly, magnificent towers collapsing onto themselves is the most sublimely terrifying thing I have ever seen.

And pilots, like fire fighters, police officers, and everyone else whose professions had been implicated, had no choice but to take things, well, personally. Four on-duty crews were victims. They were disrespected in the worst way, killed after their beloved machines were stolen from under them and driven into buildings. John Ogonowski comes to mind, the good-guy captain of American 11. Of the thousands of people victimized that day, Captain Ogonowski was figuratively, if not literally, the first of them. He lived in my home state; his funeral made the front pages, where he was eulogized for his philanthropic work with local Cambodian immigrants. Maybe it's melodramatic to say I felt a direct bond or kinship with these eight men, but I did feel an underlying and wrenching empathy.

In the ten-second bursts it took them to fall, I knew *something* about the business of flying planes would be different. It's hyperbole to speak of the world, or for that matter flying, having been "changed forever," but yes, for sure, things are different now—albeit for reasons we don't always own up to. More than any clash of civilizations, the real and lasting legacy of Mohammed Atta is something more mundane: tedium. Think about it. The long lines, searches, and pat-downs; the color-coded alerts, the litany of inconvenient rules and protocols we're now forced to follow—all this meaningless pomp in the name of security. Of all of modern life's rituals, few are marinated in boredom as much as air travel. "Flying" is what we call it. How misleading. We don't fly so much as we sit and stand around for interminable amounts of time. And most distressing of all, we seem to be okay with this. The terrorists have won, goes the refrain, and perhaps that's true. It isn't quite what they hoped to win, but they've won it nevertheless.

Why can't commercial jets be fitted with an exclusive side entrance into the cockpit, making it impossible for a potential skyjacker to gain access?

First, you can't simply cut a hole into the side of a plane and add an extra door. Doing so would require a large-scale and extremely expensive structural redesign. And you'd presumably need to add a lavatory to the cockpit. And what about rest facilities? Long-haul flights carry augmented crews working in shifts (*see crew rest, page 99*), and the off-duty pilots require a suitable place to relax. You'd be doubling or tripling the size of the average cockpit, which in turn would take up space already used for galleys, storage, and passenger seats. In addition, there are times when it's beneficial for pilots to have direct access to the cabin—for checking out certain mechanical problems, helping flight attendants deal with passenger issues, and so on.

Even if this were an easy or affordable thing to do, which it's not, would it really be worth the trouble? Strategically, the September 11 suicide takeover scheme was a one-shot, one-time formula. Hijacking protocols are different today (*see security essay, page 179*), and the awareness of passengers and crew, together with armored cockpit doors, does about as good a job as is necessary, in my opinion. Long and short: having the crew barricaded up front is going to cause more problems than it solves.

How worried should we be about shoulder-launched missiles? Should airlines install measures to defend against them?

The hazard of portable rockets—they are often referred to as MANPADS, a horrible acronym formed out of the words Man-Portable Air-Defense Systems—has become a hot topic, provoked by media stories about possible, even imminent, attacks using these weapons, which are small and easily concealed. An estimated half a million such rockets exist worldwide, with more than thirty terrorist organizations and other rogue groups possessing them. Some experts have opined that all U.S. airliners should be installed with electronic antimissile devices, as are some military and VIP planes. Systems are available for about $1 million per unit, and the U.S. government has pressed ahead with a feasibility study.

What hasn't been widely reported, for one, are the weapons' technical shortcomings. They are difficult to use, and when fired at short range are unlikely to score anything other than a close miss. Two Soviet-made Strela-2M missiles were fired from a truck at an Israeli charter plane taking off from Mombasa, Kenya, in 2002. Both missed. Even a direct hit would not necessarily destroy a plane, as proven by a DHL Airbus struck over Baghdad in 2003, and a DC-10 that survived a shot in 1984. Granted, we shouldn't disregard this or any other threat because it *probably* won't result in a disaster. Trouble is, we're again chasing the chimera of absolute security, price tag be damned. Of all the air safety ventures on which we could spend tens of billions of dollars, I don't think this is the right one in terms of cost-effectiveness and the number of lives it might save.

It has been proposed that onboard software be developed to physically prevent hijacked planes from being guided into restricted airspace or over cities.

"Soft walls," this idea is called, and it's one of those things that keeps the writers at *Popular Science* busy. More power to them, but it's on par with the idea of establishing colonies on Mars: within our engineering abilities, extremely expensive, and then only vaguely useful. Reading comments from people at work on these ideas, one is struck by how consumed and infatuated they are not with the promises of safety or practicality, but with technology alone. That's not a bad thing by itself, and it's a fine testament to anyone's devotion as a scientist or engineer, but the application of these concepts is limited. It's sci-fi show-and-tell. In another way, it gets back to our greater national fetishizing of safety. Believing we can protect ourselves from every last direction of attack, we now wish to string coils of virtual barbed wire among the clouds. To me, there's a beautiful and poetic futility to the idea of securing the very air above our heads.

Almost every high-profile airplane crash is trailed by a conspiracy theory of one sort or another. Could you clear up lingering doubts and suspicions concerning a few of these?

Where to start? Conspirobabble stretches back to the death of Dag Hammarskjöld and the heyday of the Bermuda Triangle. The modern era got going with the 1983 shoot-down of Korean Air Lines flight 007 by a Soviet fighter. Since then, the Internet has become a potent incubator of myth and misinformation, spreading pseudo-truths with the lackadaisical tap of a Send button. Five minutes with a keyboard and mouse, and you're privy to more feverish speculation than the old Grassy Knollers ever could have dreamed of.

Prior to 2001, the 1996 TWA tragedy was probably the most mulled-over disaster in the minds of the intellectually eccentric. Flight 800 blew up like a giant roman candle in the July twilight off Long Island, the result of a short circuit igniting vapors in an unused fuel tank. What came next was a sideshow of at least four books and enough web chatter to power a 747 through the sound barrier. Even mainstream commentators registered intense skepticism that flight 800 could've crashed the way it did. After all, fuel tanks don't simply explode.

Except, under very unusual circumstances, they do. It's not likely, but it's neither impossible nor unprecedented. There have been fuel tank explosions on at least thirteen commercial planes, including a Thai Airways 737 that burst into flames while parked at the gate in Bangkok, killing a flight attendant. TWA 800, an older 747-100 destined for Paris, had been baking on a hot tarmac up until departure, superheating the vapors in its empty center fuel cell (a 747 does not need full tanks to cross the Atlantic). Later, an electrical short deep in the jet's mid-fuselage bowels provided the ignition. Per FAA behest, airlines have begun phasing in a system that uses nitrogen as an inert filler in vacant tanks.

We heard more whispering after American 587 went down in New York City less than two months after the 2001 terror attacks. Officially, the crash was caused by crew error, compounded by a design quirk in the A300's rudder system, but the mongers had another idea: a bomb destroyed the plane, and the government, along with the airlines, fearing paralysis of the economy, decided to pass off the crash as an accident.

Then we have September 11 itself. If you haven't been paying attention, cyberspace is awash with claims that the attacks were an inside job. The specific assertions are too numerous and complicated to list here exhaustively. They vary website to website, overlapping, underscoring, complementing, and contradicting one another to the point of madness. The Pentagon was struck with a missile, not a 757; the planes that hit the World Trade Center were remotely controlled military craft; the real flights 11, 175, 77, and 93 never existed or were diverted to secret bases; controlled demolitions felled the Twin Towers. And so on.

The same technological magic that makes the spread of wild conjecture so effortless should, you would think, make countering and dismissing it no less easy. Strictly speaking, indeed it does. But it depends who's paying attention, and the human proclivity for *believing* in conspiracies is a lot stronger these days than our proclivity for analyzing and debating them. Maybe that's human nature, or maybe it's some perverse/inverse fallout of technology. Either way, there are lots more people around hungry to make us believe something than make us *not* believe something. A pro-conspiracy website is certainly a lot more exciting and will garner a lot more hits than an *anti*-conspiracy website. Both kinds are out there, but it's the conspiracy traffickers, regardless of their credibility, who believe more passionately in their cause and consequently garner more attention.

It's not beyond reason that *some* aspects of the 2001 attacks deserve more scrutiny than the 9/11 Commission granted them. But those who most urgently wish us to believe so have done themselves no favors by expanding the breadth of their contentions beyond all plausibility: particulars of the conspiracy theories fall anywhere from compelling to lunatic. I'm genuinely curious about why surveillance video from the Sheraton hotel near the Pentagon was confiscated and never made public—if, in fact, that's true. On the other hand, I'm told that the aircraft that struck the World Trade Center were artificial images projected by laser and that the real flights never existed. There's so much flak out there, it's difficult to tell what's genuinely mysterious and worthy of a closer look and what's nonsense. (I haven't the room for it here, but on my website, I tackle several of the airplane-related 9/11 myths, point by point.) I propose a conspiracy theory that the conspiracy theories are themselves part of a conspiracy, intended to discredit the idea of there being a conspiracy—and to divide and conquer those who might sleuth out certain facts.

I don't deny that, at times, important truths have been concealed from public view. But we also need to remember Carl Sagan's famous quip about extraordinary claims requiring extraordinary proof. It's distressing that so many people become married to a preposterous idea based on little more than erroneous interpretations of some pictures and selective, manipulative use of evidence. We see this with September 11, with the "chemtrails" theory (don't get me started on that one), and still others. And I've learned to be wary when attempting to reason with such people. Ultimately, it's like arguing religion. Evidence, or a lack of it, has little to do with what motivates many believers, and contradictory facts are simply not accepted. At the heart of their convictions is something only partially subject to reason. It's faith.

✈ *We Gaan*: The Horror and Asburdity of History's Worst Plane Crash

Most people have never heard of Tenerife, a pan-shaped speck in the Atlantic. It's one of the Canary Islands, a volcanic chain governed by the Spanish, clustered a few hundred miles off the coast of Morocco. The big town on Tenerife is Santa Cruz, and its airport, beneath a set of cascading hillsides, is called Los Rodeos. There, on March 27, 1977, two Boeing 747s—one belonging to KLM, the other to Pan Am—collided on a foggy runway. Five hundred and eighty-three people were killed in what remains the biggest air disaster in history.

The magnitude of the accident speaks for itself, but what makes it particularly unforgettable is the startling set of ironies and coincidences that preceded it. Indeed, most airplane crashes result not from a single error or failure, but from a chain of improbable errors and failures, together with a stroke or two of really bad luck. Never was this illustrated more calamitously—almost to the point of absurdity—than on that Sunday afternoon almost forty years ago.

In 1977, in only its eighth year of service, the Boeing 747 was already the biggest, the most influential, and possibly the most glamorous commercial jetliner ever built. For just those reasons, it was hard not to imagine what a story it would be—and how much carnage might result—should two of these behemoths ever hit each other. Really, though, what were the chances of *that*—a Hollywood script if ever there was one.

Imagine we're there:

Both of the 747s at Tenerife are charters. Pan Am has come from Los Angeles, after a stopover in New York, KLM from its home base in Amsterdam. As it happens, neither plane is supposed to be on Tenerife. They were scheduled to land at Las Palmas, on the nearby island of Grand Canary, where many of the passengers were on their way to meet cruise ships. After a bomb planted by Canary Island separatists

229

exploded in the Las Palmas airport flower shop, they diverted to Los Rodeos, along with several other flights, arriving around 2:00 p.m.

The Pan Am aircraft, registered N736PA, is no stranger to notoriety. In January 1970, this very same plane completed the inaugural commercial voyage of a 747, between New York's Kennedy airport and London-Heathrow. Somewhere on its nose is the dent from a champagne bottle. White with a blue window stripe, it wears the name *Clipper Victor* along the forward fuselage. The KLM 747, also blue and white, is named the *Rhine*.

Let's not forget the airlines themselves: Pan Am, the most storied franchise in the history of aviation, requires little introduction. KLM, for its part, is the oldest continuously operating airline in the world, founded in 1919 and highly regarded for its safety and punctuality.

The KLM captain, Jacob Van Zanten, whose errant take-off roll will soon kill nearly six hundred people, including himself, is the airline's top 747 instructor pilot and a KLM celebrity. If passengers recognize him, it's because his confident, square-jawed visage stares out from KLM's magazine ads. Later, when KLM executives first get word of the crash, they will attempt to contact Van Zanten in hopes of sending him to Tenerife to aid the investigation team.

The normally lazy Los Rodeos is packed with diverted flights. The *Rhine* and *Clipper Victor* sit adjacent to each other at the southeast corner of the apron, their wingtips almost touching. Finally at around four o'clock, Las Palmas begins accepting traffic again. Pan Am is quickly ready for departure, but the lack of room and the angle at which the jets face each other requires that KLM begin to taxi first.

The weather is fine until just before the accident, and if not for KLM requesting extra fuel at the last minute, both would be on their way sooner. During the delay, a heavy blanket of fog swoops down from the hills and envelopes the airport. That fuel also means extra weight, affecting how quickly the 747 is able to become airborne. For reasons you'll see in a moment, that will be critical.

Because of the tarmac congestion, the normal route to runway 30 is blocked. Departing planes will need to taxi down on the runway itself. Reaching the end, they'll make a 180-degree turn before taking off in the opposite direction. This procedure, rare at commercial airports, is called a "back-taxi." At Tenerife in '77, it will put two 747s on the same runway at the same time, invisible not only to each other, but also to the control tower. The airport has no ground tracking radar.

KLM taxis ahead and onto the runway, with the Pan Am Clipper ambling several hundred yards behind. Captain Van Zanten will steer to the end, turn around, then hold in position until authorized for takeoff. Pan Am's instructions are to turn clear along a left-side taxiway to allow the other plane's departure. Once safely off the runway, Pan Am will report so to the tower.

Unable to differentiate the taxiways in the low visibility, the Pan Am pilots miss their assigned turnoff. Continuing to the next one is no big problem, but now they're on the runway for several additional seconds.

At the same time, having wheeled into position at the end, Van Zanten comes to a stop. His first officer, Klaas Meurs, takes the radio and receives the ATC route clearance. This is not a *takeoff* clearance, but rather a procedure outlining turns, altitudes, and frequencies for use once airborne. Normally it is received well prior to an aircraft taking the runway, but the pilots have been too busy with checklists and taxi instructions until now. They are tired, annoyed, and anxious to get going. The irritability in the pilots' voices, Van Zanten's in particular, has been duly noted by the control tower and other pilots.

There are still a couple dominos yet to fall, but now the final act is in motion—literally. Because the route clearance comes where and when it does, it is mistaken for a takeoff clearance as well. First officer Meurs, sitting to Van Zanten's right, acknowledges the altitudes, headings, and fixes, then finishes off with an unusual, somewhat hesitant phrase, back-dropped by the sound of accelerating engines. "We are now, uh, at takeoff."

Van Zanten releases the brakes. "*We gaan,*" he is heard saying on the cockpit voice recorder. "Let's go." And with that, his mammoth machine begins barreling down the fog-shrouded runway, completely without permission.

"At takeoff" is not standard phraseology among pilots. But it's explicit enough to grab the attention of the Pan Am crew *and* the control tower. It's hard for either party to believe KLM is actually moving, but both reach for their microphones to make sure.

"And we're still taxiing down the runway," relays Bob Bragg, the Pan Am first officer.

At the same instant, the tower radios a message to KLM. "Okay," says the controller. "Stand by for takeoff. I will call you."

There is no reply. This silence is taken as a tacit, if not exactly proper, acknowledgment.

Either of these transmissions would be, should be, enough to stop Van Zanten cold in his tracks. He still has time to discontinue the roll. The problem is, because they occur simultaneously, they overlap.

Pilots and controllers communicate via two-way VHF radios. The process is similar to speaking over a walkie-talkie: a person activates a microphone, speaks, then releases the button and waits for an acknowledgment. It differs from using a telephone, for example, as only one party can speak at a time, and has no idea what his message actually sounds like over the air. If two or more microphones are clicked at the same instant, the transmissions cancel each other out, delivering a noisy occlusion of static or a high-pitched squeal called a heterodyne. Rarely are heterodynes dangerous. But at Tenerife this is the last straw.

Van Zanten hears only the word "okay," followed by a five-second squeal. He keeps going.

Ten seconds later there is one final exchange, clearly and maddeningly audible on the post-crash tapes. "Report when runway clear," the tower says to Pan Am.

"We'll report when we're clear," acknowledges Bob Bragg.

Focused on the takeoff, Van Zanten and his first officer apparently miss this. But the second officer, sitting behind them, does not. Alarmed, with their plane now racing forward at a hundred knots, he leans forward. "Is he not clear?" he asks. "That Pan American?"

"Oh, yes," Van Zanten answers emphatically.

In the Pan Am cockpit, nose-to-nose with the still unseen, rapidly approaching interloper, there's a growing sense that something isn't right. "Let's get the fuck out of here," Captain Victor Grubbs says nervously.

A few moments later, the lights of the KLM 747 emerge out of the grayness, dead ahead, 2,000 feet away and closing fast.

"There he is!" cries Grubbs, shoving the thrust levers to full power. "Look at him! Goddamn, that son of a bitch is coming!" He yanks the plane's steering tiller, turning left as hard as he can, toward the grass at the edge of the runway.

"Get off! Get off! Get off!" shouts Bob Bragg.

Van Zanten sees them, but it's too late. Attempting to leapfrog, he pulls back on the elevators, dragging his tail along the pavement for 70 feet in a hail of sparks. He almost makes it, but just as his plane breaks ground, its undercarriage and engines slice into the ceiling of the *Victor*, instantly demolishing its midsection and setting off a series of explosions.

Badly damaged, the *Rhine* settles back to the runway, skids hard on its belly for another thousand feet, and is consumed by fire before a single one of its 248 occupants can escape. Remarkably, of 396 passengers and crew aboard the Pan Am jumbo, 61 of them survived, including all five people in the cockpit—the three-man crew and two off-duty employees riding in the jumpseats.

☆ ☆ ☆

Over the past few years, I've been fortunate enough to meet two of those Pan Am survivors and hear their stories first-hand. I say that nonchalantly, but this is probably the closest I've ever come to meeting, for lack of a better term, a hero. Romanticizing the fiery deaths of 583 people is akin to romanticizing war, but there's a certain mystique to the Tenerife disaster, a gravity so strong that shaking these survivors' hands produced a feeling akin to that of a little kid meeting his favorite baseball player. These men were *there*, emerging from the wreckage of what, for some of us, stands as an event of mythic proportions.

One of those survivors was Bob Bragg, the Pan Am first officer. I met him in Los Angeles, on the set of a documentary being made for the thirtieth anniversary of the accident.

It was Bragg who had uttered, "And we're still taxiing down the runway"—seven easy words that should have saved the day, but instead were lost forever in the shriek and crackle of a blocked transmission. Just thinking about it gives me the chills.

But there's nothing dark about Bob Bragg—nothing that, on the surface, feels moored to the nightmare of '77. He's one of the most easygoing people you'll ever meet. Gray-haired, bespectacled, and articulate, he looks and sounds like what he is: a retired airline pilot.

God knows how many times he's recounted the collision to others. He speaks about the accident with a practiced ease, in a voice of modest detachment, as if he'd been a spectator watching from afar. You can read all the transcripts, pore over the findings, watch the documentaries a hundred times over. Not until you sit with Bob Bragg and hear the unedited account, with all of the strange and astounding details that are normally missing, do you get a full sense of what happened. The basic story is well known; it's the ancillaries that make it moving—and surreal:

Bragg describes the initial impact as little more than "a bump and some shaking." All five men in the cockpit, located at the forward end of the 747's distinctive upper-deck hump, saw the KLM jet coming and had ducked. Knowing they'd been hit, Bragg instinctively reached upward in an effort to pull the "fire handles"—a set of four overhead-mounted levers that cut off the supply of fuel, air, electricity, and hydraulics running to and from the engines. His arm groped helplessly. When he looked up, the roof was gone.

Turning around, he realized that the entire upper deck had been sheared off at a point just aft of his chair. He could see all the way aft to the tail, 200 feet behind him. The fuselage was shattered and burning. He and Captain Grubbs were alone in their seats, on a small, fully exposed perch 35 feet above the ground. Everything around them had been lifted away like a hat. The second officer and jumpseat stations, their occupants still strapped in, were hanging upside-down through what seconds earlier was the ceiling of the first class cabin.

There was no option other than to jump. Bragg stood up and hurled himself over the side. He landed in the grass three stories below, feet-first, and miraculously suffered little more than an injured ankle. Grubbs followed, and he too was mostly unharmed. The others from the cockpit would unfasten their belts and shimmy down the sidewalls to the main cabin floor before similarly leaping to safety.

Once on the ground, they faced a deafening roar. The plane had been pancaked into the grass, but because the cockpit control lines were severed, the engines were still running at full power. It took several moments before the motors began coming apart. Bragg remembers one of the engines' huge forward turbofans detaching from its shaft, falling forward onto the ground with a thud.

The fuselage was engulfed by fire. A number of passengers, most of them seated in forward portions of the cabin, had made it onto the craft's left wing, and were standing at the leading edge, about 20 feet off the ground. Bragg ran over, encouraging them to jump. A few minutes later, the plane's center fuel tank exploded, propelling a plume of flames and smoke a thousand feet into the sky.

The airport's ill-equipped rescue team, meanwhile, was over at the KLM site, the first wreckage they'd come to after learning there'd been an accident. They hadn't yet realized that *two* planes were involved, one of them with survivors. Eventually, authorities opened the airport perimeter gates, urging anybody with a vehicle to drive toward the crash scene to help. Bob Bragg tells the cracked story of standing there in fog, surrounded by stunned and bleeding survivors, watching his plane burn, when suddenly a taxicab pulls up out of nowhere.

Bragg returned to work a few months later. He eventually transferred to United when that carrier took over Pan Am's Pacific routes in the late 1980s, and retired from the company as a 747 captain. He lives in Virginia with his wife, Dorothy. (Captain Grubbs has since passed away, as has second officer George Warns.)

During the documentary shoot, I traveled with Bob Bragg and the producers to the aircraft storage yards at Mojave, California, where he was interviewed alongside a mothballed 747, describing that incredible leap from the upper-deck.

A day earlier, using a flight deck mock-up, director Phil Desjardins filmed a reenactment of the Tenerife collision, with a trio of actors sitting in as the KLM crew. To provide the actors with a helpful demo, it was suggested that Bob Bragg and I get inside the mock-up and run through a practice takeoff.

Bragg took the captain's seat, and I took the first officer's seat. We read through a makeshift checklist and went through the motions of a simulated takeoff. That's when I looked across, and all of a sudden it hit me: Here's Bob Bragg, lone surviving pilot of Tenerife, sitting in a cockpit, pretending to be Jacob Van Zanten, whose error made the whole thing happen.

Surely Bragg wanted no part of this dreary karma, and I hadn't the courage to make note of it out loud—assuming it hadn't already dawned on him. But I could barely keep the astonishment to myself. One more creepy irony in a story so full of them.

☆ ☆ ☆

Closing note: On the thirtieth anniversary of the crash, a memorial was dedicated overlooking the Tenerife airport, honoring those who perished there. The sculpture is in the shape of a helix. "A spiral staircase," the builders describe it. "[...] a symbol of infinity." Maybe, but I'm disappointed that the more obvious physical symbolism is ignored: early model 747s, including both of those in the crash, were well known for the set of spiral stairs connecting their main and upper decks (*see High Art, page 23*). In the minds of millions of international travelers, that stairway is something of a civil aviation icon. How evocative and poetically appropriate for the memorial—even if the designers weren't thinking that way.

7 THE AIRLINES WE LOVE TO HATE

THE YIN AND YANG OF AIRLINE IDENTITY

I. Logos and Liveries

There was a time, not terribly long ago, when the logo of Pan American World Airways was one of the most recognized commercial trademarks in the world. There was nothing remarkable about the symbol—a fissured blue and white globe reminiscent of a basketball—but it worked. The globe appeared in the 1950s and endured for almost half a century, right to Pam Am's final breath in 1991. Aspects of the airline's identity would change over the years, but through it all, the blue ball persevered. Had Pan Am survived, I suspect that globe would still be around.

Since the dawn of civil aviation, airlines have been devising and revising what they believe to be meaningful identities. As explored by author Keith Lovegrove in his superb volume *Airline: Identity, Design, and Culture,* the logo represents only a slice of this overall branding process, which takes place on a score of fronts, from cabin interiors to crew attire to the color of maintenance vehicles. But it's the logo—the trademark, the company emblem, reproduced on everything from stationery to boarding passes—that encapsulates identity in a single, vital aesthetic mark. Everything else revolves around this.

Many of the most renowned airline insignia incorporate national symbols or cultural associations: the shamrock of Aer Lingus, the Qantas kangaroo, the green cedar of MEA (Lebanon), the Thai Airways lotus. Subtler adaptations include Malaysia Airlines's indigenous kite design or the calligraphic brush stroke of Hong Kong's airline, Cathay Pacific. But while symbolism is optional, simplicity is a must. It has been said that the true test of a logo is this: Can it be remembered and sketched, freehand and with reasonable accuracy, by a young child? Think of the Apple apple. Pan Am's basketball fits this criterion beautifully, as does Lufthansa's crane, the Air New Zealand "Koru," and many others. They're dignified, unpretentious, and unencumbered—and, for exactly those reasons, are able to cultivate recognition the world over. Maybe they need a tweaking or two over time, but the template of such trademarks—the really good ones—remains essentially timeless.

And if you've got something like that, you dispense with it at your peril. Among the most deplorable branding moves ever made was American Airlines's decision in 2013 to abandon its venerable "AA" logo. With its proud, cross-winged eagle, this was one of the most distinctive and enduring icons in all of aviation. Created by Massimo Vignelli in 1967, it always looked modern. Its successor is almost too ugly to be described—a vertical bar of red and blue, bisected by what's supposed to be an eagle's beak. Symbolically lifeless and hideous to boot, it looks like a linoleum knife cutting through a shower curtain.

No less disappointing was the elimination of the *tsurumaru*, the red and white crane motif worn by Japan Airlines. Since 1960, every JAL aircraft featured what was possibly the most elegant airline logo ever conceived: a stylized depiction of the crane, lifting its wings into the circular suggestion of the Japanese rising sun. Beginning in 2002, this ageless symbol succumbed to what had to be the most regrettable makeover in industry history, replaced by an oversized, blood-red blob—a rising splotch—oozing across the tailfin. It was a terrible decision on aesthetic merits alone, and still worse considering the crane's cultural importance in Japan.

Apparently enough people complained, however, and the *tsurumaru* has since been resurrected. Bringing it back was an unusual move, marking one of the very few times an airline has reverted to a prior logo, but JAL couldn't have made a wiser decision. (American, are you listening?)

Not that you can't retain the outlines of a classic logo and still manage to ruin it, as demonstrated in recent years by several airlines that couldn't leave well enough alone.

Take the case of cargo giant UPS. The original United Parcel Service emblem showed a bow-tied box set atop a heraldic-style badge. The work of Paul Rand, a legendary design guru who also did logos for Westinghouse and IBM, it was a wonderful heart-and-soul manifestation of the company's core mission: delivering packages. Its replacement is a singularly bland, almost militaristic "modernization." The box and string have been deposed, swapped for a meaningless gold slash mark. If we didn't know better, UPS could be a bank or insurance company. It's the worst thing we've seen in the shipping business since the U.S. Postal Service came up with that monsterized eagle head.

A similar tragedy struck at Northwest Airlines several years ago. You might remember the carrier's circular "NW" symbol, worn in white atop the bright red tail. Unveiled in 1989, this was a work of genius. It was an N; it was a W; it was a compass pointing toward the northwest. It was all of those, and perhaps the most memorable trademark ever created by Landor Associates, one of the industry's most powerful identity creators. By 2003, it was in the waste can, bastardized into a lazy circle and small triangular arrow. Past tense, and good for that: Northwest and its ruined colophon no longer exist, having been folded into Delta Air Lines.

Delta, for its part, is owed kudos for hanging on to its famous "widget" tricorn, albeit in revised colors. The widget says one thing and says it without a hint of fuss or pretension: Delta. Aeroflot gets a mention here too. Overall, the Russian carrier's newest paint job is garishly overdone but scores big points for retaining its winged hammer and sickle, virtually unchanged since the 1940s.

And what of those logos that ought to be changed but haven't been? For starters I give you the "Sir Turtle" mascot of Cayman Airways, who looks like he just crawled out of a Bosch painting.

But needless to say, the corporate trademark is only one part of an airline's visual presentation. An airplane is a very large canvas on which to make or break your statement. Enter the paint bucket.

Decades ago, Braniff International was famous for dousing whole planes in solid colors—blues, greens, even powder pastels. In the same way, today's de rigueur relies on perception of the airplane as a whole, rather than a separate body and tail. Traditional paint jobs approached these surfaces separately, while contemporary ones strive to marry body and tail in a continuous canvas. This has brought the once familiar "cheat line"—that thin band of paint stretching across the windows from nose to tail—to the brink of extinction. There was a time when virtually every hull was decorated by horizontal striping, a custom now gone the way of drive-up stairs and fancy inflight meals.

With a stripeless fuselage, the tail becomes the focal point. Some airlines, such as Qantas, rely on powerful fin markings that carry the entire aircraft. Others, such as Emirates, balance tail and fuselage through the use of oversized, billboard-style lettering. Still others go for a flying warehouse extreme—an empty white expanse with few details aside from a capriciously placed title.

But the dominant theme in liveries these days is one of motion. There are enough streaks, swishes, arcs, twists, swirls, and curls out there to make anybody dizzy. And most of them, sadly, are indistinguishable from one another—overwrought, gimmicky, and self-conscious. See TACA, El Al, and Pakistan International for three of the worst examples. "The lowest common denominator of brand identity is something I call the 'Generic Meaningless Swoosh Thing,'" says Amanda Collier, a graphic design veteran. According to Collier, "The GMST is what happens when any corporation tries to develop a new look. The managers will talk about wanting something that shows their company is 'forward thinking' and 'in motion,' and no fewer than three of them will reference Nike, inventors of the original Swoosh. The creative types smile, nod, secretly stab themselves with their X-Acto knives."

And as a result, there are fewer lasting impressions. Airplanes blur together in a palette of motion-themed anonymity. Somewhere is a vending machine. Airline executives drop in a million dollars' worth of consulting coins and out pops another curvy-swervy variant of the GMST. With a few exceptions (Aeromexico is one), these designs are so dismally uninspired that it's hard to look at them without yawning. They are meant to be sophisticated and suggestive of movement and energy, but all they really do is make your airline indistinguishable from everybody else's. Watching from a terminal window, people are asking the one question they should never have to ask: What airline is *that*?

Keeping all of this in mind, let's critique the latest liveries of North America's ten largest airlines:

1.   United Airlines

When United and Continental Airlines announced their merger in 2010, this combination paint scheme was unveiled, marrying the Continental tail and fuselage with the United typeface. "Continented," let's call it. It's a good-looking design, and we understand the sentiment, but doing away with United's friendly and familiar "U" emblem was a mistake. The U—a feathery, truncated tulip in its final, pre-merger form—was never especially dashing, but Continental's segmented globe, now in its place, is so boring that it looks like a PowerPoint slide. Also, I miss the fully spelled "United Airlines" used in the 1990s, which had more gravity than a lackadaisical "United."

Crisp, light, ultra-corporate. Overall grade: B-plus

2.   Delta Air Lines

"Delta puts on a tux" is how one person describes it. It's a sophisticated, upmarket look. The typeface is very handsome, as is the newly textured "widget" up on the tail, now in a two-tone red (an apparent nod to Northwest, which became part of Delta in 2010). The drawback is the anemic fuselage and its scrawny blue understripe. A bolder bottom, maybe with some red accenting, would put it over the top.

Tight, confident, stylish. Overall grade: B

243

3. American Airlines

One of the few vintage holdouts, American hadn't changed its colors in forty years, hanging tough with its polished silver body, gothic tail bird, and tricolor cheat. It was never anything beautiful, but give them credit for bucking four decades of design fads. American's new look, launched in 2013, manages to be boring and garish at the same time. As already discussed, the real crime here was forsaking the ageless "AA" logo. I can live with the piano key tail and the gray typeface, but killing off that trademark was unforgiveable.

Tragic, ruinous, patriotic. Overall grade: D-minus

4. Southwest Airlines

The old Southwest used lengthwise fillets of red and orange, topped with a peculiar khaki that the airline called "desert gold." It was homely as hell, but it was unassuming and geographically correct. Having expanded far afield, the airline's look, if not its name, was thought too parochial, and so it has been, um, refreshed. Refreshed to the point that a Southwest jet looks like an amusement park ride, or an overly rich dessert concocted by a hungry child. The roof of every plane is a cotton-candy purple, delineated from a neon-red underside by a nose-to-tail ribbon of yellow. Even the cowls and wheel hubs have been splashed with confection. Who signed off on this? Next time, hide the peyote.

Exuberant, profuse, may rot your teeth. Overall grade: F

5. US Airways

Until a few years ago, US Airways had one of the best schemes in the sky, with its smoky, postapocalyptic gray and smart red accenting. The current design was unveiled in 2005, after the merger with America West, and attempted to incorporate motifs from both carriers. The flag and font are US Airways; the lightly sprayed fuselage jags are America West; the feeling is Walmart. Couldn't they just have given everybody a watch? The tuck-under at the nose is especially frivolous and ugly.

Downmarket, cheap, contrived. Overall grade: D (Note: We'll be seeing fewer of these as US Airways merges with American.)

6. Air Canada

Taking a cue from US Airways, our friends to the north ignored the if-it-ain't-broke clause and mucked up one of the strongest looks around. The maple leaf lives on, and that's a good thing, but it's been strangely pixelated. The soapy blue fuselage is—how else to put it?—unique. It does have a certain glacial pallor, I guess, in keeping with things Canadian. It also evokes the tiling in an airport men's room.

Just plain odd. Overall grade: D

7. jetBlue

jetBlue uses a grab-bag series of tail markings, with different geometric patterns painted in alternating shades of, guess what, blue. Squares, diamonds, polka dots, and plaids. There's one that looks like a circuit board. It sounds fun, but they're rather uninspired. The rest of the plane is an exercise in nothingness—a bare white top, a navy bottom, and the jetBlue name in a coy, too-small font.

Blue, bland, blah. Overall grade: C-minus

8. AirTran

I reckon there isn't an artist alive who could take white, teal green, royal blue, and candy-apple red and make them look good together, but that didn't stop AirTran from trying. In case it wasn't ugly enough, they threw in some gratuitous curves and swooshes. And while I confess to liking the big italicized A on the tail, somebody needs to rein in the tacky practice of painting website addresses on engine cowls and winglets.

Assertive, unconventional, unhinged. Overall grade: F (Note: Southwest's takeover of AirTran means this one is being phased out.)

9. Alaska Airlines

Ignoring that Alaska Airlines is actually based in Seattle, we love the parka-wearing Inuit mascot, whose smiling face graces every tail. It's a downhome—wherever home is exactly—and effective touch. Revisionists have attempted to discredit the visage by claiming it's the face of Old Man Winter, Johnny Cash, or even Che Guevara, but the airline's communications department assures me he's indigenous. In any case, he's not the problem. What sinks this scheme is the frightful fuselage writing, running billboard-style ahead of the wing. If you ever try composing the word "Alaska" on an Etch-a-Sketch while being electrocuted, this is what you'll come up with.

Folksy, ethnic, impossible to read. Overall grade: D

10. Hawaiian Airlines

It's charming that states forty-nine and fifty both have gone with faces on the tail. One a man, the other a woman, they look longingly at each other from across the vast Pacific. Both have character, but Hawaiian's island maiden is more colorful, and prettier, than Alaska's wintry Inuit. The blobbish lavender petals creeping up the rear fuselage are a touch strange, but on the whole there's a nice, even balance between front and back. The typeface is perfect.

Warm, sunny, a little sexy. Overall grade: A-minus

What can I say, I'm a tough grader. I wonder how Sister Wendy or the late Robert Hughes would feel.

Thinking back to airlines that no longer exist, one of the things I miss is the old PSA smile. California-based Pacific Southwest Airlines used to apply smile decals to the noses of its jets. It wasn't anything showy, just a thin black curve. It was a DaVincian, ambivalent kind of smile that didn't get under your skin—as if each plane were expressing contentment simply at being a plane. The PSA name, if not its good mood, has been retained by its inheritor, US Airways, and reassigned to one of their commuter affiliates. In Ohio. Deserves a frown if you ask me.

One of these days I'll put together a report card for Europe and Asia. People might assume we Americans are outstyled by our foreign competitors, but that's not necessarily true. Just to choose one, take a look some time at the newest EgyptAir paint job, a perfect example of everything that is wrong with airline branding so far in the twenty-first century. Almost unspeakably awful, it looks like the uniform for an amateur hockey team. Similarly, check out Air India's latest. They downsized the little Taj Mahalian window outlines to the point where you can't see them and threw a gaudy, sunburst-style spinning wheel up on the tail.

British Airways earned a spot in marketing infamy when, in 1997 and to considerable fanfare, it unveiled its "world images" look. A dozen or so unique patterns, each representing a different region of the world, were chosen for the tails of BA aircraft. Out went the quartered Union Jack and heraldic crest, and in came *Delftblue Daybreak*, *Wunala Dreaming*, and *Youm al-Suq*. It was all very progressive, multicultural, and revolting. Newell and Sorell, creators of the campaign, called it "a series of uplifting celebrations." A more cynical source called it "a wallpaper catalog." Margaret Thatcher once draped a handkerchief over the tail of a 747 model and said, "We fly the British flag, not these awful things." World Images was abandoned in 2001, replaced by the fleetwide red, white, and blue still in use today, and that makes every BA aircraft look like a huge can of Pepsi.

And yes, I have seen Southwest's killer whale 737, *Shamu*, and all the similar novelties. Jetliner hulls have been painted up to commemorate everything from ethnic identity to the Olympics. One of the more distinguished was an Aborigine-inspired Qantas 747 called *Nalanji Dreaming*. By the mid-1990s, this concept finally crossed an inevitable threshold, with carriers leasing out their exteriors to paying advertisers in the style of a Manhattan bus. Ryanair exploits this to boorish excess, as did the now-defunct Western Pacific Airlines, the Colorado-based operator whose "logojet" 737s advertised, among other things, hotel casinos and car rental companies. FOX-TV paid to have one of those 737s done up to promote *The Simpsons*—with Marge's blue beehive riding up the tail. Western Pacific went bust around the time that *The Simpsons* finally became unwatchable (1996 was the last tolerable season), and billboard schemes have remained, for now, the exception and not the rule. Here's hoping it stays that way.

II. Names, Slogans, and Salt Packets

Truth is, all the graphic design genius in the world will go straight into the lav when offset by a poorly chosen moniker. Branding is a lot more than visual impressions, it's about sound as well—the raw intonation of an airline's name, and those things it evokes or implies.

For the most impossible collection of tongue twisters, look no further than Russia, home to the likes of Adygheya Avia, Avialesookhrana, Aviaobshchemash, and Khalaktyrka Aviakompania. And those are the short ones. The longest have been safely locked away into abbreviations and acronyms. KMPO is all you need to know—but if you insist, it's Kazanskoe Motorostroitel'noe Proizvodstevennoe Ob'yedinenie, which is also the sound a person makes when gargling aquarium gravel. Not to be outdone, there's an airline in Kazakhstan called Zhezkazan Zhez Air. There are five Zs in that name. I'm not sure how to pronounce it, but a loud sneeze should be a close enough approximation.

The prevalent trend these days is a fondness for ultra-quirky—should I say "fun"?—monikers. We've had Zoom, Jazz, Clickair, Go Fly, Wizz Air. Enough already. Sure, it freshens things up, but can you really buy a ticket on something called Bmibaby (a regional branch of British carrier BMI) and still feel good about yourself in the morning? The idea, I think, is to personify the ease and affordability of modern air travel. That's fine, except that it also undercuts whatever shred of dignity the experience retains. Similarly, we presume the intent of Clickair is to evoke the sound one makes while conveniently booking his or her ticket online. Logical, but still annoying. Hungary's low-cost entrant Wizz Air also reminds us of a sound, though probably not the one they have in mind.

Meanwhile, regional conglomerate Mesa Air Group, whose huge fleet of RJs and turboprops provides code-share service for several majors, is having success with an alter ego it formed about five years ago. Capitalizing on a certain spirit of the times, the Mesa spinoff is dubbed—here it comes now—Freedom Airlines. Ugh. I met a Freedom Airlines pilot once at Kennedy airport. He looked about seventeen, and I was trying to figure out which company he flew for. I couldn't make sense of the star-spangled logo on his ID badge, so I asked him.

"I fly for Freedom," he said.

I wasn't sure if he was answering my question or making a political statement. I wanted to put my arm on his shoulder. "We all do, son. We all do."

Speaking of double meanings, nobody will ever outdo the hilarity of Taiwan's now-defunct U-Land Airlines, which before it was shuttered—for safety violations, no less—seemed to take the concept of the discount carrier to a whole new level. And let's not forget the nervy confidence of Russia's Kras Air, always just an H away from infamy.

Call me old-fashioned, but I've always been partial to the more thoughtful and symbolic names—those that evoke the imagery, history, or culture of their nations. Take Garuda, for instance, the national carrier of Indonesia. Borrowed from ancient Sanskrit, Garuda is the name of an eagle common to Buddhist and Hindu mythology, and one of Hinduism's animal-god trinity. It's a little perplexing in that Indonesia is the world's most populous Muslim country, but let's not bicker lest it be switched to "Air Indonesia." Likewise, Avianca is a gorgeous word; "Air Colombia" would be awful. Iberia is pleasantly rich compared to, say, "Spanish Airways," and Alitalia has a much prettier ring than "Air Italy." If you insist on directly invoking your homeland, please do it with a bit of flair. Royal Air Maroc and Royal Jordanian are acceptable examples. Even Aeromexico has a pleasant flow to it.

Qantas, by the way, is not the name of an indigenous Australian marsupial. It's an acronym for Queensland and Northern Territory Aerial Service, founded in 1920.

In 1992, an airline called Kiwi International was started up by a band of ex-Eastern pilots, operating out of Newark. No strangers to failure, Kiwi's founders tempered their upstart optimism with an ironic twist, calling their airline after a bird that can't fly. In New Zealand, a different Kiwi International launched services between Auckland and Australia. The second Kiwi was, if nothing else, more geographically correct, its flightless namesake an icon of that country, but in both cases the name had a clever mocking-of-fate quality. Alas, neither was successful for very long. You could say they asked for it.

Certain airlines cling to labels they've literally outgrown. Thirty-five years ago, Southwest was an intra-state operator confined to the boundaries of Texas. Northwest is gone now, but it retained its homey geographic association right to the end—not an easy task considering the convolution of compass points that constituted that airline. Known as Northwest Orient at the time, it merged with Republic Airlines in 1985. Republic was itself the amalgam of North Central Airlines, Southern Airways, and Hughes Airwest.

But wait a minute, isn't there a Republic out there today? Indeed there is, which brings us to the annoying phenomenon of airline name recycling:

The existing Republic, one of the biggest regional carriers in the United States, is of no relation to the original. They've merely resurrected the name (using the Airways suffix in place of Airlines). And we've seen this before. At one time or another, we had two different reincarnations of Pan Am, two of Braniff, and a Midway. All were in-name-only outfits, and none lasted very long before joining their predecessors on that big tarmac in the sky. When USAir—as US Airways was called at the time—purchased Piedmont and Pacific Southwest Airlines (PSA) in 1987, these brands had been so admired that a decision was made to keep the names alive. They were given to a pair of USAir Express affiliates. Suddenly, PSA found itself headquartered in Ohio, while at airports along the Eastern Seaboard, passengers could (and still can) once again step aboard Piedmont. Sort of.

By the way, the doppelganger Republic recently acquired struggling Frontier Airlines. Frontier is, you guessed it, another appropriated moniker. The original Frontier, based in Denver, flew from 1950 until 1986. At this point, we're getting layer upon layer of rehash.

While it might have a ripped-off name, the new Frontier uses a clever outdoors theme as an all-around marketing tool. The tails of its Airbuses depict animals and birds native to North America, from mallards to sea otters to bobcats. "A Whole Different Animal" is the airline's wily catch phrase. Bringing us to yet another facet of air carrier identity: the slogan.

As with logos or liveries, a slogan needn't be particularly ingenious to be successful, but the right combo of sentiment and lyric rhythm go a long way. "We like you too," jetBlue tells its customers—a bit presumptuous, maybe, but a capable tag for just that reason. Korean Air's "Excellence in Flight," is another of my favorites. It's pleasantly succinct and has a canny double meaning, without the pandering, we-do-it-all-for-you sentiments we expect from airlines.

We've heard some classics over the years. United scored big with the touchy-feely warmth of "Fly the Friendly Skies," while Pan Am's "The World's Most Experienced Airline" pretty much said it all. KLM's "The Reliable Dutch Airline" excelled in its plainspoken modesty. At Braniff, the most image-conscious airline of all time, it was "Coming Through with Flying Colors." Perfectly apropos considering Braniff's rainbow-painted fleet.

On the other hand, Eastern once billed itself "The Wings of Man," which was definitely over the top, as is British Airways' use of "The World's Favourite Airline." I suppose BA was under pressure to devise something with one of those cute British spellings that so charm Americans, but technically, measured by boardings, it's the world's twenty-first favourite airline.

Other unfortunate campaigns include at least two from Delta Air Lines, whose affable "Delta Is Ready When You Are" was nixed for the gross vapidity of "Good Goes Around," which sounded like the pitch for a diet cola. An earlier slogan was "We Get You There." Passengers don't anticipate much from airlines anymore, but talk about the nadir of lowered expectations.

If nothing else, be coherent. Stepping into the cabins of SAS (Scandinavian Airlines System), one is prone to notice the immaculate furnishings and tasteful, understated colors. All very Scandinavian, you could say, except for the period a few years ago when SAS chose to include a scattering of bizarrely rendered English slogans as part of

251

its décor. "There are three ways to travel," announced a placard near the forward boarding door. "In an armchair. In your imagination. Welcome to the third." What's that now? Later, when your meal arrived, the tray included conjoined packets of salt and pepper, upon which was written:

The color of snow,
The taste of tears,
The enormity of oceans.

Ah, what better for those quiet moments at 37,000 feet than the existential musing of the Scandinavian salt-poet.

And finally, advertising:

We have come a long, long way since the old National Airlines "Fly Me" campaign of the early 1970s. "I'm Lorraine," a seductively posed flight attendant would say to the camera. "Fly me to Orlando." Braniff had a similar pitch, called the "air strip," showing attractive young flight attendants changing uniforms mid-flight to the sound of suggestive music.

But possibly the most memorable airline commercial I ever saw, if not entirely for the intended reasons, was the 1989 "winking eye" spot from British Airways. Conceived by the Saatchi & Saatchi agency and directed by Hugh Hudson (*Chariots of Fire*), the commercial featured hundreds of people costumed to represent various world cultures, assembled in a dramatic landscape near Salt Lake City, Utah. The voice-over was from actor Tom Conti, and the score, from Leo Delibes's opera "Lakme," was adapted by Malcolm McLaren (of Sex Pistols and Bow Wow Wow fame). Seen from high above, the actors took on the shape of a gigantic face, which through the magic of carefully timed choreography proceeded to "wink." It was a stunning and altogether creepy 30 seconds. Impressive for sure (you can watch it on YouTube), but I get nervous when masses of oddly dressed people are winking at me. What's worse, I forever associate British Airways with footage of the crowds in North Korean stadiums forming those enormous profiles of the Dear Leader.

In the meantime, as if you need to be reminded, "DING, You Are

Now Free to Move About the Country." Southwest's TV tag, with its signature chime, is a brilliant evocation of the discount carrier's key to success: affordable fares for everybody. Unfortunately after hearing it for the five-thousandth time, it becomes grating enough to send any sensible person scurrying to a competitor. ✈

How about some thoughts on the service standards of U.S. airlines compared to those overseas?

It's no secret that U.S. carriers have a lot of catching up to do, as shown year after year in passenger surveys and industry awards. Almost everywhere—Asia, Europe, South America, even Africa—U.S. carriers are heartily outclassed by their foreign competitors. To be impartial, I might mention the knee-breaking seat pitch and treacherous cuisine of EgyptAir and Royal Air Maroc, but exceptions like these are uncommon.

How we got to such a shameful position is the subject of debate. Is it a fiscal thing? A cultural thing? A little of both? It has been a long, hard slide, and most folks agree that it began at or around the moment president Jimmy Carter attached his signature to the Airline Deregulation Act of 1979. From that moment on it was a race to the bottom, with competitive chaos inspiring a battle so fierce that, from the airlines' perspectives, undercutting the competition became more important than pleasing customers. By 2001, the few remaining extravagances were curtailed in the battening-down that began after September 11.

In my opinion, there's something systemic at hand that transcends the bottom line. It is easy to assume that with a falloff in profits comes a falloff in the quality of your product, but what we have today is the nadir of a prolonged decline that was ongoing even through the mid-1990s—the airlines' most profitable period in history. Overseas, in the meantime, even financially struggling companies are, for the most part, able to uphold their good reputations. For them, profitability and customer service are not zero-sum variables.

It has reached a point where an economy class seat in a foreign market is often on a par with a *first class* seat in the U.S. domestic market. I can vouch for that. My recent experiences aboard Korean Air, Emirates, Cathay Pacific, Turkish Airlines, Thai Airways, and LanPeru, all in economy, were as good or better than many first class segments I've flown within the United States. What made them so was a combination of things tangible and intangible; both physical comforts and onboard staff who were exceptionally attentive. We'll get to the latter in a moment. The former included things like extra-wide personal video screens with a comfortable headset, retractable footrests, seat-back USB connections, contoured tray tables, amenities kits, and full meals even on short flights. Cathay Pacific's long-haul planes have those shell-style economy seats mentioned earlier (*see cabin classes, page 166*) that even when fully reclined do not interfere with the person behind you. In Thai Airways' economy, hot towels are handed out before takeoff. They're not the cotton facecloth version like you'd get up front, but more of a heavy tissue, dispensed from a microwaveable box. It's a nice touch, and one that couldn't cost more than a few dollars per flight. And every airplane was immaculately clean, from the seat pockets to the lavatories.

None of those things, you'll notice, was especially luxurious. Honestly, in light of how inexpensive fares are, together with the razor-thin margins our airlines are forced to work with, luxury is out of the question. And that's all right. What the airlines haven't quite figured out yet, is that satisfactory service doesn't have to be elaborate. The average passenger doesn't expect to be pampered. What he or she expects and deserves are convenience, respectful employees, and a modicum of comfort. Nobody is lobbying for a return to the prissy pretensions found aboard planes in decades past. In the premium cabins, you've earned the right to some grandiloquent fun, if that's your thing, after handing over $7,000 for a sleeper seat to London or Tokyo, but a backpacking college kid in row 45 is not interested in living out a bourgeois fantasy of the 1940s. He is not covetous of a velvet-clothed cheese cart or a fussily presented plate of grilled salmon with braised fennel and leeks. What he yearns for is a clean, halfway comfortable space to sit in, something to watch or listen to, maybe a sandwich, and for God's sake an occasional bottle of water.

And something else too: workers who are polite and professional. While it may sound hackneyed, it's also patently true that passenger allegiance is ultimately earned or squandered not through material comforts, but through the attitude and dedication of your employees. I'll never say that anybody else's job in this mad business is an easy one, but if airline workers, as a group, cannot muster the necessary levels of commitment, then something is systemically wrong and needs to be fixed before any of the rest will matter. Extra legroom, on-demand video, and free drinks are much appreciated, it's true. But they're all for naught when you're dying of thirst in the middle of an overnight flight, with trash on your table from a meal that was served three time zones ago, because the flight attendants have spent the last five hours reading magazines in the galleys and ignoring the passengers. Or when a gate agent takes your boarding pass without so much as making eye contact. What I remember most about those flights aboard Korean, Cathay, Emirates, and the others was the attentiveness of the onboard crew. For the full duration of the flight, flight attendants were constantly coming up and down the aisles, asking if passengers needed water, coffee, juice, or anything else.

It is worth mentioning that in an industry where the average is six weeks, Singapore Airlines flight attendants endure *five months* of schooling. That is considerably longer than pilot training at most carriers. I am not suggesting that Singapore's model is a reasonable target for a U.S. major—it's not. For any U.S. airline, hoping to emulate the Singapores of the world would be at best quixotic and at worst financially ruinous. But the deeper point is that an airline's most valuable service asset is the professionalism, grace, and courtesy and of its staff. End of story.

And here's some advice: if you're going to do something, don't be half-assed about it. The smallest touches can leave an impression. If you're going to have pillows on your aircraft, they should be *useful* pillows. Flying across the Atlantic on Air France, economy class riders get a comfortable feather pillow wrapped in attractive fabric. It's neither a significant nor expensive item, but it's a *nice* one, and you remember it. On an American carrier, assuming there are pillows at all, they tend to be flimsy wedges of foam about the size of a slice of bread, with coverings that tear apart like tissue. Thanks for nothing. Or, if you're going to offer gratis cocktails, be dignified about it. Don't, as I heard one airline do, precede the meal service with a stern-sounding public address announcement reminding people that your generosity extends to "one, and one only, beverage per passenger." That's about as tacky as it gets. The problem isn't the one-drink rule itself, but the idea of scolding people about it as if they were children.

So which airlines are tops, exactly? Let's see what SkyTrax says. SkyTrax is a prestigious air travel advisory group that ranks carriers on a scale of one to five stars. Currently only six airlines meet the group's strict criteria for five-star status, awarded only to those "at the forefront of product and service delivery excellence, often setting trends to be followed by other airlines." They are, alphabetically:

- Asiana Airlines (South Korea)
- Cathay Pacific (Hong Kong)
- Hainan Airlines (China)
- Malaysia Airlines
- Qatar Airways
- Singapore Airlines

Dropping down a notch, thirty-two carriers manage to hit four-star status. This is where you'll find most of the mainstay Asians and Europeans: Air France, Emirates, British Airways, Lufthansa, JAL, Korean, Qantas, Thai, Turkish, and South African Airways. Plus a few surprises, such as Kazakhstan's Air Astana, Oman Air, and Canada's tiny Porter Airlines. The sole U.S. finisher is jetBlue (that's a stretch if you ask me, but for some reason, jetBlue always winds up getting its tails kissed).

The rest of the Americans are found in the three-star category, having achieved "a satisfactory standard of core product across most travel categories, but poor or less consistent standards of staff service/ product quality in selected onboard or airport features." This is the biggest group by far. Delta, United, Southwest, and American join the likes of Ethiopian Airlines, Aeroflot, Aerolineas Argentinas, Pakistan International, and China Eastern.

It could be worse. There are no Americans among the twenty-five or so names on the two-star list. Here you'll find Cubana, Sudan Airways, TAAG Angola, and Biman Bangladesh. And Ryanair.

The one-star list contains but a solitary finisher, the mysterious Air Koryo of North Korea.

I would argue that our airlines' biggest collective failure is not one of onboard service, but one of communications. Airlines have lost the ability to deliver timely or accurate information to their customers.

In spite of what most people think, airlines do not, as policy, intentionally lie or mislead. What passengers take to be lies are better described as garbles, caused by the faulty transfer of information. Such is the rigidly compartmentalized structure of airlines, where specifics of a circumstance are passed along from department to department, each with its own priorities, vernacular, and expertise. There's plenty to lose in translation, and it's not unlike that game you played in grade school, where a short anecdote is whispered around the room, growing more and more scrambled each step of the way. At the airport, the person in charge of picking up a microphone and announcing that your plane is delayed often has limited understanding of what the problem actually is.

And the various personnel can be mighty territorial. Several years ago I was the captain of a commuter plane victimized by a snowstorm. Our twenty or so passengers were confused, and the gate staff did little to make things clear. So, there in the boarding lounge, I asked for people's attention and began to explain what was happening. Maybe I got too in-depth with definitions of things like "wheels-up time," but a few seconds later came some loud footsteps and a voice booming behind me, asking, "What the hell is this asshole doing?" It was the station manager, and he didn't take kindly to a pilot usurping the role of airport customer service.

No matter the reasons, time and time again, and against their best interests, airlines fail at getting the truth out, and that's a problem.

Not only does it violate the common sense protocols of customer service, it also allows rumors, myths, and conspiracy theories to flourish unchecked. It stokes anger and distrust, and it aids and abets the fears of anxious flyers. Airlines have a terrible habit of responding to anomalies—be it a minor schedule disruption or something more serious—in one of two ways: either with total silence or, perhaps worse, resorting to hideous oversimplifications. The result is nearly total lack of respect from the public. People dislike airlines and don't believe anything they say—partly because they never actually say anything. Or, when they do, it's condescending or even terrifying:

A flight is cancelled because "it's too hot to fly." A crew aborts a landing because "a plane crossed in front of us." In Flagstaff, Arizona, one day, counter staff informed a group of delayed passengers that volunteers were needed to give up their seats. When passengers asked why, they were told, "We need to lighten the load. The plane has been having problems and we're afraid one of the engines might cut out."

Of all front-line employees, pilots are potentially the most valuable for soothing anxieties and explaining the nuances of abnormal situations. Unfortunately, thanks to fears over liability, much of this potential is squandered. Pilots are wary of saying the wrong thing, of being blamed, punished, or otherwise called to the carpet should something be misconstrued or taken from context. It's true that people write letters and threaten lawsuits over the damnedest things, but really this is an airline culture and training problem. Too often the emphasis is on how *not* to communicate—which phrases never to say, which terms and scary-sounding buzzwords to avoid. The result is a tendency to say as little as possible—a default policy of evasive simplification.

This is obviously counterproductive, and never more so than those times when minor abnormalities are made to sound harrowing: One time I was riding in economy class on a flight into Boston. Just before landing, the pilots aborted the landing and went around. There was no reason to believe anything remotely serious had occurred, but the sense of fright emanating from those around me was palpable. Eventually, one of the pilots gave an explanation. "Ah, well, sorry about that," he began. "Another plane cut in front of us on the runway, so we needed to break off the landing. We're circling back and will be landing in a few minutes."

Nothing else was offered. I sat there in silent anguish. "Please, say more," I thought. "You *need* to say more." But he didn't, and rather than quell the passengers' anxieties, he had made them worse. "A plane *cut in front of us*?" came a raised voice from a few rows down, followed by nervous laughter. A college kid sitting diagonally from me was visibly shaken. Later that evening, no doubt, he'd be regaling friends with the harrowing tale of his "near miss." Which it was not. The go-around (*see aborted landings, page 76*) was the result of a simple spacing issue—not a near miss at all, but a maneuver performed well in advance of one; indeed, to *avoid* a near miss.

"Carriers in general could do a better job of communicating," admits one airline spokesperson. "In fact, you might say it's difficult to *over* communicate." Admittedly, however, there's the proverbial can of worms when it comes to full disclosure; lawsuits can arise from what appear to be harmless, even helpful, remarks or actions. And there's little benefit to overwhelming people with the arcana of aircraft operations. Layering things in technical mumbo-jumbo can leave people suspicious and shaking their heads. "If you try to get too technical about something," adds the spokesperson, "it can come across as serious when it's actually routine. My sense is that most customers would like to have timely updates about a delay, and a general, honest sense of what caused it. Beyond that, I don't think drilling down into a lot of details adds much."

He may have a point. When those aboard jetBlue flight 292 were faced with a stuck undercarriage and an impending emergency landing back in 2005 (*see jetBlue incident, page 201*), the crew made every effort to let customers know they were in very little danger. Yet rather than accept this, according to some who were there, many passengers assumed the pilots were lying. I receive letters all the time from people accusing airline staff of falsifying the "truth" of supposedly life-threatening situations. However wrong, it's a notion that's deeply ingrained.

Perhaps at the heart of the matter, though, is the simple fact that carriers pay little penalty for acting as their own worst enemies. Fostering and reinforcing skewed perceptions of air travel has little effect on their balance sheets. Profitability is another issue altogether, but planes remain full, and a majority of people, intellectually if not emotionally, grasp that flying is safe. Why stir the pot?

Which are the largest airlines?

It depends how you measure it. The easiest method is just to tally up the number of passengers carried in a year. The trouble is, this neglects the scope of an airline's network—the number of cities it serves, how far it flies, etc.

A second calculation uses what are known as available seat-kilometers (ASK). This is the total number of seats an airline has for sale, multiplied by the total number of kilometers it flies. (ASKs are often called ASMs, using miles in lieu of kilometers.) A 777 flying from New York to London is good for approximately 1,200,000 ASKs; a 757 going from LAX to Chicago is worth about 450,000. Larger planes on longer routes, in other words, are worth more than shorter planes on shorter routes—though an airline can make up the difference by operating more flights. The problem with ASKs is that they include empty seats. A four-hundred-seat 747 scores more ASKs than a two-hundred-seat 767 over the same route, but what if the latter is full while the 747 is empty?

A third metric is the revenue passenger-kilometer, or RPK. These are basically ASKs corrected for occupancy, or "load factor" as it's called in the business. One passenger traveling one kilometer equals one RPK. To me, this is the most accurate and equitable gauge, as it takes in everything: distances flown (network size), available seats (aircraft size and fleet size), as well as the actual occupancy of those seats (passenger totals).

At the moment, Delta is the world's largest carrier in terms of both passengers boarded (164 million annually) and RPKs (310 billion). Once its merger with US Airways is complete, American Airlines will sit second, knocking United to third. As we go down the list, those measuring techniques can make a big difference. Emirates is now the world's fifth biggest carrier in RPKs, yet fails to crack the top twenty in passengers. Ryanair holds sixth place in passengers but doesn't make the top twenty-five in RPKs.

The ten largest airlines in the world, ranked by RPKs

1. Delta Air Lines
2. American Airlines (includes US Airways)
3. United Airlines
4. Southwest Airlines
5. Emirates
6. Lufthansa
7. Air France
8. China Southern
9. Qantas
10. Cathay Pacific

Looking up there at Southwest, is it not amazing that the number-four airline—number three in passengers—is one without a single widebody jet or a single route beyond U.S. borders?

Carriers swap places year to year, and by the time you're reading this, it's not out of the question that another merger will have occurred. Nevertheless, the list above is apt to look *roughly* the same for the foreseeable future. (Note: the list deducts KLM's data from that of Air France. The companies merged in 2004 but have kept separate operational structures, with independent fleets and employee groups.)

It's tempting to think of the biggest airline as the one with the most aircraft, but capacity differences make this unreasonable. American Eagle has more planes than half the names on that top-ten list, but every one of them is an RJ. For the record, the American/US Airways combo places first, with about 960 jetliners, followed by Delta at 715. China Southern's 368 aircraft represent the largest fleet outside the United States. (The numbers change as planes are bought, sold, mothballed, and retired, but as with RPKs, the field looks pretty much the same year to year.) The largest all-widebody carriers are Emirates, Cathay Pacific, and Singapore Airlines. The *smallest* plane in these airlines' fleets is the Airbus A330.

Currently, fewer than a dozen airlines worldwide are able to claim membership in what I call the "Six Continent Club"—providing scheduled service to at least one destination in each of North and South America, Europe, Asia, Africa, and Australia. At the moment, Delta and United are the U.S. representatives, alongside Emirates, British Airways, South African Airways, Singapore Airlines, Qatar Airways, Korean Air, and Etihad Airways. In terms of total number of countries served, Turkish Airlines is the winner. Turkish is a much bigger player than people realize. Its service is top-notch, and its network now extends to ninety-five countries—more than any other airline in the world.

☆ ☆ ☆

Size is one thing, profitability something else. Here are the ten best-performing airlines as of publication time, measured in net profit:

1. Japan Airlines
2. Air China
3. China Southern
4. Delta Air Lines
5. United
6. China Eastern
7. Ryanair
8. Cathay Pacific
9. Aeroflot
10. Emirates

Plenty of stars on that list, but not many stars and stripes. To be fair, American carriers *do* earn periodic profits, but we seem to have a much harder and inconsistent time of it. The reasons for this would require an entire book of its own to conclusively discuss. Competitive environment, state ownership and subsidies, and the price of labor all play a role.

Of the airlines above, not all of them are privately run, which brings up the issue of governments providing tax breaks, subsidies, and other favors for airlines they sometimes own outright. Consider the words of Tim Clark, president of Dubai-based Emirates, which has quickly become one of the fastest-growing and most profitable airlines in the world: "The Dubai government's progressive and unrelenting policy support for aviation is at the heart of this steady, long-term growth," Clark said at an industry luncheon in 2012. The U.S. government, for its part, does much to hinder and handicap its own commercial aviation infrastructure. But we're foolish to go searching overseas for answers. The real problem isn't between U.S. airlines and those in other countries; it's between the U.S. airlines themselves.

Even before September 11, the largest U.S. carriers were suffering from the effects of overcapacity and a dragging economy. Then came the toxic ramifications of terrorism and war, unprecedented spikes in the price of fuel, and a pummeling recession. Between 2001 and 2012, United, Delta, Northwest, American, and US Airways all declared bankruptcy—the latter twice. Losses were in the billions, layoffs in the tens of thousands.

For the most part, that bleeding has stopped, but while the entrenched old-timers were left to shed costs, reshape their business models, and return to profitability—a decade-long process that ultimately resulted in three mega-mergers—opportunistic low-cost carriers (LCCs) like jetBlue, Southwest, Spirit, and AirTran seized the opportunity. Unencumbered by high labor costs or the need to support complex fleets and decades-old infrastructures, these adaptable youngsters were able to offer streamlined service and irresistibly cheap tickets, rapidly winning over a huge segment of the domestic U.S. market. The proliferation of the LCC, more than any other factor, has radically transformed the competitive dynamic.

And this isn't just a U.S. phenomenon. See Europe, where LCCs like Ryanair and easyJet are giving mainstay carriers a literal run for their money. The Brazilian airline Gol now carries more people annually than British Airways. The ever-expanding AirAsia carries more people than Singapore Airlines, Thai, or Korean Air. Other LCCs have sprung up in Australia, Kuwait, Hungary, Mexico, Canada, and Slovakia, just to name a few.

For the legacies, one survival tactic has been the outsourcing of routes to regional jet operators. RJs today are responsible for a whopping 53 percent of all domestic departures in the United States. At first, their deployment tended to mirror that of their predecessor turboprops—"commuter planes" we used to call them— going hub-and-spoke on routes 300 miles or shorter. But larger, second-generation RJs proved able to capitalize on longer runs previously the sole domain of Airbuses and Boeings. Whether Chicago–Peoria or Chicago–New York, regional planes are profitable across a wide swath of markets.

At any large airport today, legacy jets sit tethered to the gate looking wounded and worried. All around them maneuver nimble packs of RJs and LCCs, either circling voraciously or going happily about their business, depending how you see it.

Has intense competition not provided an upside for the consumer, however?

Passengers have reaped the benefit of dirt-cheap tickets, for one. As I mentioned in this book's introduction, in 1939, it cost the equivalent of over $6,000 for a round-trip ticket between New York and France. As recently as the 1970s, flying from New York to Hawaii cost nearly $3,000. On my bookshelf at home is an old American Airlines ticket receipt. It's a flea market find dating from 1946. That year, somebody named James Connors paid $334 to fly each direction between Ireland and New York. That's equal to $3,690 today—*one way.* In 2013, you can pick up an off-season round-trip on that route for less than $600.

The real cost of air travel—the price of a ticket adjusted for inflation—has fallen sharply in the years since deregulation, despite tremendous surges in the cost of oil. Between 2005 and 2010, with airlines struggling and fuel prices soaring, the average economy class fare was the cheapest it had ever been. Things have changed little as we move into the next decade, even when factoring in those add-on fees passengers so despise (*see next question*). Amenities and customer service aren't what they used to be, but what do you expect when profit margins come down to a few pennies per passenger? Airlines sell what their customers want. And more than anything else, they want rock-bottom fares.

If flying *seems* expensive, one factor might be the myriad of taxes added to your fare. There's a domestic flight segment tax, a security surcharge, a passenger facility charge, a jet fuel tax, international departure and arrival taxes, customs fees—and those are just some of them. The U.S. government adds seventeen unique taxes and fees to airline tickets, accounting for a quarter or more of the total cost of a ticket, depending on fare. (On a $300 round trip, they add up to about $60.) Percentage-wise, these taxes are often more than double those carried by tobacco, firearms, or alcohol—products carrying so-called sin taxes meant to *dissuade* use.

In addition to affordable fares, another seldom-acknowledged benefit of modern-day air travel can be seen in the airlines' route networks. One can travel between almost any two airports in America with, at worst, a single stopover. A few decades ago, flying even halfway across the country often entailed awkward transfers through two or more cities. Traveling to Europe or Asia once meant having to depart from one of a small handful of U.S. gateway cities; today, you can fly directly from many smaller hubs (Pittsburgh, Portland, Charlotte), saving considerable amounts of time.

Please address the growing practice of airlines charging for things that used to be free. Checked bags, food, a blanket...

As everyone knows, airlines are resorting to the practice known as "unbundling" as a means of increasing revenue. Flying has gone à la carte: $50 for a second piece of luggage; $20 for a take-home fleece blanket and hypoallergenic pillow; that old beef-or-chicken entrée is now a $6 sandwich wrap.

But these ancillaries were never "free." They were included in the price of your ticket. And that price used to be higher. It's impossible to have a rational discussion about unbundling without first acknowledging that fares are as low as they are. It's amusing to hear a passenger whine about the cost of checking in a bag after paying $159 to fly cross-country. And although unbundling can leave customers feeling nickel-and-dimed, it's a smart idea in that those looking for perks can have them, absorbing a higher share of the cost. Is it not better to charge a premium for specific items, not all of which everybody wants, rather than raise prices across the board?

Nonetheless, it's a practice that should only be taken so far. In 2010, in a move that ignited controversy, Fort Lauderdale–based Spirit Airlines began charging up to $45 for *carry-on bags*. This pushes the concept to the edge of the envelope—beyond it, really, and against the spirit (pardon the pun) of unbundling. Let's be realistic: a carry-on bag is not an optional item, not when the airline already charges for checked bags.

How far will airlines go to maximize revenue? The same month that Spirit unveiled its carry-on fees, Europe's Ryanair announced it would start charging 1 euro for the use of a lavatory. (The company eventually backed off, but Ryanair's cost-saving gimmicks are legendary and not to be underestimated.) I once joked that airlines would soon be selling advertising space on their overhead bins and tray tables. No sooner had I opened my mouth when, riding on a US Airways jet, I folded down my tray table and discovered a cell phone ad staring me in the face. Call me a romantic, but perhaps airlines wouldn't have so much trouble earning respect if they weren't so willing to sell their souls.

We hear about nightmare delays in which people are stuck on planes for hours at a time. Why does this happen, and what can be done about it?

Marathon tarmac strandings receive tremendous attention and are great for stoking the public's implacable hatred for airlines. In the grand scheme of things, they are extremely uncommon. Annually, around 1,500 flights in the United States face delays exceeding three hours; that seems like a lot until you remember there are close to ten million departures each year, 85 percent of which arrive on time or earlier. Even so, there are no good excuses as to why the simple act of getting people off a plane and into a terminal, or getting food and water out to a stranded aircraft, has been, at times, such an ordeal. In 2007, after a midwinter snow and ice storm slammed the Northeastern United States, hundreds of jetBlue passengers in New York were stranded aboard grounded planes for as long as ten hours. A few months earlier, an American Airlines jet sat on the ground in Austin, Texas, for more than eight hours. And most memorable of all, in 2000, thousands were stuck aboard Northwest Airlines planes for up to eleven hours during a New Year's weekend blizzard in Detroit.

These public relations disasters were symptomatic of, among other problems, airlines' general reluctance to think outside the box, and a failure to adequately empower their employees—captains, station managers, and others in the chain of command—to make critical operational decisions. Get a stairway. Get a bus. Let people deplane on the apron if you have to.

You could say they had it coming, and since 2010, U.S. airlines are now legally beholden to a maximum three-hour constraint for departure delays, or a maximum of ninety minutes for arrival delays. Passengers *must* be allowed to deplane before exceeding those limits. Failure to comply means fines up to $27,000 per passenger. The rule, a key component of what is sometimes referred to as the Passenger Bill of Rights, is exactly the sort of get-tough measure that people have been screaming for. But was it necessary, and will it work? And beware of unintended consequences:

Picture yourself on a delayed airplane going from New York to San Francisco. Parked out on the taxiway in a snowstorm, your assigned ATC wheels-up time is only twenty minutes away. But because the three-hour tarmac limit is about to elapse, the plane is compelled to return to the gate. After docking, several passengers, having missed their connections, choose to get off and go home. This means their luggage too needs to come off. And because going back and forth to the terminal burned a substantial amount of fuel, the jet also must be refueled. Coordinating all of this will involve a large number of personnel—most of whom are, at the moment, dealing with other flights—and a whole new flight plan will need to be worked up and printed. Let's be conservative and say that everything takes an hour. You're now a minimum of thirty minutes later than you would have been *without* returning to the gate. Throw in the need to de-ice, or the possibility of crew replacement because of duty time regulations, and it's substantially worse. And missing that wheels-up time means you'll be assigned a new one, and lo and behold it's another two hours away. Your three-hour delay just became a five-hour delay.

What the better solution might be, I don't know. But I do know that airline delays are complex and fickle—the types of situations that don't respond well to regulation based on arbitrary time limits. Like the mandatory sentencing guidelines so despised by many judges and public defenders, these rules can cause more problems than they solve.

Cynical flyers sometimes contend that pilots and cabin attendants actually delight in long delays because we're able to collect overtime pay. Without getting into the nitty-gritty of how crews are (or aren't) compensated, this is nonsense. If you're envisioning a pair of pilots up there in the cockpit, rubbing their hands and making that annoying cash register sound, believe me, that's not what's happening. We don't enjoy these situations any more than you do. Unfortunately, we are more or less at the mercy of staff overseeing and coordinating things, often from afar. Short of declaring an emergency, something for which he'd need to answer both to the FAA and his superiors, the captain cannot unilaterally decide to let people off the airplane and out onto a taxiway or an icy apron. Neither can he simply drive the plane up to the terminal and open the doors.

As for the idea of passengers taking matters into their own hands and initiating their own evacuation, as is sometimes suggested, I reckon that half of them would wind up breaking their legs or clobbering themselves with their carry-ons as they plummet down the escape slides. Those slides can be two stories tall, and they are *very* steep. They are not designed with convenience in mind. They are there to get a planeload of people out of and away from the aircraft as quickly as possible during an emergency—without their belongings.

Please talk for a minute about the success of Southwest Airlines. Why does its less refined product consistently do so well?

Southwest is the most perennially profitable U.S. airline, and the last of a nearly vanished breed: an airline with a true personality that large numbers of flyers have a genuine fondness for. Returning the favor, Southwest's logo features a winged heart, and its three-letter stock ticker code is LUV (taken from its home base of Love Field, Dallas). This is an airline whose founder, Herb Kelleher, rode a Harley, swigged whiskey from a flask, and once took on a rival in an arm-wrestling match (he lost). LUV them or hate them, we owe Southwest a toast—something domestic, cheap, and served in aluminum.

It's easy to say that Southwest owes its success to the fact that people don't expect much of them. The airline is nothing if not unpretentious, having mastered the art of get-what-you-pay-for satisfaction. But of the things people *do* expect, the airline delivers almost every time, and that, more than anything, is what wins them such loyalty. Specifically, customers appreciate its first-come, first-serve seating policy, the upbeat tenor of its staff, and its flexible ticketing and refund policies. To describe Southwest's mojo in three words, you might go with these: easy, friendly, and above all else, predictable. On that last point, its competitors can be all over the place; one flight is pleasant, the next is awful.

Remember too that in most people's minds the air travel experience is measured curbside to curbside, not takeoff to landing. Southwest reaps the advantage of not only how it flies, but where. Aiming off-center in many markets, it allows customers to savor the logistical ease of a Manchester, Islip, or Providence, instead of the hectic snarls of a Boston, Newark, or La Guardia. The legacy giants, with their reliance on mega-hub feed, can't succeed this way. Southwest is the closest thing we've got to an official airline of the suburbs.

Its streamlined operational structure is another asset. Southwest flies only one type of aircraft, the 737, specializing in ultra-fast turnarounds in a domestic-only market. It's apples and oranges when you start making comparisons with the network carriers, which have immensely different and far more expansive operating structures. Consistency and predictability are a lot harder when you've got four hubs and a fleet of six hundred aircraft serving six continents.

Southwest has always bristled at the idea of adapting its model beyond American borders, and probably smartly so. Cheap tickets, high frequencies, and all-economy services don't lend themselves to long-distance operations and foreign accents.

Just ask Freddie Laker. The inimitable Sir Freddie, who passed away in 2006, was a high school dropout who showed the same kind of entrepreneurial panache that would later make Richard Branson famous (both received knighthoods). He launched the Laker Airways "SkyTrain" between London and New York in 1977. President Carter, prepping for his deregulation move, gave his blessing after Laker spent six years petitioning. Although people stood in line for hours to buy a $236 round trip, the SkyTrain's margins were microscopic and its success short-lived. PeoplExpress and Tower Air were two others that tried and failed in the no-frills, long-haul arena.

☆ ☆ ☆

If Southwest Airlines represents, for better or worse, the Walmartification of flight, then what can we say of Hooters Air? Yes, I'm talking about the restaurant, which for a time was flying a foursome of leased Boeings out of a base in Myrtle Beach. Operations have since ceased, but the venture deserves a posthumous mention if for no other reason than to savor one of those only-in-America sighs.

The first Hooters Air joke I heard was this: "In the unlikely event of a water landing, your flight attendant may be used as a flotation device." Two token "Hooters Girls," loaned from the chain's franchises, were strategically carried on every flight. Their aircraft were set up with blue leather seats and generous legroom. The company called it "Club Class," which is a brand once used by British Airways for its business class. Hooters Air was about as far from British Airways as a Hooters restaurant is from a banquet at Buckingham Palace, but their planes were probably more comfortable than most. Hooters Air reported large numbers of passengers requesting aisle seats and claimed this was "for the scenery." Those at the windows had a view of mountains, while on the aisles... Well, only one of the views was real.

Which is the oldest airline?

Airline genealogies can be complicated. Many carriers have changed names and identities or have blurred their pedigrees through mergers and acquisitions. But most airline historians—there really are such people—agree that the world's oldest existing airline is Amsterdam-based KLM. That's *Koninklijke Luchtvaart Maatschappij* for those of you speaking Dutch, or Royal Dutch Airlines in English. It was founded in 1919. Here are the five oldest still flying under their original monikers:

- KLM (1919)
- Qantas (1920)
- Aeroflot (1923)
- CSA Czech Airlines (1923)
- Finnair (1923)

If we allow for name changes and mergers, Colombia's Avianca would be up there at number two, having started out in 1919 as something called SCADTA. It's a shame to see Mexicana (previously in third place) gone from the list. The airline ceased flying in 2010 after eighty-seven years. If you're surprised that places like Mexico, Colombia, Russia, or Australia have such a long aviation heritage, remember that rugged terrain, lack of roads, and vast distances made these countries natural spots for aviation to take hold.

In the United States, Delta is the eldest, harking to 1928.

With all this talk of code-sharing between airlines, what, exactly, *is* a code-share?

Code-sharing is the widespread practice whereby an airline sells seats, under its own name, on *another* carrier's airplane. It's a way for partner airlines to share passengers and revenue. The financial intricacies of these arrangements isn't something we have room to get into, and from the flyer's perspective it's not important. What *is* important is knowing which airline you're actually flying on. Waiting in a concourse in Boston one night, a man walked up to me in a state of obvious fluster, trying to find his gate. He was traveling on Qantas, he told me. I asked to see his ticket, which sure enough was emblazoned with that airline's familiar red kangaroo. The problem here is that Qantas doesn't fly to Boston and never has, despite lighted signs and announcements on the airport bus to the contrary. "No," I explained. "You're looking for American."

All but a few of the biggest carriers are in cahoots with at least one other airline, and many are hooked up in huge supranational alliances, namely SkyTeam, Star Alliance, and OneWorld. The idea is to cover as much real estate as possible, with at least one participant from each of the United States, Europe, Asia, and South America.

And just as you can code-share your way to Paris, Frankfurt, or Mumbai in a 777, you can do so to Syracuse, Montgomery, or Eugene in an RJ. Virtually every "Connection" or "Express" flight is a code-share operated by an independent regional carrier on behalf of a major airline. Call United to book a trip from Newark to Buffalo, and you'll find yourself delivered to the door of an RJ flown by ExpressJet. Delta's popular shuttle routes from LaGuardia to Boston and Washington are flown by a company called Shuttle America. And so on. Full disclosure of exactly whose metal you'll be riding on is required. Check the fine print on your ticket. Or look at the flight number. With rare exception, any four-digit flight numbers beginning with the number 3 or higher signifies a code-share operator. If you bought your ticket from United and the flight number is 201, you're flying on a United aircraft flown by a United crew. If the flight number is, say, 5201, it'll be a carrier operating *on behalf* of United.

Where do flight numbers come from? Is there any rhyme or reason to them?

Ordinarily, flights going eastbound are assigned even numbers; those headed westbound get odd numbers. Another habit is giving lower, one- or two-digit numbers to an airline's more prestigious, long-distance routes. If there's a flight 1 in an airline's timetable, it's the stuff of London–New York. Numbers might also be grouped geographically. At United, transpacific flights use three-digit numbers beginning with 8, which is considered a lucky number in many Asian cultures. As discussed in the last question, four-digit sequences starting with 3 or higher are, most of the time, indications of a code-share flight.

Technically a flight number is a combination of numbers and letters, prefaced with the carrier's two-letter IATA code. Every airline has one of these codes. For Delta, American, and United, it's DL, AA, and UA, respectively. For jetBlue, it's B6. Lufthansa uses LH; Singapore uses SQ. In the United States, we tend to ignore these prefixes, but overseas they are used consistently. In Europe or Asia, the airport departure screen might show, for instance, flights LH105 or TG207. That's Lufthansa and Thai Airways. (When filling in your immigration forms before landing, you should use the full designator where it asks for the flight number.)

Flight numbers along a given route can remain unchanged for many years. American's morning departure from Boston to Los Angeles had been flight AA11 as far back as the 1960s. That ended on September 11, 2001. After an incident, one of the first things an airline does is change the number of the affected flight.

Why do flights from the United States to Europe always depart in the evening and land in the morning, plunking down their exhausted passengers at the crack of dawn?

Mostly it's about two things: passenger connections and aircraft utilization. Flying from New York to Paris, for instance, a sizeable percentage of passengers will be continuing onward to places elsewhere in Europe, Asia, the Middle East, Africa, etc. Arrivals are timed to dovetail with these connections. Not to mention many of the folks who boarded that evening in New York actually began their journey much earlier—in, say, Salt Lake City, San Diego, or New Orleans; Syracuse, Roanoke, or Harrisburg. Returning westbound, same thing: landing in New York (or Chicago, or Houston, or Dallas, or Miami) in the afternoon leaves ample time for connections to points throughout North America.

It's similar with flights to Asia. Flying from Chicago to Tokyo, you will take off in the morning and arrive in the afternoon. Later, a bank of departures will leave Tokyo destined to cities deeper in Asia. Say to Bangkok, for instance, where you'll touch down about 11:00 p.m. That aircraft spends the night, then returns to Tokyo early the next morning, landing at midday and allowing easy connections back to North America.

This way, too, the aircraft spends minimal time on the ground. Lease payments on a widebody jetliner are in the hundreds of thousands of dollars per month, and a plane can't make money resting idle on the tarmac. Airlines strive to keep their jets in the air as much as possible, scheduling the quickest feasible turnaround times (figure ninety minutes, minimum, for an international flight).

One wrinkle is with flights to and from South America, where service is often an all-nighter on both ends. An aircraft arriving after sunrise in Buenos Aires can't turn around and fly back to New York, or it will get there after dark with few opportunities for connections. Many airlines bite the bullet, letting their aircraft sit for ten or twelve hours before heading back again in the evening. (My carrier often uses this opportunity to deep-clean its interiors. Even our normally filthy cockpits come back scrubbed and vacuumed.)

Some carriers do provide limited service focusing on what's called origin-and-destination (O&D) traffic, suited for flyers who aren't connecting. British Airways, for example, has traditionally offered daytime flights to London from a few U.S. cities. Leave New York at around nine in the morning, and you'll reach Heathrow around 8:00 p.m.

On a given flight, half or more of the passengers might be continuing on from their first stop. Some well-known carriers wouldn't be half the size they are if not for the number of transfer passengers moving through their hubs. Indeed, some of our largest and most profitable airlines hail from city-states with relatively tiny populations, where O&D traffic is only a portion of the total. Singapore Airlines and Emirates, for example. Singapore has one of the world's largest all-widebody fleets, hubbed in a country smaller than metro Philadelphia. Emirates, with a population base half the size of Massachusetts, flies close to two hundred widebodies, with fifty-plus Airbus A380s still on order. It comes down to strategic position, literally. Their success is less about carrying people *to* Singapore or Dubai, but carrying them *through* Singapore or Dubai. By fortune of geography these countries make excellent transit hubs along some of the busiest long-haul routes. They also invest heavily in their aviation infrastructures.

Traveling from Dallas to Chicago, I was surprised to find myself aboard a 777. Why would such a huge, long-range plane be deployed along such a short route?

One night at the airport in Luxor, Egypt, I boarded an Airbus A340, a four-engine widebody capable of reaching almost halfway around the globe. Where was I going? Cairo, about sixty minutes away. Why would EgyptAir relegate its most long-legged plane to a nothing flight up the Nile? For any number of reasons. It's about capacity, positioning, and schedule more than outright capabilities of the machine.

Certain short-haul markets demand large planes because there is so much traffic. All Nippon and JAL fly 747s on some of their busiest Japanese domestic runs because that's the choicest plane into which they can wedge an industry-leading, if that's the right word, 563 seats. In other cases, shorter trips dovetail advantageously between long-haul assignments. Let's say a plane arrives from Europe at noontime and won't be headed back again until 8:00 p.m. Those hours in between allow it to pull valuable double-duty on a busy domestic segment. Similarly, a plane from South America that arrives in Atlanta in the morning might be scheduled for a European trip out of New York later that evening. The Atlanta-New York segment is, in effect, a repositioning run.

And don't forget freight. Airlines derive money not only from seats, but also from the pallets and containers beneath them. One plane might be best suited for a route specifically because its belly space is most advantageous. A 747 has 6,000 cubic feet of cargo space in addition to four hundred seats on the main deck.

What are the longest nonstop flights?

Back in chapter one, I explained that hours aloft, rather than distances covered, is the more accurate way of measuring aircraft range. But flying times are fickle, so nautical mileage is the best metric for this question.

Until recently, Singapore Airlines held the number-one and number-two slots, using an all-business class configured Airbus A340-500 from Singapore to Newark (8,290 miles) and Los Angeles (7,260 miles). These are the longest scheduled nonstops on record. (Yes, Newark and LAX are 2,100 miles apart, but their distance from Singapore differs by only half that much—a function of great circle trigonometry. *See great circles, page 88.*) They were discontinued in 2013, however, and the baton passed to Qantas and its 7,455-mile nonstop between Sydney and Dallas–Ft. Worth.

The following list is subject to change as airlines revise their schedules, but here are the longest scheduled passenger flights at press time, measured in nautical miles. Bring a favorite book (preferably this one), and leave your circadian rhythms at home:

1. Sydney–Dallas: 7,455 (Qantas)
2. Atlanta–Johannesburg: 7,335 (Delta)
3. Dubai–Los Angeles: 7,245 (Emirates)
4. Manila–Toronto: 7,145 (Philippine Airlines)

5. Dubai–Houston: 7,095 (Emirates)
6. Dubai–San Francisco: 7,040 (Emirates)
7. New York–Hong Kong: 7,015 (Cathay Pacific, United)
8. Doha–Houston: 6,995 (Qatar Airways)
9. Dubai–Dallas: 6,990 (Emirates)
10. New York–Johannesburg: 6,925 (South African Airways)

Notice that three of the top ten are flights between Texas and the Middle East. That's oil for you.

Quaint seem the days, forty or so years ago, when Pan Am executives sat in their Park Avenue skyscraper, scratching their heads over ways to make a 747 reach Tokyo without refueling. Thanks to aircraft like the 777 and A340 (*see long-range jetliners, page 12*), almost any two commercial air markets in the world are linkable in a single fell swoop. We haven't just closed the technological gap, we've closed the imagination gap as well.

One holdout, at just under 10,000 nautical miles, is London–Sydney, called the "grail route" in some circles. Using a 747-400, Qantas once tinkered with this elusive prize and discovered it could, under optimum conditions, make the run without having to pit stop. But this was so pushing the envelope that it proved a real teeth-chatterer for the carrier's crews and dispatchers, who were forced to juggle the logistics of fuel, weather, and diversion planning with utmost attention and accuracy. Not to mention it being untenable for advertising: "Qantas to London. Nonstop. Sometimes."

Boeing's 777-LR once made an 11,600-mile promotional flight, and on paper would seem capable of handling the journey. But just because a plane can do such things in a publicity stunt doesn't mean it can do them in regular scheduled service. You have ETOPS restrictions (extended range operational legalities for twin-engine planes) to deal with, local airspace constraints, wind patterns, seasonal weather variations, and so on, all affecting flight times. And that two cities *can* be connected means little to an airline unless there is an exploitable market to justify connecting them. London–Sydney is not the longest possible flight, but it may be the longest possible flight guaranteed to provide a steady supply of passengers. More formidable pairings are at least conceivable, should demand exist. The most intriguing of these are São Paulo–Tokyo, Auckland–London, and Buenos Aires–Tokyo, all clocking in at a shade under 10,000 nautical miles. Shattering the 10,000 frontier—Buenos Aires–Seoul, anyone?—remains, let's just say, a long-haul longshot.

My personal record for time spent on a plane is a relatively modest fourteen hours and forty-six minutes, aboard South African Airways flight SA202 from JFK to Johannesburg in May 2000. SAA uses an A340 on that route today, but it was a 747 at the time. I know the flight was exactly fourteen hours and forty-six minutes long because there was a digital timer bolted to the bulkhead, triggered by retraction of the landing gear to provide a minute-by-minute update. Watching the hours tick by seemed a tortuous proposition, until a certain passenger was bold enough to tape a piece of paper over the clock.

I flew aboard an airplane that had a name painted near its nose. Apparently planes are sometimes named individually, like ships or boats?

All airliners wear registrations (numbers or letters that also indicate a plane's nation of origin) on the rear fuselage, but some also carry names. If a plane has been christened in honor of a place, person, or thing, look for titles on the forward fuselage. I'm quite fond of this practice. It makes flying a touch less impersonal and a touch more dignified. And any airline that bothers to name its planes, I feel, is one that takes its mission to heart.

Turkish Airlines names its spotless Boeings and Airbuses after Anatolian cities. You can ride aboard the *Konya*, the *Goreme*, or the *Isparta*. Flying Virgin Atlantic, which styles itself a bit more provocatively, you might have a seat on the *Tubular Belle*, the *Barbarella*, or maybe the *Varga Girl*. You can ride the *St. Patrick* to Dublin on Aer Lingus, no surprise there, or try your luck on a Syrianair 747 called *Arab Solidarity*. For a while, Air Namibia was flying a 747 named *Welwitschia*, homage to a strange desert succulent that grows in the Namibian wilds and can live for centuries. On that fifteen-hour South African Airways flight to Johannesburg that I described earlier, I rode the *Durban*, then the *Bloemfonetein* on my return (cities in South Africa). If unsure, I needed only to check the wooden plaque near the upper deck stairs emblazoned with a crest and scroll. I thought the plaque added an elegant, ocean liner sort of touch.

I miss the Austrian carrier Lauda Air, now part of Austrian Airlines, which remembered artists and musicians with the *Gustav Klimt*, the *Miles Davis*, and a 737 named *Frank Zappa*. KLM is probably the closest in terms of creativity: cities, birds, authors, and explorers all have their namesake blue-and-white Boeing, while the airline's MD-11s are named for famous women, including the *Florence Nightingale*, the *Marie Curie*, and the *Audrey Hepburn*.

On the other hand, enough already with jetBlue's insufferable, too-cute riffs on the color blue. I don't advocate hurling tomatoes at Airbuses, but here are some deserving targets. I can live with *Idlewild Blue* and even *Betty Blue*, but *That's What I Like About Blue*, *Fancy Meeting Blue Here*, or *Bippity Boppity Blue* are too much to take. What was I just saying about dignity?

Some years back, United named several jets in honor of its highest-mileage frequent flyers. Imagine *not* getting an upgrade on the very plane with your name on its nose.

At Pan Am, each aircraft sported a distinctive *Clipper* designation, a carryover from the airline's grandiose earlier years when its flying boats pioneered routes across the oceans. There were nautical references—*Sea Serpent*, *Mermaid*, *Gem of the Ocean*—including a particular fascination with waves—*Crest of the Wave*, *Dashing Wave*, *Wild Wave*. There were nods to Greek and Roman mythology,—*Jupiter*, *Mercury*, *Argonaut*—and the inevitable heaping of faux-inspirational piffle—*Empress of the Skies*, *Glory of the Skies*, *Freedom*. A few of them made you wonder if Juan Trippe and his boys weren't tippling too much scotch in the boardrooms over on Park Avenue: *Water Witch? Neptune's Car? Nonpareil? Young Brander?* Turns out those were taken from old sailing vessels.

When Pan Am 103 was blown up over Scotland in 1988, the only part to remain somewhat intact was the forward fuselage, from the nose to roughly the first set of cabin doors. It was crushed when it landed, on its side, but still looked like a piece of an airplane, which is more than you can say for the rest of the jet. This piece was widely photographed and became a news icon in the days and weeks that followed. There it was, on the front of every newspaper and on the cover of *Time* and *Newsweek*, and it is easily found on the Internet today. The photo shows detritus and debris everywhere, wires and scraps of metal, all surrounding this impossibly still-dignified chunk of a Boeing 747, dead as a doornail. There's the blue stripe, the paint barely scratched. And there, just above the oval cabin windows in frilly blue lettering, you can still read clearly the words *Clipper Maid of the Seas.*

HOW TO SPEAK AIRLINE

A Glossary for Travelers

The experience of air travel is unique in that people subject themselves to a long string of mostly anonymous authorities. From the moment you step through the terminal doors, you're hit with orders—stand here, take your shoes off there, put your seat belt on, do this, put away that—and a flurry of information. Most of it comes not face-to-face, but over a microphone, delivered by employees, seen and unseen, in a vernacular that binges on jargon, acronyms, and confusing euphemisms. There are people who make dozens of air journeys annually and still have only a vague understanding of many terms. To help, I've compiled a glossary, focusing on those expressions most easily misunderstood or not understood at all. In no special order:

Doors to arrival and crosscheck

Example: *"Flight attendants, doors to arrival and crosscheck."*

Meaning: Occasionally heard as "disarm your doors and crosscheck" and announced by the lead flight attendant or purser as a plane approaches the gate. The intent is to verify disarming of the emergency escape slides attached to the doors. When armed, a slide will automatically deploy the instant its door is opened. Disarmed, it needs to be deployed manually. On departure, the slides are armed to facilitate an emergency evacuation. (You might hear this as "doors to automatic.") Upon docking, they're disarmed to keep them from billowing into the boarding tunnel or onto the apron during servicing. Crosscheck is a generic term used by pilots and flight attendants meaning that one person has verified the task of another. In the cabin, flight attendants cross-check one another's stations to make sure the doors are armed or disarmed as necessary.

All-call

Example: *"Flight attendants, doors to arrival, crosscheck and all-call."*

Meaning: Often part of the arming/disarming procedure, this is a request that each flight attendant reports via intercom from his or her station—a sort of flight attendant conference call.

Last-minute paperwork

Example: *"We're just finishing up some last-minute paperwork and should be under way shortly..."*

Meaning: Everything is buttoned up and the flight is ready for pushback. Then comes the wait for "last-minute paperwork," which winds up taking half an hour. Usually it's something to do with the weight-and-balance record, a revision to the flight plan (*see flight plans, page 69*), or waiting for the maintenance guys to deal with a write-up and get the logbook in order.

Flight deck

Meaning: the cockpit.

First officer (also, copilot)

Meaning: The first officer is second in command on the flight deck. He or she sits on the right and is fully qualified to operate the aircraft in all stages of flight, including takeoffs and landings, and does so in alternating turns with the captain (*see pilots and copilots, page 98*).

Flight level

Example: *"We've now reached our cruising altitude of flight level three-three-zero. I'll go ahead and turn off the seat belt sign..."*

Meaning: There's a technical definition of flight level, but I'm not going to bore you with it. Basically, this is a fancy way of telling you how many thousands of feet you are above sea level. Just add a couple of zeroes. Flight level three-three-zero is 33,000 feet.

Holding pattern

Meaning: A racetrack-shaped course flown during weather or traffic delays. Published holding patterns are depicted on aeronautical charts, but one can be improvised almost anywhere.

Ground stop

Example: *"Sorry folks, but there's a ground stop on all flights headed south from here."*
Meaning: This is when departures to one or more destination are curtailed by ATC, usually due to a traffic backlog.

EFC time

Example: *"Good news, we've been given an EFC time of 30 minutes after the hour."*
Meaning: The expect further clearance (EFC) time, sometimes called a release time, is the point at which a crew expects to be set free from a holding pattern or exempted from a ground stop.

Wheels-up time

Meaning: Similar to the EFC time, except it refers to the point when a ground-stopped plane is expected to be fully airborne. The crew must plan to be at or near the runway as close to this time as possible.

Area of weather

Example: *"Due to an area of weather over New Jersey, we'll be turning southbound toward Philadelphia…"*
Meaning: Typically, thunderstorms or a zone of heavy precipitation.

Air pocket

Meaning: Colloquial for a transient jolt of turbulence (*see turbulence, page 32*).

Final approach

Example: *"Ladies and gentlemen, we are now on our final approach into Miami."*

Meaning: For pilots, an airplane is on final approach when it has reached the last, straight-in segment of the landing pattern—that is, aligned with the extended centerline of the runway, requiring no additional turns or maneuvering. Flight attendants speak of final approach on their own more general terms, in reference to the latter portion of the descent.

The full upright and locked position

Meaning: upright.

Tampering with, disabling, or destroying

Example: *"Federal law prohibits tampering with, disabling, or destroying a lavatory smoke detector."*

Meaning: tampering with.

The off position

Meaning: off.

Deplane

Example: *"Please remember to take all of your belongings before deplaning."*

Meaning: Deplane is used to describe the opposite of boarding an aircraft. There are those who feel the root "plane" should not be used as a verb, fearing a chain-reaction of abominable copycats. Imagine "decar" for getting out of your car, or "debed" for waking up. In fact, dictionaries date "deplane" to the 1920s, and while it's not the slickest-sounding word, I'm known to employ it myself. Like "stewardess," it's a term of occasional convenience. There are few snappy, PA-friendly options with the same useful meaning. "Disembark" is the most elegant one available, and it's rather clumsy.

Deadhead

Meaning: A deadheading pilot or flight attendant is one repositioning as part of an on-duty assignment. This is not the same as commuting to work (*see commuting, page 113*) or engaging in personal travel.

Equipment

Example: *"Due to an equipment change, departure for Heathrow is delayed three hours."*

Meaning: an airplane. (Is there not something strange about the refusal to call the focal object of the entire industry by its real name?)

Direct flight

Meaning: Technically, a direct flight is a routing along which the flight number does not change; it has nothing to do with whether the plane stops. This is a carryover from the days when flights between major cities routinely made intermediate stops, sometimes several of them. Most airline staff are smart enough to realize that if a passenger asks if a flight is "direct," he or she wants to know if it stops, but check the fine print when booking.

Nonstop

Meaning: That's the one that doesn't stop.

Gatehouse

Example: *"If there is a passenger Patrick Smith in the gatehouse, please approach the podium."*

Meaning: An idiosyncratic way of saying the gate area or boarding lounge. Gatehouse has a folksy touch that I really like. They should use it more often.

Pre-board

Example: *"We would now like to pre-board those passengers requiring special assistance."*

Meaning: This one, on the other hand, has no charm. It means to board. Except, to board first.

Final and immediate boarding call

Meaning: A flamboyant way of telling slow-moving passengers to get their asses in gear. It provides more urgency than just "final call" or "last call."

In range

Example: *"The flight has called in range, and we expect to begin boarding in approximately forty minutes."*

Meaning: This is a common gatehouse announcement during delays, when the plane you're waiting to board hasn't yet landed. Somewhere around the start of descent, the pilots will send an electronic "in range" message to let everybody know they'll be arriving shortly. How shortly is tough to tell, as the message is sent prior to any low-altitude sequencing and assumes no inbound taxi congestion. What they're giving you at the gate is a best-case time for boarding. As a rule of thumb, add twenty minutes.

Ramp

Example: *"We're sorry; your suitcase was crushed by a 747 out on the ramp."*

Meaning: Ramp refers to the aircraft and ground vehicle movement areas closest to the terminal—the aircraft parking zones and surrounds. In the early days of aviation, many aircraft were amphibious seaplanes or floatplanes. If a plane wasn't flying, it was either in the water or "on the ramp."

Alley

Example: *"It'll be just a second, folks. We're waiting for another aircraft to move out of the alley."*

Meaning: A taxiway or passageway between terminals or ramps.

Apron

Meaning: Similar to ramp, this is basically any expanse of tarmac that is not a runway or taxiway—areas where planes park or are otherwise serviced.

Tarmac

Meaning: A portmanteau for "tar-penetration macadam," a highway surfacing material patented in Britain in 1901. Eventually, it came to mean any sort of asphalt or blacktop. You hear it in reference to airports all the time, even though almost no ramp, apron, runway, or taxiway is actually surfaced with the stuff. Real tarmac becomes soft in hot weather and would turn to mush under the wheels of a heavy jet. (I think of Paul Weller's invocation of "sticky black tarmac" in the gorgeous Jam song "That's Entertainment!") Like many words, it has outgrown its specificity, and there are linguistic traditionalists who are bothered by this. I am not one of them.

At this time

Example: *"At this time, we ask that you please put away all electronic devices."*
Meaning: now, or presently. This is air travel's signature euphemism.

Do

Example: *"We do appreciate you choosing American." Or, "We do remind you that smoking is not permitted."*
Meaning: An irritating emphatic, otherwise with no grammatical justification. What's wrong with "Thank you for choosing American" or "Smoking is not permitted"? People wonder if this is how airline employees talk to one another. "I do love you, Steve, but I cannot marry you at this time."

INDEX

Index

297

Index

Index

UPS (United Parcel Service), 110, 119, 199–200, 241
upside down flying, 7
US Airways, 49, 124–127, 150, 163, 197, 244, 246, 250, 261, 263, 266
US Airways Flight 1549, 49, 124–127
USAir, 52, 250
USB connections, 170, 254
UTA Flight 772, 187, 194

V

V1 (takeoff decision speed), 72–73
ValuJet, 146, 163
Van Zanten, Jacob, 230–231, 232–234, 237
vapor/mist trails, 38, 45
vapor pressure, 15
Venezuelan oil fields, 175
VOR (very high-frequency omnidirectional range), 88
Vickers VC-10, 21
views, airplane, 47–48, 157–158, 153, 173–177
views, airport, 65–66
Vincennes disaster, 205
Vignelli, Massimo, 240
Virgin Atlantic, 18, 166, 167, 278
visibility, 52, 77, 78–79, 81, 127, 231–232
Vonnegut, Kurt, 146, 174
vortices, 36–37, 38, 45

W

wake turbulence, 36–37
walk arounds, 54–55, 143
Wallace, Foster 3–4
Warns, George, 237
watches, 129
weather
  contrails, 15, 16
  cumulus clouds, 34–35, 122
  dangerous airports, 76
  delays, 81–85, 87, 257, 258, 266–268, 283
  glories, 158
  heat, 14–15, 132–133, 159, 227, 258
  instrument landing systems, 78–79, 105
  lightning, 46
  missed approaches, 77
  snow and ice, 49–53, 76, 81, 266–268
  thunderstorms, 34, 38, 46, 283
  visibility, 52, 77, 78–79, 81, 127, 231–232
  See also turbulence; wind
weight-and-balance, 13–14, 43, 144, 282

weight penalties, 14–15
Weller, Paul, 287
West Africa, xiii
Western Pacific Airlines, 247
wheels-up time, 81, 283
widebodies, 6, 30, 261, 275
widget (Delta logo), 241, 243
wind, 9–10, 70–71, 79, 152
  See also landings, crosswind; turbulence; windshear
Window Seat (Dicum), 158
window shades, 149, 155
windows, airplane, 47–48, 51, 157–158, 173–177
windows, airport, 65–66
windshear, 38–39, 77, 105
wing
  aerodynamics, 1–3, 4–7, 12, 35, 36, 37, 70–71
  deicing. *See* deicing and deicing fluid
  winglets, 5–6, 37, 47
Wired magazine, 120
Witcher, Brian, 126
Wizz Air, 248
Wright brothers, 1, 18–19

X

Xiamen Airlines, 194
x-ray screenings, 179, 181–182

Y

Yankee Clipper restaurant, 63–64
yaw, 3, 4, 5, 127
yaw damper, 4
Yemenia, 209
Yousef, Ramzi, 181, 195
Yugoslav Airlines (JAT), 192

Z

Zantop, 57
ZED (Zonal Employee Discount) fares, 133
Zen Arcade (Hüsker Dü), 20
Zhezkazan Zhez Air, 248
zone seating, 171
Zukowsky, John, 59

About the Author

Patrick Smith is an airline pilot and the host of www.askthepilot.com. For ten years, he was the author of Salon.com's popular Ask the Pilot air travel series, from which portions of this book are taken. He has appeared on more than two hundred radio and television outlets, and his work is cited regularly in print publications worldwide.

Patrick took his first flying lesson at age fourteen. His first job with an airline came in 1990, when he was hired as a copilot on fifteen-passenger turboprops, earning $850 a month. He has since flown cargo and passenger jets on both domestic and intercontinental routes.

The author's self-published punk rock fanzines and poetry journals of the 1980s and '90s are considered among the more curious works of literature ever produced by a native of Revere, Massachusetts.

Patrick travels extensively in his spare time and has visited more than seventy countries. He lives near Boston.